WHITE WALL OF SPAIN

WHITE WALL OF SPAIN:
THE MYSTERIES OF ANDALUSIAN CULTURE

ALLEN JOSEPHS

IOWA STATE UNIVERSITY PRESS • AMES

FOR LAURA, ANNA, AND MARI
y para el pueblo andaluz

FRONTISPIECE: *Homage to Picasso: A Village in the Province of Malaga. 1978.* By Allen Josephs.

"The Andalusian Picasso," by Allen Josephs, © *New Boston Review,* Nov./Dec. 1980 is reprinted by permission.

First edition, 1983

Library of Congress Cataloging in Publication Data
Josephs, Allen.
   White wall of Spain.

   Includes bibliographical references and index.
   1. Andalusia (Spain) – Civilization.   I.   Title
DP 302.A467 J67   1983   946′.8   83-311
ISBN 0-1838-1921-0

C O N T E N T S

Foreword by James A. Michener   ix

Preface   xi

Acknowledgments   xii

ONE   **CULTURE OF DEATH**   3

TWO   **SHIPS OF TARSHISH**   31

THREE   **PIGS OF THE SEA**   53

FOUR   **DANCER OF GADES**   67

FIVE   **GODDESS**   101

SIX   **MATADOR**   133

CODA   **THE ANDALUSIAN PICASSO**   163

Notes   173

Index   179

F O R E W O R D

The virtue of this book, and it is considerable, is that Dr. Josephs relates one of the most ancient and interesting areas of Spain to the classical history of which it was a distinguished part. His wealth of illustrative material is rewarding, and his allusions to learned materials from a wide range of writing are provocative. Few experts on Spain will fail to learn something new from these pages. His heroes are Richard Ford, José Ortega y Gasset, and Federico García Lorca, and it would be difficult to find more capable cicerones. This book will offer many surprises to those who think they know Andalucía. Read the chapter on Tarshish and you'll see what I mean.

James A. Michener

PREFACE

The great Andalusian poet, Federico García Lorca, once evoked with stark perfection a timeless and universal image of the south of Spain:

> *¡Oh blanco muro de España!*
> *¡Oh negro toro de pena!*
>
> Oh white wall of Spain!
> Oh black bull of pain!

The historical and cultural reality behind that unmistakable image, which is at once suggestive of Andalucía and of Andalucía's pervasive influence on the rest of Spain, is the subject of this book.

No traveler can spend much time in Andalucía without encountering certain things that seem almost inexplicable in the Western world. The frenzy of tuna fishing off the coast of Cádiz, the music and dance known as *flamenco,* religious celebrations such as Holy Week in Sevilla or the pilgrimage called the Rocío, and, of course, *toreo,* which we erroneously call "bullfighting"—these are unique phenomena which are native to southern Spain and have virtually no counterpart in our culture.

These rites are the mysteries of Andalucía because they are radically unfamiliar to most Westerners and because they stem in no small part from the ancient mysteries of the East. Unraveling their development is equivalent to undertaking a quest to the center of the human psyche, both psychologically and historically, in an attempt to understand a culture that has baffled and fascinated observers since the days of the Romans.

To enter the Andalusian labyrinth, to explore these mysteries, to trace them from their origins in antiquity to the present, is to rediscover a primordial way of life. That rediscovery is my primary purpose. I also hope this book will foster an understanding of the brilliance and originality of Andalusian culture and help to protect that culture — on paper and in fact — from the colorless homogeneity of the future.

Editorial practices: To hold notes to a minimum, I have first cited a complete bibliographical reference, followed thereafter by volume and page numbers in parentheses with short titles or authors' names when necessary. Unless otherwise indicated, classical citations are from the Loeb Classical Library (Harvard University Press). All other translations are mine except when otherwise indicated.

The University of West Florida, June, 1982

A C K N O W L E D G M E N T S

I am indebted to the National Endowment for the Arts for a Creative Writing Fellowship Grant; to the National Endowment for the Humanities for a Summer Seminar Grant; and to the University of West Florida for a summer research grant and a sabbatical leave. I am also grateful to the University of West Florida for research time and to colleagues for encouragement and support.

Many people helped me with this book, many more than I could name. The following deserve special mention for their assistance, their generosity, and their encouragement: Rafael and Maritere Aguilar, Antonio Bojollo, Gerald Brenan, Juan A. Caballero, J. M. Caballero Bonald, José Luis Cano, Juan de Mata Carriazo, Frank N. Dauster, Gustavo and Marilí Domínguez, Daniel Eisenberg, José Esteban, Alfonso de Franciscis, Federico Fulton, John Fulton, Isabel García Lorca, Alberto García Ulecia, Bodil H. Gilliam, Ángel González, Antonio González, Alfonso Grosso, David and Margaret

Gullette, José Heredia Maya, Serafín Herrera Vílchez, Perdita Hordern, Alfred Kazin, Richard P. Kinkade, Glenn and Patty Lipskey, José Ramón Marra-López, John McCormick, Stanton Millet, Eduardo Molina Fajardo, Timothy and Jo Anne Murad, José Luis Núñez-Lagos, Fernando and Matilde Pérez Camacho, Donn and Luisa Pohren, Alberto and Catherine Portera, Fernando Quiñones, Norman Rabkin (and members of his 1979 seminar on tragedy at Berkeley), Daniel and Nancy Reedy, Luis Rosales, Francisco Solano, Edward F. Stanton, Lee and Pilar Turner, Robert Vavra, and Frederick S. Wildman, Jr.

Above all, I would like to thank my friend and fellow Hispanophile, Douglas Day, upon whose assistance, advice, and collaboration I greatly depended.

The first chapter of this book is an expanded version of "Homage to Andalucía," which first appeared in *The Virginia Quarterly Review* (Summer 1979). I am grateful for permission to reprint this material.

LA MANCHA

SPAIN

RA MORENA

GUADALQUIVIR (Tartessos);

Baetis)

Desfiladero de Despeñapernos

RDOBA

Porcuna

Galera

Cueva de los Letreros

Cabra

Lucena

Moclín

Baza

Guadix

Antequera

Granada

SIERRA NEVADA

El Gárcel

Los Millares

La(s) Alpujarra(s)

RONDA

Mainake

Almuñécar (Sexi)

Almería

MÁLAGA (MALACA)

DEL

SOL

ANDALUCÍA

CHAPTER ONE

CULTURE OF DEATH

The civilization of Andalucía is the oldest in the Western world. A thriving native culture along the lower reaches of the Guadalquivir River traded regularly with Phoenicia and occasionally with the Israel of Solomon some thousand years before Christ. Strong evidence exists that this culture, known as Tarshish in the Old Testament and as Tartessos in the Greek texts, ranges well back into the second millennium to the time of the Minoans, while some of the most recent evidence involving revised radiocarbon dating indicates megalithic cultures in an even earlier age. Perhaps more striking than its remote antiquity is the extent to which that ancient culture has continued to survive in certain demonstrable ways up to the twentieth century and the extent to which that sense of antiquity has remained a part of the sensibility of the Andalusian people. Certain geographical, historical, political, and cultural factors caused an agricultural Mediterranean way of life to develop early and to remain, in many respects, unchanged in Andalucía at least through the generation born before the Spanish Civil War.

The traveler who emerges from Despeñaperros, the spectacular defile separating Andalucía from the monotony of La Mancha, becomes immediately aware that he is in another world. The famous pass, where Christians and Moslems threw each other off the cliffs and where the ancient Iberians worshiped their gods, forms a natural gateway through the Sierra Morena to an older and a not altogether

---

AN OLD WOMAN AND A CHILD ascend the whitewashed street of an Andalusian village, the kind of village which the distinguished Spanish ethnologist Julio Caro Baroja described as a living museum stretching from the Neolithic to the present. *Photograph by Allen Josephs.*

3

European world. It is precisely this non-European, or more specifically non-Indo-European, cast that comprises both the source of Andalucía's atavistic culture and the source of much misunderstanding of that culture.

In the broadest terms, the south of Spain was settled by the Iberians, a "Mediterranean" type of uncertain origin. The north was settled by the Indo-European Celts, the same tribes that settled over much of northern Europe. In the center of Spain the groups mixed forming the so-called Celtiberians. From the beginning there emerged a pattern of a Mediterranean bias in Andalucía and a European bias in the north that was to be repeated time and again.

In 1927 José Ortega y Gasset, the most sharply honed Spanish thinker of his time, wrote an essay, "Theory of Andalucía," which is still hotly discussed today by Andalusians. Typical of Ortega, the article is in some respects brilliantly original and in others somewhat uneven. The first half of the essay, which Ortega calls "Prelude," is particularly of interest as it makes certain points about Andalucía, including a quite correct as well as original explanation of the most irritating and persistent problem plaguing any student of Andalucía or, for that matter, of Spain.[1]

That problem is the Spanish, and particularly the Andalusian, stereotype: Carmen dancing with a rose in her teeth and a dagger in her garter while bullfighters and bandits alternately duel with each other and swoon at her feet: the "multi-colored farce," as Ortega calls it, that the inhabitants of Andalucía perform for the benefit of tourists. He makes the point that the Andalusians enjoy presenting themselves as a spectacle, and he believes, quite accurately, that the travelers in Sevilla can suspect they are witnessing the presentation of a magnificent ballet called *Sevilla*. Ortega believes the propensity to play a part and to mime themselves shows a surprising collective narcissism. In order to imitate himself, one must become the spectator of his own persona and must be habituated to watching himself, in fact to contemplating himself and taking delight in his own figure. Sometimes, Ortega surmises, the effect produced is one of lamentable mannerisms. And from these mannerisms, I might add, emerges the continuation of the old stereotype.

Yet the mannerisms, the narcissism, the self-stylization are only part of the story. There is another dimension involved. The mannerisms also reveal, as Ortega notes, a profound self-awareness or self-knowledge. Perhaps no other culture, he muses, possesses such a clear consciousness of its own style and character, a consciousness that allows the Andalusians to maintain themselves invariably within their millenary profile, faithful to their destiny and the cultivation of their exclusive culture. Ortega believes, and this is the crux of the matter, that the self-awareness is precisely the product of the antiquity of the culture. It should not be forgotten, he admonishes, that they are the oldest *pueblo* of the Mediterranean, older than the Greeks or the Romans.

If we follow Ortega's logic, which I believe to be essentially correct, then the antiquity of Andalusian culture and the Andalusian stereotype are two sides of the same coin. On one side we have the *Ballet of Sevilla,* on the other the millenary profile. Quite probably, then, the annoyingly persistent superficiality of the stereotype can be interpreted in part as confirmation of Andalucía's antiquity, and we can forget about its brilliant but skin-deep reflection for the moment.

The other important point Ortega makes is that Andalusian culture is a *cultura campesina,* that it is deeply rooted in the land, the soil, the *campo* of Andalucía. This chthonian quality—and that is the only word that expresses the concept—is of utmost importance since it is the basis for the radical conservatism of Andalusian culture, particularly the aspects we shall examine. *Chthon* in Greek meant "earth," and particularly "earth" in a pantheistic, pre-Christian sense. Ortega compares Andalusian history to Chinese history and makes the precise point that Andalucía was invaded over and again by practically all the violent cultures of the Mediterranean without ever putting up any real resistance. Yet just as the Chinese did, the Andalusians, by their superior, more refined culture, successfully "conquered" their invaders by receiving them passively.

It is easy enough to quarrel with Ortega or to point out that similar phenomena have occurred at times elsewhere, for example in Greece. But I want to agree with him, especially since this passive reception of other cultures, with their rapid absorption into the Andalusian mainstream, seems one of the best explanations for the syncretism of Andalusian culture. Not just once, but many times over, Andalucía received and passively conquered other cultures. Andalusian culture, then, is ancient and self-aware, passive and agricultural, chthonian and extremely conservative. The narcissistic stereotype reveals the sense of antiquity; history bears out the passivity and agricultural nature of the culture; and the lack of change, the essentially conservative nature with its absorptive, syncretistic tendency, is everywhere evident in this *tierra de María Santísima,* as the Andalusians call it, the "biblical" nature of which cannot fail to strike even the casual visitor who ventures into the rural landscape. As Ortega concluded, the Andalusian olive branch is both a symbol of peace as a cultural norm and a principle of the culture.

Ortega was not the only one, nor the first one, to propose such theories. Richard Ford in his *Hand-book for Travellers in Spain,* which described brilliantly the Spain of the 1830s, wrote that Spain was "a land *bottled* for antiquarians."[2] Andalucía, where he had lived and traveled extensively between 1830 and 1833, was quite obviously his favorite country, and he never tired of pointing out the Oriental, pagan, or ancient nature of its culture. On several occasions he quoted Livy, who described the Andalusians as *"Omnium Hispanorum maxime imbelles,"* "Of all the Spaniards the most unwarlike," to which Ford added: "nor are they at all changed" (p. 222). That is, Ford meant, not at all changed since the days of Livy some two millenniums ago.

Richard Ford, upon whose usually sagacious and profusely documented opinions I shall rely in more than one instance, brings up an interesting problem which I call the Hispanophile Imperative, a problem that returns to the prickliest part of the Andalusian stereotype. The Hispanophile Imperative is the utter inability to avoid writing books about Spain. It flourished in Roman times, during the Romantic period, and again in the twentieth century. What is worst about the Hispanophile Imperative is that it has produced a steady stream of terrible books about Spain — usually the worse the book the more it propagates the superficiality of the stereotype. What is best about it are the superb books that explain Spain's radically different culture, heritage, and history to unenlightened Westerners.

The Hispanophile Imperative exists because over the centuries Spain, and particularly Andalucía, has fascinated the travelers who ventured there. Spain, as James Michener sagely points out at the beginning of *Iberia,* intrudes into the imagination.[3] Some love it and some despise it, but few visitors remain unaffected or neutral. Our American literature is colored by what Hemingway has written on Spain. And in England the tradition of traveling to Spain, that curiously chauvinistic habit the English have of going *out,* as they put it, for the exotic experience, goes back at least to the time when Dr. Johnson told Boswell, "There is a good deal of Spain that has not been perambulated. I would have you go thither."[4]

The modern Hispanophile Imperative developed from the Romantic movement. Spain was the only near, still geographically European place one could visit with the assurance of encountering the bizarre, the exotic, the Oriental, precisely what the Romantic imagination craved and fed on when it could. And the farther south the traveler ventured the more bizarre things generally became. The Romantics and their modern followers went purposely to Spain seeking, and finding, a peculiar exoticism that was understood by few of them. Andalucía was particularly different. They described it as "exotic," "strange," "quaint," and "primitive."

Misunderstanding arose not so much from actual cultural difference but from a too facile explanation of the difference, even by the Andalusians themselves, who lamentably often merely dressed the old stereotype in a new "suit of lights" and staged another performance of the *Ballet of Sevilla*. Richard Ford, George Borrow, Alexandre Dumas, Gustave Doré, Rilke, Mérimée, Bizet, Byron, Washington Irving, to name a few of the most famous, found a world in Andalucía that they reflected with varying fortune, sometimes to the detriment of our understanding of that culture. Maugham, Montherlant, Hemingway, Dos Passos, Malraux, Walter Starkie, Gerald Brenan, and Michener, again to pick but a few, continued the tradition, often in great style but not in every instance with the greatest accuracy. Dumas had declared roundly that Africa began at the Pyrenees. Maugham believed all Andalusians to be potential bullfighters, thought the key to Andalusian beauty was nothing less than the six thousand *sevillanas* on display at the Tobacco Factory, and maintained that Spaniards were cruel to animals (but the English to their wives and children). Hemingway's worst gaffe was inadvertently to give María, his heroine in *For Whom the Bell Tolls* who was so pure that not even rape by the fascists could spoil her, an obscene nickname.[5] Yet amusing as some of these faux pas, commonplaces, exaggerations, and clichés are, they also reveal the difficulty some of the best non-Spanish artists have in dealing with all of Spain, and especially Andalucía.

The blame does not belong merely to the foreigners. At least since Cervantes wrote the line,

> *Cuando Preciosa el panderete toca*
> When Preciosa plays the tambourine[6]

which gives us the quintessential vision of the Gypsy girl and her tambourine, there has existed a similar propensity among Spaniards, especially non-Andalusians, to misinterpret or make dreadful generalizations about Andalucía. Everyone does it. It seems as difficult to avoid as it is necessary to recognize and admit. Even Ortega in his essay on Andalucía shows the insensitivity, not to say gaucheness, to call *cante jondo,* the best of *flamenco,* which he included mistakenly in the *Ballet of Sevilla, "quincalla meridional,"* or "southern frippery" (6:112). In spite of everyone's ardent desire to express the truth about Andalucía, the *pandereta* (as it is spelled today), the symbol for the worst of the old stereotype, remains with us, threatening to drown out in its jingles and seductive beat anything of value we have to say.

An understanding of the *pandereta,* however, lets us identify it and ward off its evil effects when we think misinterpretation is possible. Often such a misinterpretation has been the cause of larger misunderstanding. Because we fear falling into the trap of dealing with "Romantic Spain," we avoid altogether the most interesting and complex issues which Andalusian culture presents for our enrichment.

Orientalism, by which I mean the cultural and ethnological influence of the eastern Mediterranean and the Near East, is such a phenomenon. Dumas could get away with saying that Africa began at the Pyrenees only if he meant that Europe stopped there. If Africa began at the Pyrenees, it was because French influence proved insufficient to overcome Spain's ancient heritage, not because Spain is African. Yet Andalucía, while not African, is nevertheless the most Oriental land in western Europe. To deny the importance of African and Oriental influence in Andalucía is to fail to read history, but to claim that all Spain was African is equally myopic, not to say brutish. The journey to Santiago was for centuries, and still is, as holy a pilgrimage as a journey to Rome, and in the twelfth century the Christian struggle against the Moslems was declared a Crusade.

The Africanization, or Europeanization, of Spain brings up a division as ancient as Celts and Iberians, and one that seems to need constant reinterpretation by each generation. While we cannot solve the conflict, we can examine briefly the extent to which Andalucía was influenced by Africa and the Near East. If we bear in mind that Andalucía sometimes exceeded its boundaries geographically and that it often extended its sphere of influence far beyond those boundaries, then we can understand why the Andalusian stereotype, the *pandereta,* is so often, and so fallaciously, taken to represent all of Spain. The cultural sphere of Andalucía was at times so pervasive that the part colored the whole. Yet such has been the prejudice against the East, the Moslem, the African, the Oriental, that the interpretation of that influence has largely been ignored or tossed off as exoticism and relegated to the brilliant superficiality of the *pandereta.*

The traveler sees the *pandereta,* the *Ballet of Sevilla,* the dark-eyed women, and takes the superficial part for the whole, accepting the shallowest synecdoche as proof of what he came seeking in the first place. And many Spaniards, embarrassed by the "exotic" image of their country, and ashamed at their lack of "progress," ignore or deny the complex cultural heritage—the oldest in the Western world—that lies beneath the glittering exterior, and thus do little to explain it or understand it themselves. Worse yet, they often package that glittering exterior and sell it to tourists, thereby perpetuating the worst in themselves by turning their culture into an article for consumption and indirectly insulting the misguided tourists, who remain unaware of the insult and quite happy with gay Spain, especially Andalucía.

How many tourists leave Córdoba aware that St. Thomas of Aquinas could probably never have begun to solve the eternally vexing problem of faith and reason without the philosophical commentaries of two of her sons, Maimonides, a Jew, and Averroes, a Moslem? And how many understand that the so-called Renaissance began in Andalucía long before it did in Italy? Looking at the layers of Oriental culture in Andalucía, we can understand why it is so different and why it has been so misunderstood or misinterpreted.

The Moslems were the largest Orientalizing group in Andalucía, although they are usually thought of as the only one. Actually, the Moslems reintroduced an Arabic or Semitic tongue into Andalucía just as they reintroduced the influence of the Near East into a culture that had already been substantially Orientalized for at least two millenniums.

The Iberians were a "Mediterranean" type of uncertain origin, and, although there is some reason to believe they may have come, at least in part, from the East, no evidence exists that allows us to be certain. On the other hand, Eastern contacts with Andalucía during the third millennium are certain, and early Aegeans began arriv-

ing at Almería in the fourth or fifth millennium. During the Bronze
Age of the second millennium, trade strengthened since Andalucía
was, and is, very rich in copper, a commodity scarce in the eastern
Mediterranean. Whether Tartessos already existed as a loose tribal
kingdom or federation stretching from the Algarve in the south of
Portugal to Almería in eastern Andalucía or whether this Eastern
trade served to stimulate the formation of Tartessos is open to debate,
but close parallels in jewelry, swords, daggers, and other pieces
establish beyond doubt strong contacts between early Andalusian
cultures and early Aegean cultures.

The mineral wealth of Andalucía not only attracted the attention of the early Aegeans, it also drew the Phoenicians and the
Israelites of Solomon, who had established a bond with Hiram, king
of Tyre. The Phoenicians established at least a trading post at Gadir,
today Cádiz, before 1000 B.C., and may have been trading long
before that as a cylinder seal found near Málaga and dated about
1400 B.C. suggests. The historical date of the founding of the city
is about 1100 B.C., and, although substantial archaeological evidence
is lacking until the eighth century, the date 1100 B.C. is generally
believed to be accurate. From the eighth century, in any case, the
archaeological evidence shows a number of Phoenician and Greek
settlements on the Atlantic and on the Mediterranean coasts of Spain.
It also indicates that Andalucía, although probably not the rest of
Spain, was greatly influenced by these Semitic traders and colonizers,
as well as to a lesser extent by the Greeks, particularly the Phocaeans
from Asia Minor, who traded in Andalucía until the Carthaginians
forced them out around 535 B.C.

The Phoenicians, especially the Tyrians and their colonists, the
Carthaginians, settled and traded in Andalucía until the Romans
finally took Andalucía from Carthage in 206 B.C. Such was their
influence that by Roman times little was left of the indigenous
tongues, and from Cádiz to Almería the inhabitants spoke a Semitic
language, at first Canaanitic or Phoenician, followed by a Carthaginian dialect. Semitic writing was used into Roman times, as coins
from the area clearly substantiate.

The Carthaginian Empire across the north of Africa, which connected Egypt and the East with the western Mediterranean, also introduced another Semitic element into Spain. By the fourth century
B.C., the Jews, already well dispersed, were firmly established as
traders throughout the Carthaginian territory, including Gadir and

the Mediterranean coast of Spain. Under the Romans a large Jewish colony of wine and olive growers flourished in Andalucía. In time these Jews, known as Sephardim, became, especially under the tolerant Moslems, one of the most important Jewish populations of Europe.

During Roman times the Oriental and African nature of Andalucía, which the Romans called Baetica, was quite evident. Gadir, the Punic city, became Gades, Roman in name but retaining much of her Eastern identity. As Ford wrote, "It is quite clear that Cadiz was the eldest daughter of Tyre" (p. 323). While Gades became thoroughly Romanized, she was no mere copy of Rome. Ford waxes eloquent as he gives away the Roman propensity for the Hispanophile Imperative: "Gades was the great lie and lion of antiquity; nothing was too absurd for the classical handbooks. It was their Venice, or Paris; the centre of sensual civilization, the purveyor of gastronomy, etc. Italy imported from it those *improbae Gaditanae,* whose lascivious dances were of Oriental origin, and still exist in the *Romalis* of the Andalucian gypsies" (p. 315). The Roman poet Avienus, writing around A.D. 400, tells of still seeing the yearly rites of Hercules performed there, an allusion to the famous temple near Cádiz dedicated to the Phoenician Hercules, often called Melkart.[7] There were also temples to Astarte, the Phoenician fertility goddess, known as Tanit by the Carthaginians, and to Baal-Hammon, named Kronos by the Greeks and Saturn by the Romans. All over Andalucía existed shrines and temples to Eastern divinities, including among many others the Egyptian Isis, the Asian Earth Mother Cybele, and Mithra, the great Persian god whose cult rivaled the popularity of Christianity in the late years of the Empire.

Strabo, citing earlier sources from the first century B.C., calls the people from Cádiz, Phoenicians (3. 5. 8); the people living along what is today the Costa del Sol were sometimes referred to as Blastophoenicians or Libyophoenicians. Málaga, according to Strabo, had a Phoenician plan and a large market that traded with Numidians and other nomads from Africa (3. 4. 2). Málaga also had a large Syrian colony and during the Roman Empire carried on an intense trade with Syria and Palestine and other points south and east, as did Cádiz.

By the beginning of Christian times, Andalucía was a land of diversity. As Julio Caro Baroja, the great Spanish ethnologist, has indicated, it comprised Africans, Phoenicians, Romans, Greeks, and

indigenous tribes, including Celts. He makes the important observation that while ethnically Andalucía has long been a mixture of
European, African, and Asian elements, both the historical sources
and the archaeological finds reflect the higher cultures of the latter
groups. In his fundamental ethnological essay, *Los pueblos de
España,* he also insists on two points which concern us and which
are in basic agreement with Ortega's thesis. He points out how little
the Andalucía of our times differs in many regards from the Andalucía of antiquity, and he stresses the power of absorption of the
original culture of Andalucía.[8] Thus constant contact with later "barbarian" cultures did not cause the diminution of the older, higher
culture but rather its diffusion in such a way that the original culture
was continued and amplified. In our own culture, which believes that
material progress is the best measure of worth, this radical Andalusian conservatism may seem incomprehensible or, at best, stymied;
yet that is precisely what gives it its unique identity. As Caro Baroja
eloquently expresses it, an Andalusian village is a living museum
stretching from the Neolithic to the present (2. 133). Cave cultures,
latifundismo, the Andalusian farms known as *cortijos,* the dancing
of those *improbae Gaditanae* Ford mentioned (literally, the wicked
girls of Cádiz), the architecture and way of life of remote areas such
as the Alpujarras, or the twisting villages of the mountains around
Ronda, the bandits who roamed those mountains, the peculiar
customs and folklore, including "pagan" practices, the religious processions and pilgrimages, the ritual of *toreo,* the methods of fishing
in the Mediterranean and the Atlantic, even the peculiar beliefs about
courtship that exist in rural areas today—all these elements existed
in one fashion or another and are documentable from antiquity.
Finally he concludes that rather than the later African influences,
by which he means Berber, what is at work in Andalucía that we
notice as peculiar to Andalucía, is the survival of many traces of
earlier Semitic and eastern Mediterranean cultures. As Ford wrote,
"nowhere is *race* more evident" (p. 220).

Andalucía suffered rather less than most of Europe during the
invasions of Germanic barbarians. Although the Vandals and the
Alans passed through on their way to North Africa, none of the tribes
remained in Andalucía for long. The Visigoths, who were the most
Romanized and the least uncivilized of all the Germanic tribes, took
over most of Spain. But they did not penetrate Andalucía to any
degree until 571, when they took Córdoba, and they did not com-

plete their conquest (if indeed it can be called a conquest) until about 616, less than a century before the Moslem invasion.

In the meantime Roman Andalucía continued to survive, and the Byzantines used parts of Andalucía as a base to try to recapture the Western Empire from 554 until the Visigoths finally expelled them in 631. During this period, Andalucía remained one of the most civilized parts of western Europe, maintaining trade and close association with North Africa and the Eastern Empire. As usual the Andalusians looked not to the north but to Africa and Asia for commerce and culture. Although the old Roman structure of governance collapsed and the populace found itself huddling around the great surviving Roman *latifundia* for protection, the Andalusians did not suffer the ravages of the barbarians nor mix with them to any appreciable degree.

From 711 to 714 the Moslems conquered Spain and threatened Europe; finally in 732 at Poitiers the Franks delivered the Moslems a decisive defeat. Within Spain the Visigothic superstructure collapsed at once, and in Andalucía the Romanized population and the Hispanic Jews openly welcomed and collaborated with the new invaders. All over Spain much of the population converted to the Moslem religion, but, as we might expect, the highest number of conversions — the majority of the population — occurred in Andalucía. There the Moslems, initially under the enlightened leadership of the aristocratic Umayyad dynasty, set about creating, or recreating, the highest culture in the West, the only high culture in Europe at the time and one that rivaled those of Constantinople, Damascus, and Bagdad. In al-Andalus, which extended its influence as far as Toledo, Zaragoza, and Valencia, there were no "Dark Ages," and Córdoba, the new Moslem capital, became one of the most splendid and enlightened cities in the world. From the beginning of the eighth century until the end of the fifteenth, the Moslem culture of al-Andalus introduced into Europe major advances in philosophy, theology, astronomy, mathematics, economics, agriculture, architecture, medicine, and science that became standards for European culture. Al-Andalus, especially in the tenth, eleventh, and twelfth centuries, was no mere western extremity of Islam; rather it was the western core of the main high culture of its time. As Baetica had been one of the centers of culture of the Roman Empire, in spite of its extreme geographical position, so al-Andalus became a center of learning and culture for Islam and the world.

But the mere brilliance of Hispano-Moslem civilization is not the main point, and it is well enough known not to need extensive argument. On the other hand, the fact that an Oriental civilization in the extreme West was settled upon a land already Orientalized for an indeterminately long time, but historically verifiable from about 1000 B.C. on, is not sufficiently appreciated. Professor Stanley Payne reasons in his excellent history of Spain that the Hispanic peninsula was the only major part of Europe that was Islamized, "torn out of the matrix of western Christendom," as he phrases it.[9] And he believes that all the culture, including religion, was not only completely Oriental but that it lacked any Hispanic precedents. While that may be true enough of most of Spain, surely the early Aegean, the Phoenician, the Carthaginian, the Jewish, and the Byzantine layers of what was to become the heart of al-Andalus provide unparalleled Oriental precedents. Professor Payne believes the culture of al-Andalus was derivative and completely Oriental in inspiration. Perhaps it was, at least to the extent that the *jihad,* the peculiar and dynamic crusade of the Moslems, provided the impetus for the push into Europe. Yet the unique nature of the culture of al-Andalus, the peculiar flowering of the Caliphate of Córdoba, and the later exquisite refinements of the civilization of the Nasrids of Granada in the fourteenth and fifteenth centuries do not seem to be merely derivative and inspired from the other end of the Mediterranean. Surely it is not just accidental that the finest culture of Islam outside the Near East occurred precisely in the most western, yet highly Orientalized, territory that the Moslems conquered.

Some six hundred years before successive Moslem *razzias* reached Europe, Juvenal had written:

> *Omnibus in terris quae sunt a Gadibus usque*
> *Auroram et Gangem. . . .*
>
> In all the lands which reach from Gades
> to the Ganges and the dawn. . . .[10]

The power of Islam reached from Cádiz to the Ganges, from the dawn to the place where the ancients thought the sun sank hissing into the ocean. Of all that land why was al-Andalus so favored? Richard Ford knew and expressed it in his characteristic style, an inimitable mixture of classical erudition and Romantic charm:

> . . . the land overflows with oil and wine. The vines of Xerez,
> the olives of Seville, and the fruits of Malaga are unequalled.

The yellow plains, girdled by the green sea, bask in the sunshine, like a topaz set around with emeralds. Strabo could find
not better panegyric for the Elysian fields of Andalucía, than
by quoting the charming description of the father of poetry
('Od.' Δ, 563): and here the classics following his example, placed
the Gardens of the Blessed, and these afterwards became the
real paradise, the new and favored world of the Oriental. Here
the children of Damascus rioted in a European Arabia Felix.
On the fame of the conquest reaching the East, many tribes
abandoned Syria to settle in Andalucía, just as the Spaniards
afterwards emigrated to the golden S. America.

. . . it was here, in a congenial soil, that the Oriental took
the deepest root. Here he has left the noblest traces of power,
taste, and intelligence — here he made his last desperate struggle. [P. 225]

As Caro Baroja so wisely pointed out, there is more to the notion
of "congenial soil" than first glance would reveal. The Moslem occupation of the south of Spain by Arabs, Syrians, and Berbers merely
added more layers of Eastern culture upon an already thoroughly
Orientalized land. If Eastern ideas took root it was because the soil
had been prepared over and again.

From the time the Christian conquest of al-Andalus was com-
pleted up until quite recently, there existed a strong bias against
anything Eastern that extended as far back as investigation had taken
place. In *South from Granada,* Gerald Brenan, the most perceptive
English Hispanophile of the twentieth century, writes, for example,
of the bitter complaints of the great Belgian archaeologist, Louis
Siret, who spent fifty years digging in the province of Almería:

Denigration of the Phoenicians, he declared, had become a
mania with some people. One could call it the anti-Semitism
of the learned. And it was useless to argue about it. The only
facts to which archeologists paid any attention were their own
envies and jealousies. *"Ce n'est pas une science, l'archéologie,
c'est un combat à mort."*[11]

This anti-Eastern bias was both Spanish and Catholic within
Spain and European and Christian without. Hispano-Moslem culture
became one of the main targets for the expanding Spanish Christians. What for centuries had been a relationship of rivalry and
exchange — in the eleventh century many of the vassals of El Cid and
many of his personal friends were Moslems — turned sour and became
a so-called Holy War to rid Spain of the Moslem plague. The
Castilian society that waged this nationalistic crusade employed the

Inquisition for the same nationalistic ends in persecuting the Hispanic Jews. The *moriscos,* as the Moslems who converted and attempted to live under Christian rule were called, and the *marranos,* as the Jews who pretended to convert to Christianity were known (the word actually means "pig"), became the special scapegoats apparently necessary for Castilian supremacy in Spain. The Semitic and Hamito-Semitic blood of the exiled and the burned, the persecuted and the slaughtered, became the agglutinant that held together the Spanish Empire until it fell of its own weight, in part because it had destroyed its tradesmen, merchants, and economists in the purges of non-Christian elements.

From a historical and Andalusian point of view, the splendid Oriental society stretching from the time of Tartessos to that of the Nasrids and bridging nearly three millenniums, ended in 1492 when the Catholic sovereigns, Fernando and Isabel, took Granada and began, under the guidance of Cardinal Cisneros, to force the population to become Christian. The point is not the persecution, which must be understood, and is understood today largely owing to the heroic scholarship of Américo Castro, but the concurrent lack of esteem that all things Eastern, Semitic, Arabic, or Moorish suffered as a result of this double persecution, which ultimately contributed substantially to the wrecking of the largest empire ever assembled and to the downfall of the first nationalistic power in Europe. Renewed persecutions of the Jews and the rise of the Turks, a new Eastern menace, helped extend the prejudice all across Europe. The peculiar animosity between the British and the Spanish aggravated the situation, and accusations about Spanish cruelty, which grew into a kind of Hispanophobia known as the "Black Legend," made the Spaniards even more determined to demonstrate the purity, with no Eastern taint, of their "old Christian" blood.

There are some intriguing ironies which render this story more tolerable, not the least amusing of which is the probability, explored minutely by Gerald Brenan in his study *St. John of the Cross,* that both Saint John and Saint Teresa, the great Spanish mystics, were of Jewish origin. Yet surely the greatest irony is the one that Américo Castro proposes in all of his work, which radically reoriented Spanish historical and cultural studies. Spain, as a nation, cannot be understood properly, Castro believed, either in medieval times or today without taking fully into account precisely those elements which the Spanish nation began systematically purging in 1492. Since 1492 Christian Spain had vainly attempted to explain itself without those non-Christian elements, as though they had existed only for conquering and purging. Castro showed, intuitively at times, and tenaciously over his long and distinguished career, that Christian Spain, all Spain, owed its character, its definition as a nation and as a people, to all three "peoples of the Book": Christians, Moslems, and Jews.[12] What makes Spain so radically different from the rest of Europe is precisely that extra element of Orientalism that held sway in the southern part for so long. Foreign writers recognized at once what was different although they often did not understand why: thus Dumas's "Africa begins at the Pyrenees." Richard Ford, on the other hand, was able to understand, sometimes with amazing lucidity, what nationalism and conservative Catholicism kept many Spaniards blind to for centuries.

Castro did not, and I do not, make the point that all Spanish civilization is due to Oriental influence. I do believe that the decisive Oriental influence in Andalucía, still largely misunderstood or overlooked, especially as that Oriental influence can be interpreted as conservative and syncretistic, needs a great deal more attention. The main point about Moslem culture—and Castro does not make this point—is not that it was the major Oriental influence in Andalucía. The main point is that, since it was an Oriental culture superimposed on an old civilization already extensively Orientalized, it did not in the process of that superimposition eradicate the culture which was already established there. Andalucía, syncretistic, absorptive, already old, passive (as Ortega says), absorbed and enriched the new culture even when that culture became at times violent, puritanical, and ruthless, as in the case of the African invasions by the Almoravids and Almohads in the eleventh and twelfth centuries.

One reason for the brilliance of al-Andalus was surely the implanation of a dynamic society on an old and sophisticated culture. Al-Andalus did not destroy that existing culture; it revitalized it in a synergistic process responsible for a civilization unique in its time. When the seeds of Islam fell on the sands of the desert, they grew because they were hardy, young, and dynamic, but when they fell on the already fertile ground of Andalucía they created the anomaly of an autochthonous flowering in the West of an Eastern civilization.

The final layer of Oriental influence has caused much controversy and more misunderstanding, yet in some ways it proves the

perseverance of the previous layers. Sometime in the late 1400s
caravans of Gypsies, dark-eyed and dark-skinned nomads of uncertain but most likely Hindu provenance, speaking a primitive and still
pure form of Sanskrit, wandered into Spain. Eventually thousands
of them ended their mysterious and still unexplained *Völkerwan-
derung,* from India and the dawn to Andalucía, by forgetting their
own tongue and settling down, anathema to their nomadic race, in
the caves of Granada and Guadix and the Gypsy quarters of Sevilla,
Jerez, and Cádiz.[13] The Gypsies spread over Europe and eventually
over the globe, yet the Andalusian Gypsies became more sedentary
than the rest, and subsequently famous as *flamenco* artists.

Gypsies in Andalucía are more assimilated than anywhere in
the world; they have become so much a part of Andalucía, so much
like Andalusians and so unlike other Gypsies, that some authorities
think they have been in Andalucía longer than Gypsies in other parts
of Spain, having arrived in earlier migrations. Some colorful theories
have been engendered by such speculation, the most colorful of which
is surely that the Andalusian Gypsies are Sumerians or Hittites
displaced by the Sea Peoples and brought to Gadir by the Phoenicians.[14] Such speculation, far-fetched as it is, illustrates the extent
to which Andalusian Gypsies are considered an ancient and integral
part of Andalusian culture. Many believe there was an earlier African
migration of Gypsies, but we have yet to see much evidence for that
theory. In all probability they arrived in Andalucía in the late 1400s
and found themselves at home in a land they had never seen before.
The Gypsies put down roots in Andalucía precisely because it was
the most Oriental and atavistic place they had seen since they left
the Orient.

Although they were officially persecuted, they remained in Andalucía and became so integral a part of the culture that they gave
up their language — today many Andalusian Gypsies only know a
few words of even their Spanish dialect, *caló* — and their nomadic
ways. They also mixed with the Andalusians to such an extent that
many Gypsies are indistinguishable from Andalusians. What is
perhaps more revealing is that many Andalusians who are *not* Gypsies, resemble Gypsies.

Consideration of the Gypsies brings us back, full circle, to the
pandereta. What is difficult to ascertain is the extent to which the
Gypsy has become "Andalusianized" and the extent to which the Andalusian has become "Gypsified." Ricardo Molina, the late poet and
erudite student of Andalucía, Gypsies, and *flamenco,* believed the

peculiar style the Andalusians developed, particularly by the nineteenth century, took on a Gypsy cast. The Gypsies, he wrote, identified so thoroughly with Andalucía and with the Andalusian way
of life that they became more Andalusian than the Andalusians.[15]
In other words, they stylized and externalized, particularly in *flamenco*, the ancient sense of life latent, or dormant, in Andalusian culture
from its beginning. This idea meshes with Ortega's theory perfectly,
yet Ortega failed to make the Gypsy connection. He knew that
popular theater and *toreo* in the eighteenth and nineteenth centuries
were the source for the superbly popular sense of style, known as
majismo, in the people of Madrid, but he did not realize, or admit,
that *flamenco* and *toreo* in Andalucía formed an identical and more
primary source.[16]

   In the eighteenth and nineteenth centuries the Spanish aristocracy and court lacked initiative and vitality, and Spanish high culture
became at best a poor copy of *le beau monde* across the Pyrenees.
While the aristocracy danced the latest minuet from Versailles, the
common people, especially in Madrid, created an inimitable spectacle in the streets which was to define their character. Lacking
models from above they created their own style and their own popular heroes, the *majos,* so characteristically painted by Goya.
Cloaked in heavy, tasseled capes and wide-brimmed hats, arrogant
and elegant in their tight pants and long black curls, these *majos*
were at once the Romantic archetype of the Spaniard and the collective response of the lower classes to a sterile society above them.
Ortega believed correctly that the models for these types came from
popular theater and from the *toreros.* Yet he failed to realize that
many of the *toreros* were Andalusians who had been in close association with *flamencos,* (in other words, with the Andalusian Gypsies),
in Sevilla, in Ronda, and in Jerez. He knew and wrote with great
intuition that those who did not understand the sociohistorical significance of *toreo,* could not understand Spanish history or culture
from 1650 to the present (6:588). Yet somehow he failed to realize
that *toreo* and *flamenco* had the same inseparable source in Andalusian culture and that a few select families of Gypsies had become
the finest stylists not just of *flamenco* but of *toreo* as well. The
majismo of Madrid undoubtedly drew from the Andalusian sense
of *majismo,* and if Ricardo Molina is correct that Andalusian
popular culture took on a Gypsy color, then it is no less true that
popular culture all over Spain became somewhat *flamenca.*

   Ortega could see that Andalusian culture always tended to re-

duce itself to its original essence, and he could see just how popular
and stylized Spanish culture had become. But he refused to make,
or merely did not see, the connection between the two. Yet the connection between the original essence of the culture and the stylized
nature of that culture was ironically tantamount to what he posited
in his "Theory of Andalucía" as the *Ballet of Sevilla* and the
"millenary profile." When the Gypsies arrived in Andalucía they
found an already ancient sense of style at work that must have appealed to them or been very familiar to them at least. To that sense
of style, millenary, atavistic, and Oriental, some of them added their
own profound sense of style — and the interpretative ability for which
they are famous everywhere — which was also millenary, atavistic,
and Oriental. Certain groups of these Gypsies, a small artistic minori-
ty to be sure, but a pervasively influential one nevertheless, stylized
the already stylized culture of Andalucía. This quintessentialized style
lies at the core of the Hispanic sense of popular art. Its misinterpretation or misunderstanding, so frequently the case, produces
endless variations of the *pandereta*. Its rare proper interpretation produces in *toreo* and in *flamenco* the possibility for a kind of
catharsis, perhaps the only true catharsis left in modern Western
culture.

Substantial sociohistorical reasons for this aesthetic phenomenon exist, the major one being the stagnant nature of Andalusian
culture from the 1500s on. We have seen the extent to which Andalusian culture from its beginnings to 1492 was influenced from the
East. After 1492 it was Christianized and Westernized, at least in
theory. In fact, little happened, especially in rural regions, and in
mountainous zones such as the Serranía de Cádiz and the Serranía
de Ronda and in the high mountains of the Alpujarra on the south
flank of the Sierra Nevada, clandestine groups formed and hid out,
living their lives in a kind of hybrid underground culture. Many of
them were Gypsies who refused to abandon their nomadic ways and
tried to escape constant persecutions. Some were *moriscos* who went
underground after 1609 when they were all ordered deported. Some
were New Christians, Jews who had converted but were suspected
of being secret Judaizers. Others were mere adventurers or bandits,
even — according to some of the promulgations against them — monks
and nuns who had abandoned their religious callings to take up the
unorthodox life of renegades. Out of this underground culture of
Gypsies, bandits, smugglers, and adventurers and out of the Gypsy

quarters of Sevilla, Jerez, Cádiz, and Granada, grew the popular music — the ageless folk music of the Andalusians ranging back to the time of Gadir and Tartessos, especially as interpreted and modified by the Gypsies — known as *flamenco*. The British sociologist Julian Pitt-Rivers did a sociological study, published in 1954, of a mountain town of the Serranía de Ronda — Grazalema — which today is considered a classic. *The People of the Sierra* made quite clear that the social structure of this *pueblo* still possessed many tribal qualities and that in many respects its governance was closer to an ancient Greek *polis* than to a modern town. The most germane facet of the study was Pitt-Rivers's contention that despite the radical changes in Spain between 1752 and 1952 (he used the censuses of 1752, 1852, and 1952 for his statistics), in the *pueblo* virtually nothing had changed. The same ancient authority was still based on collective social values, the acceptance of custom, and sanction by public criticism. Contained within a system of self-governance independent of and at times in conflict with the normative external laws of the national system, it still provided (as it had two hundred years before, or had the *pueblo* existed then, two thousand years before), the basis for social conduct. The Spanish sociologist Álvaro Fernández Suárez, in his study *España: Árbol vivo,* came to similar conclusions about Andalucía, the sociology of which depended on attitudes formed, in his opinion, by superimposing one culture upon another in a chain reaching back to the earliest Mediterranean civilizations. Gerald Brenan, not unlike his predecessor Richard Ford, although without Ford's occasional exaggerations, observed, discussed, and documented in some detail in his *South from Granada* the extent to which pagan and ancient customs still exist in Andalucía.[17]

From the Middle Ages to the twentieth century, there was probably less material progress per capita in Andalucía than anywhere in Europe. When Fernando III and other Castilian kings won large areas from the Moslems, they tended to give away province-sized estates to their ablest knights. Much of Andalucía, as a consequence, was colonized rather than settled by Castilla, and the resulting *latifundia,* passed down by primogeniture, remained a constant factor in the life of the Andalusian peasants, keeping them in continual and often devastating poverty.

The lower classes (the great majority of the population) remained alienated from their Castilian conquerors and ignored as much as possible the subsequent laws that the Church-State (as unified in the Castilian mind as they are separate in the Anglo-Saxon) imposed upon them. The landowners, the Church, and the government elicited no sympathy, and quite frequently they elicited hatred and opposition. The substructure of Andalucía became amenable to, and often openly (or covertly when necessary) sympathetic to, the culture of bandits, smugglers, Gypsies, and adventurers who, particularly in the eighteenth and nineteenth centuries, became famous as the Romantics flocked to Spain to observe them and spread their misunderstood and usually superficial image abroad in the rest of Europe.

One thing many Andalusians had in common, aside from their ancient cultural heritage, was poverty or a lack of material well-being, often accompanied by persecution. Yet what they lacked in material goods they seem to have made up for in a peculiarly tenacious sense of personal worth and individualism that made them seem especially "noble" or "dignified." Ford does not hesitate in describing the Spanish peasantry as a "gay, good-humored, temperate peasantry, the finest in the world, free, manly, and independent" (p. 120), while at the same time maintaining that Andalucía is the seat of all matters in popular culture: "Andalucia is the headquarters of all this, and the cradle of the most eminent professors, who in the other provinces become stars, patterns, models, the observed of all observers, and the envy and admiration of their applauding countrymen" (p. 223).

The kind of class war and purgation that occurred in France did not take place in Spain. The French Revolution frightened the Spanish monarchy and aristocracy badly, and instead of reform the Spaniards got political persecution and occupation by the armies of the Holy Alliance to wipe out opposition. Nor did Spain undergo the Industrial Revolution. The collapse of the Empire bankrupted the country, and virtually no middle class emerged, except in the largest cities. Even agrarian reform usually backfired, especially in Andalucía where it was needed most, serving to make the rich richer and the poor poorer. No progress came to Andalucía and the land of *María Santísima* remained much as it had always been, a pristine paradise owned and ruled by an often absent handful of landed aristocrats.

As a result of all these factors — centuries of Eastern cultural and ethnographical influence, persecutions, poverty, and the lack of any material progress — Andalucía became a kind of continuum for a way of life that had ceased to exist in the modern world. Little wonder then that the Romantics were so attracted to it, so compelled to write about it, correctly or incorrectly, so fascinated by its charm, its paradoxes, and its delights. And little wonder that the Andalusians themselves created their own popular culture. As Europe moved from the Enlightenment into the modern age, Spain remained constant and Andalucía seemed, perhaps only by contrast, but perhaps by some collective cultural instinct, almost to move backward.

As Europe and the United States developed materialist societies and notions of progress, inventing machinery, revolutionizing agriculture, building opera houses, writing grand novels for the new and prospering bourgeoisie, Spain stood still, and the Andalusian people created or re-created out of the atavistic recesses of their cultural consciousness a new ritual slaying of the bull-god and the cathartic liturgy of *cante jondo,* creations which in time came to affect the whole country and fix a particular image of Spain in the mind of the rest of the world. The Andalusian peasantry and urban lower classes, and certain of the Gypsies and the bandits, became the self-conscious creators of, and simultaneously the subjects of, a unique popular style and art.

Ortega notwithstanding, these creative processes were intimately bound together, as Richard Ford had recognized a century before. Telling of the *ladrones,* "highwaymen," he wrote:

> Their dress is for the most part very rich and in the highest style of *"aficion,"* "the fancy;" they are the envy and models of the lower classes of Andalucians, being arrayed after the fashion of the smuggler, *"contrabandista,"* or the bull-fighter, *"torero,"* or in a word, the *"majo,"* or dandy, who, being peculiar to the south of Spain, will be more properly described in the section on Andalucia, which is the home and headquarters of all those who aspire to the elegant accomplishments and professions to which we have just alluded. [P. 64]

Ford's recognition of this Andalusian phenomenon and his understanding and ability to write of it were not the product of superficial observation. In spite of occasional exaggeration and certain flights of fancy or language, Ford knew extremely well what he was writing about. Gerald Brenan has accorded him the singular honor of naming him, in his prologue to a Spanish edition of Ford's work, *el primer hispanófilo.*[18]

Ford was not the only observer of the peculiar nature of the Andalusian genius. Not surprisingly, the Andalusian artists, especially the poets and painters of our century, have understood perfectly the recondite nature of their culture and its transcendent and universal meaning. Historically, Andalucía's older culture has produced an understandably high proportion of great artists. And the same holds true in our time. The great poet Antonio Machado came from Sevilla. Juan Ramón Jiménez, who was awarded a Nobel Prize in Literature in 1956, was from the province of Huelva. Picasso came from Málaga, as did Vicente Aleixandre, Spain's newest Nobel laureate. And Federico García Lorca, who is gradually becoming appreciated as one of the consummate artists of our time, was born near Granada.

The preponderance of artists from Andalucía was so great during the brilliant period of the late 1920s in Madrid that it caused some resentment among the non-Andalusians. In its title, *Un Chien andalou,* Salvador Dalí and Luis Buñuel's surrealist film reveals some of that resentment. In spite of the bad feelings, the artists of Andalucía, and others who were not Andalusian but who were nonetheless appreciative, celebrated its ancient, pantheistic, unmodern, non-Western way of life. In the sense that artists are seers, they saw the dangers inherent in what had become the Western way of life and were glad in some ways not to be a part of it. Shortly after the announcement of his Nobel Prize, Aleixandre said that he had never felt Castilian, in spite of having spent his whole adult life in Madrid, but Andalusian and Mediterranean. Much of modern Spanish art has been pointedly antirational and antimaterialistic, but the works of Lorca, of Aleixandre, of Picasso have been especially so.

Lorca's sense of art was hieratic, sensual, and mythic, and his work, including several superb essays on *flamenco* and the Andalusian sense of art, is the finest embodiment we have of the entire Andalusian phenomenon. His exaggerated and exquisitely attuned sense of life and death enabled him to stylize brilliantly the Andalusian sense of high art, poetry, music, and theater. And he made the popular arts, with which he was also perfectly in touch, one of his most characteristic subjects. Risking criticism and risking the dangerous stereotype of the *pandereta,* he presented Andalucía as a mythical and magic world that reverberated with all the ancient echoes his poetic genius could conjure. *Toreo* became an "authentic religous drama."[19] *Cante jondo* was folksong submerged in an ancient people's "river of voice" (1:1066), which he likened to a "blind nightingale" plaining in the infinite "blue night" of the Andalusian countryside (1:1015). The Gypsies, elevated to their highest artistic abstraction by his mythical touch, became the most profound and aristocratic element of Andalucía, the most representative of the Andalusian way of being, the guardians of "the embers, the blood and the alphabet of universal and Andalusian truth" (1:1114).

Lorca, Picasso, Aleixandre, Juan Ramón Jiménez and others dug beneath the glittering superficiality of the *pandereta*. What they found and what they expressed was nothing more nor less than the Andalusian earth itself, the unchanged fertile land of Andalucía — source and substance of everything they were — preserved, to use Caro Baroja's words, like a living museum.

Anyone who looks at Picasso's art in this light, or delves into the pantheistic world of Aleixandre's poetry, or the theogonic universe of Lorca's creations, cannot fail to be impressed with the sense of chthonian reality which surfaces within their works. As Andalucía's great and universal artists, they were naturally enough Andalucía's great and universal interpreters, a fact of which they were all very well aware. Juan Ramón Jiménez wrote once to Lorca's sister, Isabel, that the Andalusians need to love Andalucía so much that Andalucía spills over into the rest of the world, not to universalize Andalucía but to "Andalusicize" the rest.[20]

In 1937, the year after Lorca was assassinated, Aleixandre wrote a superb description portraying Lorca precisely in the chthonian terms which characterized Lorca's work as well as Aleixandre's own thoroughly Andalusian sense of art. His description of Lorca is unmatchable precisely because he understood the nature of Lorca's genius from the inside:

> I have seen him in the latest nights suddenly looming over some mysterious rail, when the moon conformed with him and silvered his face; and I felt that his arms were propped in the air, but that his feet were sunken in time, in the centuries, in the remotest roots of the Spanish earth — I do not know how deep — in search of that profound wisdom which flamed in his eyes, which burned on his lips, which turned his brow incandescent with inspiration. No, he was no child then. How old, how old and how "ancient," how fabled and mythic! I mean no irreverence by this comparison: only some old *flamenco* singer, only some ancient dancer, already turned into statues of stone, could be compared to him. Only an ageless, remote Andalu-

sian mountain, looming against a noctural sky, could be likened
to him. . . .
I spoke before of his nocturnal visage steeped in moonlight,
turning almost yellow like stone, petrified as though by some
ancient grief. "What ails you, my son?" the moon would seem
to ask. "The earth ails me, the earth and men, human flesh and
the human soul, mine and those of others, which are one with
mine." . . .
The poet is perhaps the being who lacks corporal limits. His
long and sudden silences had about them something of the
silence of a river, and in the late hour, dark as a broad river
you could sense flowing, flowing, passing through him, through
his body and soul, blood, remembrances, grief, the beating of
other hearts and other beings that were he himself in that instant, the way the river is all the waters that give it body but
not limit. The mute hour of Federico was the hour of the poet,
the hour of solitude, of the generous solitude when the poet
senses he is the expression of all men.[21]

What is perhaps most surprising from the point of view of our
culture is that Aleixandre was not so much poeticizing his description of Lorca as he was attempting to describe the precise process
of creation that characterized Lorca's personality and his work. Odd
as it may sound, Lorca affirmed and often reiterated the *realistic*
aspects of his works, and he maintained firmly that all his poetic
creations were based on real people. What may seem fanciful and
often quite Romantic to us now, in rural Andalucía at the turn of
the century when Lorca was growing up was the stuff of everyday life.

Pedro Salinas, a poet and critic of Lorca's and Aleixandre's
group, has written an excellent description of that peculiar reality
on which Lorca drew so heavily for his creations. Although Salinas
intentionally and correctly refers to Spain in his essay, "Lorca and
the Poetry of Death," it is clear enough that he did not consider the
capital of this special culture to be Madrid. In comparing the matter of death in the poetry of Rilke and of Lorca, he wrote:

But Lorca, who expresses the same feeling for death with an
undoubted originality and personal accent, has not had to search
for it through processes of intellectual speculation along the innermost galleries of the soul. He discovers it all around him,
in the native air that gives him breath, in the singing of the servants in his house, in books written in his tongue, in the churches
of his city; he finds it in all his individual personality that has
to do with people, with the inheritance of the past. Lorca was
born in a country that for centuries has been living out a special
kind of culture that I call the "culture of death."[22]

Salinas had in mind no cult of death, nor denial of life. Quite the contrary, it is precisely the positive and constant acceptance of death that creates the awareness of life and gives it its fullest meaning. In discussing this culture of death he cited as the best examples of its popular spirit Holy Week and the Fair as celebrated in Sevilla:

> The first is a religious festival of extraordinary pomp and beauty. The images . . . that are kept in the churches go forth into the city in processions, carried on litters, and at a slow pace they pass through the streets, where they are admired by a large crowd. And one of those images, one of those splendid seventeenth-century wood carvings, is of Christ on the cross. It is impressive to see, over the heads of the people, the naked body of the dying Christ, proceeding step by step in the night. Anyone who might regard this spectacle as indelicate morbidity, as pleasure taken in the funereal symbol of a dying body, would be wrong. No, as far as the people are concerned, in the death of that God-man, everlasting life is actually being achieved. [Pp. 11–12]

Holy Friday is, in fact, the most important feast of the year — Easter morning, by contrast, is quiet and somber. But that same afternoon the *clarines* sound the ancient ritual sacrifice of the bull-god. Not long after, the Feria begins with *corridas* every day, yet Easter Sunday's *corrida* is always considered the first of the celebration of that special culture of death. Lorca himself had written that "the innumerable rites of Holy Friday along with the most cultured *fiesta* of the bulls form the popular triumph of Spanish death" (1:1105).

If we keep in mind that the culture of death is, as Salinas and Lorca remind us, essentially popular, then I believe we can take it as the phrase that best defines the culture of Andalucía, that best calls to mind all the qualities I have attempted to bring together to arrive at the essence of that culture. The essential paradox that a culture of death is actually a culture of life fits the Andalusian and Spanish character perfectly. That the consciousness of death is very Spanish and Hispanic as well, indicates the extent to which Andalusian culture is central rather than peripheral in Spanish and Hispanic culture. The use of the word *death,* the mention or discussion of which borders on anathema in our own culture, reminds us to what an extent this historical culture of Andalucía has been un-Western, nonmodern, antirational, nonviolent, and antimaterialist, and instead Eastern, consciously stylized, radically conservative, spiritual often in a somewhat Dionysian manner, atavistic, aesthetic, and visionary. And, finally, the mortality implied by the phrase confronts us with the fact that our own materialistic culture is rapidly over-coming and absorbing everything we have examined. Andalucía sur-vived and assimilated into a strikingly original culture a whole series of invaders from at least the Phoenicians on down, but the sweep-ing technical advances of our culture are inevitably making Andalucía much like the rest of the modern world.

In particular when the generation of rural Andalusians born be-fore the Civil War, to pick a not altogether arbitrary period, dies out, the unbroken chain of civilizations stretching back to the Tarshish of Solomon's time may well have ended. Perhaps some ex-planation of that culture of death — that culture of life — can forestall the damage to which it is being subjected. Such an explanation is the subject of this book. It is also the least and most humble homage I can pay Andalucía's living museum.

EXOTIC BEAUTY and intriguing syncretism make the "Carriazo Bronze" (575 B.C.), which portrays a fertility goddess, one of the finest pieces we have from the ancient Andalusian culture known to the Greeks as Tartessos and to the Old Testament Hebrews as Tarshish. *Foto-arte Palau.*

CHAPTER TWO
SHIPS OF TARSHISH

In the beginning—before the written word—fable, legend, oral history, myth, and religion were so intertwined that we can seldom separate their individual threads. So it was with Andalucía, known to the Hebrews as Tarshish and to the Greeks as Tartessos. Tarshish-Tartessos was a city, a river and a kingdom, a mythic place, land's end, a country of fabled resources. It was famous enough that trading ships became known to the Hebrews as "ships of Tarshish." The Greeks equated it with the Elysian Fields. It was the end of the world where the sun sank into the ocean, a mythic kingdom near Hades visited by Hercules in his trials. It has been said, not without reason, that it was the El Dorado of the ancient world. At least one archaeologist, Adolph Schulten, sought to discover in it a Western Troy. Unlike Schliemann, Schulten never found his fabled city, and no ruins have revealed to us layer by layer the secrets of the ancient Western world.

Even though we have not found the city that the ancient texts tell us existed, we hear about it from a wide variety of sources. The Old Testament echoes the name Tarshish—which modern biblical scholars now agree was Tartessos—from Genesis to Jonah, and while the earliest references may or may not have been to Spain, the later ones indicate a land that could only have been Andalucía.

Long before the Hebrews were aware of Tarshish, Aegean sailors had discovered the mineral riches that the indigenous people of Andalucía were exploiting and employing in the development of their already somewhat civilized and urban way of life. Throughout the second millennium Aegeans, Cretans, Cypriots, and Northwest Semites traded with these Bronze Age Andalusians who undoubtedly absorbed in turn part of their way of life from their Oriental visitors.

Certainly by the time of Solomon at the beginning of the first millennium, and perhaps well before that, they had organized into a kingdom or federation of towns and were engaged in extensive trading with the Orient and with the Atlantic coastal settlements as far away as Britain and possibly Denmark.

The catalyst for this unprecedented development was metal: silver, gold, and copper existed in Andalucía in quantities unknown in the rest of the ancient world, and tin was imported from northern Spain and, probably, Cornwall. Copper and tin were the necessary ingredients for the making of bronze, and both were in short supply in the eastern Mediterranean. Tarshish, or Tartessos, capital of the kingdom of Andalucía, or the kingdom itself, became a principal supplier of these metals for the East. In the process of developing into the main emporium of the West, it also became a link between the eastern Mediterranean and northern Europe, between the Indo-European Celts and the Mediterranean peoples of the Levant.

By the beginning of the first millennium, and perhaps earlier, the Phoenicians had established regular trade with Tarshish. After the destruction of Minoan thalassocracy and the collapse of Mycenaean power, the way lay open for the Phoenician city-states, especially Tyre, to dominate the maritime routes established in the second millennium. Since we are now dealing with an increasingly historical period, we have substantial documentation to prove what archaeology has been unable, so far, to verify in much depth until a later period. Strabo, for example, wrote that the Phoenicians explored the regions beyond the Pillars of Hercules shortly after the Trojan War and founded cities there and along the coast of Africa (1.3.2). Velleius Paterculus appeared to know in the first century A.D., practically the year in question for the founding of Gadir. *"Anno octogesimo post Troia,"* he wrote, "eighty years after the fall of Troy," traditionally held to be 1184 B.C. (*Historiae Romanae* 1.2.1 and 2.2.3).

Although the writers of Roman times, approximately a millennium after the fact, might have mistaken legend for history, we gather from sources in the Old Testament that the Phoenicians were carrying on active commerce with Tarshish during the reign of Solomon around 950 B.C. In 1 Kings 10:22 we read of an alliance between Solomon and Hiram, the ruler of Tyre: "For the king had at sea a navy of Tarshish with the navy of Hiram: once in three years came the navy of Tarshish, bringing gold, and silver, ivory, and apes, and peacocks." Second Chronicles 9:21, written somewhat later, gives slightly more specific wording: "For the king's ships went to Tarshish with the servants of Hiram: every three years once came the ships of Tarshish bringing gold, and silver, ivory, and apes, and peacocks." The ivory and the apes could easily have been brought to Tarshish from North Africa, and, of course, apes are native to Gibraltar even today. Although the peacocks (assuming that is the correct translation of the term) are something of a mystery, the gold and the silver point more convincingly to southern Spain than to any other site.

The mineral wealth of southern Spain, especially gold, silver, and copper, is usually described as astounding or legendary or fabulous. It increased in fame throughout the ancient world, starting as early as the Minoans and continuing to grow up through Roman times until the discovery of America. For the Romans, Spanish gold made up the most important source of mineral income in the entire Empire. Strabo informs us specifically of Andalucía that "up to the present moment, in fact, neither gold nor silver, nor yet copper, nor iron, has been found anywhere in the world, in a natural state, either in such quantity or of such good quality" (3.2.8).

These riches undoubtedly meant a great deal to the Tyrians who first exploited them. We hear often in the Old Testament of the extent of that wealth and its importance to the merchants of Tyre. Jeremiah 10:9 has this to say: "Silver spread into plates is brought from Tarshish, and gold from Uphaz, the work of the workman, and of the hands of the founder: blue and purple is their clothing: they are all the work of cunning men." (Uphaz is thought to have been on the northern coast of Africa.) Ezekiel 27:12, 25 is even more explicit. Speaking directly to Tyre and ironically singing her riches in anticipation of her fall, he proclaims: "Tarshish was thy merchant by reason of the multitude of all kind of riches; with silver, iron, tin and lead, they traded in thy fairs. The ships of Tarshish did sing of thee in thy market: and thou wast replenished, and made very glorious in the midst of the seas." And in his prophecy against Gog, ruler of the symbolic kingdom of Magog, Ezekiel (38:13) asks: "Sheba, and Dedan, and the merchants of Tarshish, with all the young lions thereof, shall say unto thee, Art thou come to take a spoil? hast thou gathered thy company to take a prey? to carry away silver and gold, to take away cattle and goods, to take a great spoil?" Cumulatively these references, all of which mention Tarshish in the context of mineral wealth, show the extent to which the Hebrews, who were never sailors and who lived at the opposite end of the Mediterranean, were aware of the wealth, both real and symbolic, of Tarshish.

In Psalm 48, a psalm of liberation, the power of the Lord is expressed in the seventh verse: "Thou breakest the ships of Tarshish with an east wind." In Psalm 72, a psalm which predicts the coming of a messianic king, we read beginning in the eighth verse: "He shall have dominion also from sea to sea, and from the river unto the ends of the earth. They that dwell in the wilderness shall bow before him; and his enemies shall lick the dust. The kings of Tarshish and of the isles shall bring presents. . . ." It is evident from these verses that the ships of Tarshish, ships for sailing to Tarshish, were the vessels of power and wealth for the Hebrews' neighbors in Tyre and the adjoining city-states, and that Tarshish itself represented the ends of the earth.

Jonah, who was trying to escape from the Lord, naturally tried to get as far away as he could. In Jonah 1:3, we learn his destination: "But Jonah rose up to flee unto Tarshish from the presence of the Lord, and went down to Joppa; and he found a ship going to Tarshish: so he paid the fare thereof, and went down into it, to go with them into Tarshish from the presence of the Lord." It is interesting that Jonah, who probably lived as early as the eighth century, although the book of Jonah was written later, should apparently have had so little difficulty in finding a ship bound for the opposite end of the "Great Sea," as the Hebrews and indeed all Mediterraneans thought of "their sea."

The earliest of the Old Testament prophets to speak of Tarshish, and in some ways the most eloquent, is Isaiah, especially in chapter 23, verses 1–14. Written in the latter part of the eighth century B.C., these verses prophesy the downfall of Tyre when it was the richest of the Phoenician cities, the richest precisely because of its commerce and its colonies throughout the Mediterranean, symbolized in these passages about Tarshish:

> The burden [prophecy] of Tyre. Howl, ye ships of Tarshish; for it is laid waste, so that there is no house, no entering in. . . .
> Pass ye over to Tarshish; howl, ye inhabitants of the isle [of Tyre]. . . .
> Pass through thy land as a river, O daughter of Tarshish: there is no more strength. . . .
> Howl, ye ships of Tarshish: for your strength is laid waste.

At the end of Isaiah (60:9), the prophet foretells the messianic kingdom and the conversion of the Gentiles: "Surely the isles shall wait for me, and the ships of Tarshish first, to bring thy sons from far, their silver and their gold with them. . . ."

The symbolic importance of Tarshish is evident. The most representative part, the area richest in metals and therefore richest in fame, was taken somewhat poetically to represent all of Phoenician commerce. Of course Tarshish was not Phoenician. And Gadir, the Phoenician colony established near Tarshish to ply that trade, is never mentioned. The writers of the books of prophecy seem not concerned so much with the realistic details or the actual names of their neighbors' colonies—Gadir, Lixus, Utica, Carthage, Nora are not the names the prophets employ—preferring instead the power and the poetry of Magog and Tarshish.

While the Hebrews give us a splendidly vague idea of the legendary or fabulous wealth represented by Tarshish, the Greeks, who began to compete with the Phoenicians for that trade, give us more realistic and detailed accounts. As the Greeks expanded toward the west, following the Phoenician routes when they were able, they incorporated new expanses of the Mediterranean into their stories and myths. As a result, we first read allusions to southern Spain in Homer and in Hesiod.

In the *Iliad* and the *Odyssey* there are vague references to places, often described in mythic rather than realistic terms, that may lie beyond the Pillars of Hercules. Whatever the veracity of those allusions, they at least convinced Strabo, who wrote in his *Geography,* first published around 7 B.C., that Homer probably knew of Tartessos, since it was known by hearsay in Homer's time as " 'Farthermost in the west,' where . . . falls into Oceanus 'the sun's bright light, drawing black night over earth, the grain-giver' " (3.2.12). Strabo's reasoning regarding Homer, although not necessarily accurate, sheds light on the historical view of Andalucía in Roman times:

> In the first place, the expeditions of Heracles and of the Phoenicians, since they both reached as far as Iberia, suggested to Homer that the people of Iberia were in some way rich, and led a life of ease. Indeed, these people became so utterly subject to the Phoenicians that the greater number of the cities in Turdetania [Andalucía] and of the neighboring places are now inhabited by the Phoenicians. Secondly the expedition of

Odysseus, as it seems to me, since it actually had been made
to Iberia, and since Homer had learned about it through in-
quiry, gave him an historical pretext; and so he also transferred
the *Odyssey,* just as he had already transferred the *Iliad,* from
the domain of historical fact to that of creative art, and to that
of mythical invention so familiar to the poets. [3.2.13]

Strabo apparently believed Homer's allusions to be based on concrete information. Although we may be reluctant to accept such a
literal point of view, Homer's description as interpreted by Strabo
could well describe Andalucía:

So then, the poet, informed through his inquiries of so many
expeditions to the outermost limits of Iberia, and learning by
hearsay about the wealth and the other good attributes of the
country (for the Phoenicians were making these facts known),
in fancy placed the abode of the blest there, and also the Elysian Plain, where Proteus says Menelaus will go and make his
home: "But the deathless gods will escort thee to the Elysian
Plain and the ends of the earth, where is Rhadamanthys of the
fair hair, where life is easiest. No snow is there, nor yet great
storm, nor ever any rain; but always Oceanus sendeth forth the
Breezes of clear-blowing Zephyrus." For both the pure air and
the gentle breezes of Zephyrus properly belong to it, where
Hades has been "mythically placed" as we say. . . . Further-
more, the poets who came after Homer keep dinning into our
ears similar stories: the expedition of Heracles in quest of the
kine of Geryon and likewise the expedition which he made in
quest of the golden apples of the Hesperides — even calling by
name certain Isles of the Blest, which, as we know, are still now
pointed out, not very far from the headlands of Maurusia that
lie opposite to Gades. [3.2.13]

Strabo's commentary does not prove that Homer had in mind all
that Strabo ascribed to him, but it does portray in no uncertain terms
what Tartessos and the south of Spain suggested to the cultured mind
of antiquity.

The story of Geryon to which Strabo refers is somewhat less
problematical than Homer's allusions, although we are still in the
realm of myth. Hesiod, in his *Theogony,* written around 700 B.C.,
is the first to mention the three-headed figure: "But Chrysaor was
joined in love to Callirrhoë, the daughter of glorious Ocean, and
begot three-headed Geryones. Him mighty Heracles slew in sea-girt
Erythea by his shambling oxen on that day when he drove the wide-
browed oxen to holy Tiryns, and had crossed the ford of Ocean and

killed Orthus and Eurytion the herdsman in the dim stead out beyond glorious Ocean" (lines 287–94).

The island of Erythea, Ocean (to the Greeks the Atlantic), and the cattle – the same region still produces Spain's finest bulls – bring southern Spain to mind, although Hesiod never explicitly makes it clear. Subsequent writers, however, leave us no doubt about where Geryon reigned. Stesichorus, the first western Greek poet, who lived and wrote at Himera on the north coast of Sicily around 600 B.C., may have been responsible for westernizing some of the myths and specifically for transferring parts of the myth of Hercules, which was of particular importance to the western Greeks, to known parts of Iberia. From a lost poem called the *Geryoneis,* we have this significant fragment quoted by Strabo, who is describing the Baetis (today the Guadalquivir) River:

> The ancients seem to have called the Baetis River "Tartessus"; and to have called Gades and the adjoining islands "Erytheia"; and this is supposed to be the reason why Stesichorus spoke as he did about the neat-herd of Geryon, namely, that he was born "about opposite famous Erytheia, beside the unlimited, silver-rooted springs of the river Tartessus, in a cavern of a cliff." Since the river had two mouths, a city was planted on the intervening territory in former times, it is said, – a city which was called "Tartessus," after the name of the river; and the country, which is now occupied by Turdulians [Turdetani, i.e., Andalusians], was called "Tartessis." [3.2.11]

Any of these ancient mythical references has inherent problems of interpretation, and taken all together they begin to form at best what Richard Ford called "the uncertain geography of the ancients" (p. 330). Nevertheless, the fragment from Stesichorus, and Strabo's comment on it, fit exactly what historical sources verify. Although it appears in myth, Stesichorus's felicitous phrase may have been a surprisingly accurate description, as we shall see.

Early poets were not the only ones to allude to this area. Herodotus recounts several very germane episodes. In the first place, he confirms the geography, which is quite accurate, of the myth of Geryon, the details of which were familiar to him by around 450 B.C.: "Geryones dwelt westward of the Pontus, being settled in the island called by the Greeks Erythea, on the shore of the Ocean near Gadira, outside the Pillars of Hercules" (4.8).

But of even greater interest are the accounts he gives of a Greek sailor named Colaeus and of the voyages of the Phocaeans. Colaeus, who was sailing from his home port of Samos off Asia Minor for Egypt, was blown off course by a ferocious easterly wind which, according to Herodotus, "ceased not till they had passed through the Pillars of Heracles and came (by heaven's providence) to Tartessus. Now this was at that time a virgin port [for the Greeks]; wherefore the Samians brought back from it so great a profit on their wares as no Greeks ever did . . ." (4.152).

It is difficult to believe these experienced sailors could have been blown all the way across the Mediterranean by accident. Probably the account is a tale, possibly influenced by similar malevolent winds in Homer, which covers up a clever commercial venture by the Samians. No one doubts that Herodotus heard such a story, but the Samians who first told it were probably careful to conceal their true and thoroughly calculated motives.

The Phocaeans, also Ionians from Asia Minor, were the Greeks who most successfully attempted to vie with the Phoenicians for the rich trade of Andalucía, eventually establishing a town called Mainake near Málaga. Herodotus again is the primary source regarding such ventures:

> The Phocaeans were the earliest of the Greeks to make long sea-voyages: it was they who discovered the Adriatic Sea, and Tyrrhenia, and Iberia, and Tartessus, not sailing in round freight-ships but in fifty-oared vessels. When they came to Tartessus they made friends with the king of the Tartessians, whose name was Arganthonius; he ruled Tartessus for eighty years and lived a hundred and twenty. The Phocaeans so won this man's friendship that he first entreated them to leave Ionia and settle in his country where they would; and then, when he could not persuade them to that, and learnt from them how the Median [Persian] power was increasing, he gave them money to build a wall round their city therewith. Without stint he gave it; for the circuit of the wall is of many furlongs, and all this is made of great stones well fitted together. [1.163]

Arganthonius became, through Herodotus, the first and only historical king of Tartessos. The famous lyric poet Anacreon, who lived for a while in Samos, may have heard of Arganthonius there. Strabo, speaking of the wealth of southern Spain, cities an apparently well-known phrase of Anacreon as proof of what he is explaining:

> The wealth of Iberia is further evidenced by the following facts: the Carthaginians who . . . made a campaign against Iberia

found the people in Turdetania, as the historians tell us, using
silver feeding-troughs and wine jars. And one might assume that
it was from their great prosperity that the people there got the
additional name of "Macraeones" [long livers], and particularly the chieftans; and that is why Anacreon said as follows: "I,
for my part, should neither wish the horn of Amaltheia [a cor-
nucopia], nor to be king of Tartessus for one hundred and fifty
years"; and why Herodotus recorded even the name of the king,
whom he called Arganthonius. [3.2.14]

The quote reveals indirectly that Anacreon expects his audience
(around 530 B.C.) to be familiar with his allusion to Tartessos and
its king. If the horn of Amaltheia, from which flowed nectar and
ambrosia, was the symbol of plenty, the parallel symbol for longevity
was apparently to be the king of Tartessos.

Adolph Schulten, the German archaeologist who dedicated
thirty years of his life to the search for Tartessos, studied all the
ancient sources, indefatigably seeking the location of the city Arganthonius had ruled. In the process he edited the collection of sources
known as *Fontes Hispaniae Antiquae,* the first two volumes of which
comprise all the sources relating to ancient Spain, from an Assyrian
inscription dating from the third millennium to the time of Caesar.[1]
The great majority of sources refer to Andalucía, particularly to the
Phoenician and Greek colonies there, to Tartessos, and to the
Carthaginian and Roman occupations of Spain, especially in
Andalucía. The index of these volumes reads like a compendium of
antiquity with hundreds of names from Aristophanes to Xenophon,
including citations from such unlikely sounding sources as Aeschylus,
Aristotle, Euripides, and Thucydides. Yet Schulten's most important, and most vexing, source was a late Roman poet named Rufus
Festus Avienus who wrote a long geographical work in verse known
as the *Ora Maritima,* which conserved fragments of a Massiliote
periplus (Massilia was a colony of Phocaea, modern Marseilles). According to Schulten, this description of the coast was written around
520 B.C., possibly by a certain Euthymenes, who was thought to have
written a description of western seas.

Schulten believed that Euthymenes had written a periplus in
prose which was put into poetry and interpolated by an unknown
Greek around 100 B.C. Part of the interpolations were by the
unknown Greek himself, and part came from the geographer

Ephorus, working in turn from eleven authors of the sixth and fifth centuries B.C. Avienus translated the manuscript of the unknown Greek into Latin around A.D. 400 and added his own interpolations, some of which seemed to Schulten to be correct, others fallacious. Why did Schulten pay critical attention to such an obviously indirect and unlikely source? Euthymenes, or whoever the Massiliote was who wrote the original periplus, had been in Tartessos. His description was an eyewitness account and a firsthand record of what the Tartessians had told him about sailing the Atlantic up to Brittany, Ireland, and Great Britain.

Much of the work lacks interest except as a curiosity, but lines 261–317 created, especially after Schulten's commentaries on them, enormous interest. The text described in a garbled fashion, due to the often incorrect interpolations of Avienus, how Tartessos looked. The most important phrases—what Schulten thought were the buried keys to the ancient city—are these:

> Next there is a promontory of a temple and at a distance a place which has an ancient Greek name, the citadel of Geron. For we have received the report that once upon a time Geryon was named from it. Here over a long distance is the shore of the Tartessian bay. . . . Here is the town called Gadir for it means in the language of the Carthaginians "fenced-in place." It was formerly called Tartessus. [The false notion that Gadir and Tartessos were in the same place was common in Roman times, a confusion undoubtedly due to one of Avienus's "corrections."]
>
> But the Tartessus river, spread through open spaces from the Ligustine lake, binds an island on all sides with its lapping. Nor does the river flow through with a simple course or singly cleave the underlying earth. Rather on the eastern side, it brings three mouths into the fields, and it washes the south part of the city with four mouths. . . . As we said above, salt water in the middle separates the citadel of Geron and the promontory of the temple, and a bay recedes between the heights of the crags. At the second ridge, an ample river flows out. Then the mountain of the Tartessians rises up, dark with forests. Next is the island of Erythia, spread in its land and once under Punic sway. . . . Erythia is cut off from the mainland by the intervening sea. . . .

Schulten believed he could untangle and decipher this improbable geography, some of which was quite correct. Erythia was obviously Gadir, which in antiquity was an island. Yet Avienus makes the common mistake of confusing Gadir and Tartessos. There were forests in those days, but nothing near Cádiz ever resembled a mountain — *Tartesiorum mons,* as Avienus had written.

After a remarkable amount of work on the text Schulten believed he could separate the ancient, correct parts from the rest. The descriptions of the island in the multi-forked river did not correspond to any geography Avienus could have seen, but they sounded very much like what Strabo had recorded, working from earlier sources. There was, for example, the phrase of Ephorus regarding the illustrious market beyond Gades, two days sailing from the Pillars, named Tartessos, washed by a river which bore vast amounts of tin, gold, and copper from Celtic lands (*Fontes* 2:54–56, 210–13). Working from these and similar sources, often obscure and contradictory ones, not the least confusing of which was Plato's assertion that Atlantis was beyond the Pillars and near Gadir (*Critias* 114), Schulten formulated a theory which placed Tartessos in the delta of the Guadalquivir, in the marshland on the north bank known today as the Coto de Doñana. After years of excavation the only physical proof he could show was a Greek ring from approximately the time the Phocaeans had been trading in the markets of Tartessos. No Western Troy lay beneath the shallow marshes, despite Schulten's singular conviction that it did.

Compared to Schliemann, Schulten failed: he excavated no city. Yet he is the true discoverer of Tartessos, and all who now seek the buried city do so because Schulten showed in his studies of the texts that Tartessos was no philosopher's chimera. By singularly diligent work, he proved beyond any doubt that a city of some description lay beyond the Straits of Gibraltar in the double disemboguement of a river (or the separate mouths of two nearly contiguous rivers) emptying into the Atlantic. The city, the river, and the country around it were known by the same name — Tartessos in Greek and Tarshish in Phoenician and Hebrew — to the early traders, both Phoenician and Ionian Greek, who went there seeking the rich metals, principally silver, gold, copper, and tin, which abounded there and which, along with its location in the extreme West, lent Tartessos a legendary reputation. That much seems certain. Schulten had discovered Tartessos, but he had failed to determine its exact location.[2]

After Schulten have come a group of distinguished investigators who have added substantially to what we know about Tartessos. No one has figured out yet exactly where it was, or ought to have been, but the strongest cases are made for the delta of the Guadalquivir, upriver from where Schulten dug, perhaps nearly as far up as Sevilla, and for the area of Huelva near the confluence of the Odiel and the Tinto. The Guadalquivir seems the stronger choice, but the mineral riches of the mountains above Huelva, which are still actively mined today, provide a powerful counter to the more traditional Guadalquiver thesis.

Even though we cannot pinpoint the location of the city itself, we can, thanks to the work of Schulten and his followers, make certain generalizations about Tartessos that establish it beyond doubt as the oldest center of trade and civilization in western Europe. Out of the amalgamated ancient cultures of Andalucía—the builders of the megaliths and the passage graves, and the Bell Beaker cultures—there arose, sometime in the Bronze Age of the second millenium, a superior culture in Andalucía. This culture was located especially west of and along the lower Guadalquivir River. By virtue of its metallurgical resources it was well known to sailors from the eastern Mediterranean. Very probably trading went on also. This proto-Tartessian period ended with the collapse of Minoan and Mycenaean power and the turmoil the invasion of the "sea peoples" caused in the eastern Mediterranean around 1200 B.C.

About 1100 B.C. the Phoenicians began trading in this market, in the process founding a factory which in time became the city of Gadir. The Phoenicians, especially from Tyre, kept up active trade here until at least the seventh century, when Tyre fell under Assyrian sway, although the trade with Tartessos may have continued sporadically afterwards. This is the period referred to in the Old Testament and in the early Greek myths.

By tradition, Elissa, Princess of Tyre, fled from her brother Pygmalion and founded Carthage in 814 B.C. From about that time until 535 B.C., Tartessos was an open market trading with Ionian Greeks, Cypriots, Etruscans, Phoenicians, and Carthaginians, as well as the Celtic tribesmen of Spain and Celts from the north of Europe. Tartessian ships were plying the North Atlantic for tin and amber and her fishermen were ranging the banks off the Canaries and the west coast of Africa. It was the apogee of Tartessos, culminating in the long and peaceful reign of the philhellene monarch, Arganthonius. This prosperity came to an end around 535 B.C. when the Carthaginians destroyed most of the Phocaeans' ships off Alalia, their

colony in Corsica, and closed the western Mediterranean to all but
Punic ships.

From 535 until 206 B.C., the Carthaginians made the western
Mediterranean their own. They dominated the western maritime
routes, as their treaties with Rome make perfectly clear, and kept
the Straits of Gibraltar closed. During this period Tartessos declined
or, as Schulten believed, was destroyed by the Carthaginians. When
the Romans took Gadir in 206 B.C., they erroneously identified the
once legendary city of Tartessos with the Punic city. By this time
the Andalusians called themselves Turdetani, although the Romans
frequently invoked the name Tartessos for poetic reasons.

The lion's share of the credit for the reconstruction of this brief
history goes to Adolph Schulten. Although he failed to realize his
dream of excavating Tartessos's ruins, he began a systematic turning around — especially through his work on Avienus's text — of the
history of western Europe.

Since the much revised second edition of Schulten's *Tartessos*
was published in Madrid in 1945, archaeologists have made some
remarkable finds. Although the city itself still eludes us, the scintil-
lating culture of Tartessos has been brought to light repeatedly.
Schulten had written at the end of the introduction to his second
edition that the most important mission of Spanish archaeology was
precisely the investigation of the kingdom of Tartessos. What archaeologists have found in the brief years since constitutes glittering proof of the legendary fame of the wealth of Tartessos. Myth,
legend, story, and the echoes of early history stretching back three
thousand years began to take shape as the fertile soil of Andalucía
yielded up her treasures.

The kingdom of Tartessos in Arganthonius's time contained as
many as two hundred settlements; thus even if the capital city could
not be positively located, other sites which would shed light on
Tartessian culture could profitably be excavated. So reasoned the
archaeologists who began to concentrate less on discovering the location of the lost city and more on defining, excavating, and dating
the material culture of the area known to have been greater Tartessos.
The change of critical direction was sound indeed. Although only
a handful of sites have been excavated, the results have been positive
enough that some older finds, previously considered Phoenician, have

had to be reclassified as possibly Tartessian with a strong Oriental influence.

In 1957 Juan de Mata Carriazo, historian, archaeologist, chaired professor at the University of Sevilla, and specialist on Tartessos, purchased purely by chance — just happened to see it glint, as he tells it — one of the singular pieces in Spanish archaeology from a trinket merchant at the open air *jueves* flea market in Sevilla. Now known as the *bronce de Carriazo,* the "Carriazo Bronze," the piece, which represents a fertility goddess, displays precisely the syncretistic character that is the hallmark of Tartessian work. The Hathor hairstyle is clearly Egyptianizing. The face is very similar to a carved Phoenician Astarte from Nimrud. The double birds and the pendants which surely swung from the holes in the bottom have a clear parallel in the Aegina Treasure pendant from Crete, as Carriazo has pointed out. The fertility symbol of the delta is generalized over all the Mediterranean. The stylized lotus flowers on her breast point again to the East. And finally, the "boat" formed by the aquatic birds is common in Hallstattan, which is to say Celtic or continental European, cultures, except that the Carriazo Bronze shows much finer workmanship (Carriazo has published a Hallstattan parallel from the British Museum).[3]

Given the intriguingly syncretistic nature of the piece, largely but not entirely Phoenician, which matches rather precisely the ethnic and cultural agglomeration of Tartessos, and the fact that the bronze turned up within the geographical area that once comprised Tartessos, it is implausible to consider it imported. Carriazo positively identifies it as Tartessian, and the distinguished historian Juan Maluquer, of the University of Barcelona, calls it patent proof of the technical originality, beauty, and symbolism of Tartessian metallurgy (Carriazo *Tartessos y el Carambolo* p. 44). With its strikingly exotic beauty and its perfectly assimilated cultural crosscurrents, the *bronce de Carriazo,* dated by Maluquer at about 575 B.C., constitutes the finest single representation of the apogee of Tartessian culture we have to date.

In recent times mining companies in the province of Huelva have been going back through the slag heaps and reopening the ancient galleries and veins with electrical equipment to get the gold and silver that ancient miners had failed to remove. Thus it was in 1961 that the Tharsis Mining Company — the name is modern but nonetheless evocative — summoned Professor Carriazo to examine a stone sculpture which had been discovered at one of the recently opened veins. After careful examination, Carriazo, who called the piece the *máscara de Tharsis,* the "Mask of Tharsis," came to the following conclusions. The piece was sculpted from local stone. It showed Greek and Phoenician influences, yet it was, he believed, like the *bronce de Carriazo,* another example of indigenous art. In spite of Eastern influences and a "hieratic rictus," it was an original piece with a decidedly Western sense of realism. Carriazo dated it at about the end of the seventh century and speculated in an appropriately poetic way that, given the mask's majestic and profound expression, it probably represented a priest or a king. Since we believe this mining area was one of the main sources of the wealth of Tartessos, it was not out of the question, Carriazo reasoned, to think that the mask was a portrait in stone of the "opulent, longevous and magnanimous Arganthonius" (pp. 21-30).

Just west of Sevilla across the Guadalquivir the land rises in a series of small hills which mark the beginning of the low plateau known as the Aljarafe. On El Carambolo, the first and highest of the hills, the Real Sociedad de Tiro de Pichón de Sevilla (the pigeon-shooting club) has its facilities, which in 1958 they decided to enlarge. As Carriazo tells the story, the architect decided at the last moment to lower the level of the new terrace by another fifteen centimeters. Had he not made such a decision, one of the most unusual treasures of antiquity probably would have been paved over forever.

Around noon that day, September 30, 1958, a worker's hoe digging that extra fifteen centimeters struck a metallic object. When the whole lot had been unearthed, the spectacular results added up to twenty-one pieces of 24-carat gold jewelry—a necklace, two bracelets, two pectorals, and sixteen plates—weighing six and a half pounds. The pieces are all of a style obviously done by the same craftsman or craftsmen in one shop. The designs are exclusively geometric—the complete absence of figurative design is highly noticeable—as are all the designs on the accompanying pottery which Carriazo later excavated from the remains of a town at the base of the same hill. As Carriazo later pointed out, the *tesoro,* "the treasure," *del Carambolo* fits perfectly into the geometric style generalized all over the Mediterranean area, yet the uniquely geometric design is as original as it is calculated (pp. 125-61, 665-81).

The treasure imparts an impression of mass, of weight, and of a kind of primitively self-confident unity and mastery of technique.

There is an almost barbarian splendor in so much gold, perfectly in keeping with the idea of Tartessos as an El Dorado in the West. Andalucía's mineral wealth could hardly be more magnificently embodied than by this unique hoard of gold pieces destined surely for a high priest or king, or, as in many ancient cultures, some fastuous combination of the two. Not only does this treasure constitute an ensemble unique in antiquity, it also makes us wonder how many other treasures lie still undiscovered in the rich Andalusian soil.

Professor Maluquer has dated the "Carambolo treasure" to the sixth century, to the time of the reign of Arganthonius.[4] Not two months after its discovery, another treasure began coming to light on the Ébora estate near Sanlúcar de Barrameda. When it was finally dug up, the *tesoro de Ébora,* which is still probably incomplete, contained ninety-three gold pieces and forty-three pieces of carnelian. Much smaller in size and more delicate, this jewelry was probably intended to be worn by women. The most spectacular piece is an exquisite diadem much like earlier diadems from treasures previously thought to be imported from Phoenicia but now believed possibly indigenous with a strong Phoenician influence. Carriazo dates the treasure—the largest in number of pieces yet found—from the fifth century down to the third, corresponding to the Turdetanian period.

Taken together these discoveries provide us with virtual proof of the riches of Tartessos, especially the gold. But these fascinating objects make up only the pieces most illustrative of the brilliance of early Andalusian culture. The archaeological museums of Spain now contain literally thousands of related pieces—pottery, jewelry, sculpture, glass, hardware, arms, armor, to name a few categories— which we would have to examine in their entirety in order to fully appreciate the sophistication of the early cultures of Andalucía. The gold of the treasures best reflects the myths of the Greeks and the lamentations of the prophets, but the thousands of more mundane pieces are the ultimate proof of the extent, specifically of Tartessian and, in general, of greater Andalusian culture, which at the height of Tartessos in the sixth century spread its direct sphere of influence from the Portuguese Atlantic to Almería.

The complete archaeology of Andalucía comprises much more than we wish to examine, but the mining country in the mountains of Huelva bears examination since it amounts to the chief source of wealth, especially silver, which Tartessos possessed. Silver was first mined in the eastern province of Almería, but the process used

there was relatively primitive. In the western province of Huelva a
far more complex kind of silver mining took place at the hill known
as Monte Salomón, the source of the Río Tinto. The Ríotinto district
was heavily mined in Roman times from Tharsis to Ríotinto to
Niebla, but "Solomon's Mountain" showed clear evidence of a large
pre-Roman population as well. When it was uncovered, the pre-
Roman town at Monte Salomón extended over the hill for nearly
a kilometer. The great quantity of mixed native and Phoenician pottery going back at least to the eighth century provides splendid
evidence of the extent of the activity of this early settlement. The
mining evidence is more striking yet. The Phoenicians and the natives
dug here for silver principally, and at Ríotinto alone, left some 20
million tons of slag as proof of their diligence. As a result of the
excavation, Ríotinto became a kind of magical name in the world
of mining. At almost no other place on the earth had such richness
and variety of minerals been uncovered.[5]

Such a place — a virtual geologist's paradise — would have been
quite famous in antiquity. Strabo may not have been exaggerating
when he mentioned that the people in Turdetania were "using silver
feeding-troughs and wine jars" (3.2.14). In the *Liber de mirabilibus
auscultationibus,* attributed to Aristotle (but probably by Timaeus),
the author claimed that the first Phoenicians who traded at Tartessos
had such a load of silver to bring back that they melted it down and
cast it for use in lieu of anchors (*Fontes* 2:220). Diordorus, who wrote
that "this land possesses, we may venture to say, the most abundant
and most excellent known sources of silver," alleged a very similar
procedure for the Phoenician merchants: ". . . in case their boats
were fully laden and there still remained a great amount of silver,
they would hammer the lead off the anchors and have the silver perform the service of the lead" (5.35.1 and 4).

Diodorus, working from older sources, especially from Polybius
who had been in Andalucía, has much to say about these extraordinary mines of antiquity, not the least interesting phrase of which
is the following: "And now and then, as they go down deep, they
come upon flowing subterranean rivers" (5.37.3). Just such a river
was the Río Tinto itself, which, in the days before modern mining
changed the topography, began in a subterranean cave inside the
Monte Salomón. The inside of the cave, which was destroyed in the
seventeenth century, was supposed to have been visible from remotest
antiquity. It was said to have mineral veins in it that stood out like

the veins in a dissected body. Ford described the river as flowing "out of the bowels of the mountain" and heard that it was "connected with some internal undiscovered ancient conduit." In his day "the shafts and galleries" of the ancients were "constantly being discovered" (p. 434). In light of that description, Stesichorus's phrase, "the unlimited silver-rooted springs of the River Tartessus, in a cavern of a cliff," sounds like a perfect description of the source of the Río Tinto.

Stesichorus's description may only be a coincidence, yet it is a highly suggestive one. The myth, the ancient histories, archaeology, even the evocative toponym, Monte Salomón, all point to precisely the same concrete reality that is today still being exploited. Even the root of the name of the only historical Tartessian figure, Arganthonius, sounds "silver-rooted." We may never be able to untangle all the threads, to separate history from myth, coincidence from fact, reality from fabrication. Yet all those threads lead to the same ancient labyrinth which day by day the archaeologists are discovering in the pliant vault of the Andalusian earth. They may never complete the reconstruction of that labyrinth because the actual lair may never be found, but since Schulten's time they have uncovered enough evidence to begin a different orientation of the ancient world.

What did happen to Tartessos? Once we are certain of its existence, how do we account for its disappearance? Schulten was fairly positive that the Carthaginians razed the city, yet we have no evidence that the Carthaginians, despite their aggressiveness, did to the Tartessians what the Romans would methodically do in turn to them. It is more probable that the Phoenicians of Gadir and the Carthaginians really had nothing to fear from the Tartessians and nothing to gain from their destruction. It is quite possible that no one destroyed the city, and that in time the kingdom broke up owing to internal decadence, caused by an untenable economic situation. After the battle of Alalia, when the Carthaginians and Etruscans destroyed the majority of the Phocaeans' ships and the Carthaginians closed the Straits of Gibraltar, Greek commerce with Tartessos undoubtedly dwindled. Gadir, now a flourishing monopoly, probably took over the commerce with Carthaginian assistance and made the Tartessian monarchy subservient.

Arganthonius's long reign may well have been followed, as has so often been the case, by a breaking up of the larger kingdom into local city-states. In Andalusian history this is a phenomenon that has repeated itself time and again. Probably eastern and western Andalucía split, as they were often wont to do, into two separate spheres of influence. If this was the case, it establishes a pattern of separation into city-states — large *pueblos* with their surrounding fields — which has become the classic pattern of fragmented local power still evident today. In any case, when the Carthaginians attempted in the third century B.C. to unify greater Andalucía by force, it cost them a great many lives, including the life of their great general Hamilcar Barca, father of Hannibal and of Flaubert's heroine Salammbo.

Rome conquered a fragmented and war-weary Andalucía. Yet even under such conditions the high culture of the Andalusians struck the Romans, who duly recorded their praise. Tartessos had disappeared, but it had left an appreciable legacy. Strabo, who never went to Spain but who was very careful about his sources, wrote in no uncertain terms about the country around the Guadalquivir which held "pre-eminence in comparison with the entire inhabited world in respect of fertility and of the goodly products of land and sea." He also had high praise for the people, the Turdetani: "The Turdetanians are ranked as the wisest of the Iberians; and they make use of an alphabet, and possess records of their ancient history, poems, and laws written in verse that are six thousand years old, as they assert" (3.1.6). Although the phrase "six thousand years old" has been discounted as factual error, the rest of the description accurately reflects Roman opinion.

Clearly the higher culture of Andalucía, especially the greater Guadalquivir area inhabited by the Turdetani and called Baetica by the Romans, influenced the intense relationship of trade and culture between Rome and the south of Spain. Along with Strabo's description one should bear in mind Livy's phrase of which Richard Ford was so fond, *"Omnium Hispanorum maxime imbelles,"* "Of all the Spaniards, the most unwarlike" (p. 222). They were the least bellicose and most cultured in Roman times because they were the oldest, having already suffered one full eclipse of their civilization, a civilization of which they were eminently aware, as their boasting of the antiquity of their history, their literature, and their laws bears out, especially in what looks suspiciously like a rather familiar pattern of exaggeration and stylization already at work.

Tartessos, already a millennium old, had gone through a classic cycle of rise, fall, and decadence before the Romans ever set foot in Spain. We really do not know how far back the chain of cultures stretches unbroken and within a somewhat civilized framework, but it is at least intriguing to note that there are dolmens within a few kilometers of El Carambolo that date as far back as 4000 B.C. What I am suggesting does not prove that Strabo's figure of six thousand years is correct — no one believes it accurate. Yet at the same time, there is little denying what archaeological studies are making more plain all the time. Andalucía was inhabited by a culture of megalith builders at a very early date. From the beginning of that culture up to Roman times amounts to twice the time from the Romans to the present. Many mysteries remain to be solved in those very early periods about which we know so little, but it is easy enough to understand why the Romans spoke admiringly of the people they found in Andalucía.

The Romans even encountered a type of local theogony or mythology which thanks to Justinus was preserved.[6] The Tartessian wood was first peopled by the Curetes — the mythic guardians of Zeus who taught the Cretans agriculture and metallurgy — of whom the oldest king was Gargoris, who taught the art of beekeeping and who had by his daughter a son named Habis whom he ordered abandoned on a mountain. Habis was suckled by wild beasts and survived all manner of disasters including being thrown into the sea, from which he emerged in a little boat. Raised by a deer, he became a hero and civilized his people, giving them laws and teaching them to cultivate the earth. He also prohibited the nobles from working and was succeeded by his heirs who ruled Tartessos for many centuries.

As Julio Caro Baroja has indicated, this myth contains enormously interesting ethnological material. Not only does it have obvious ancient parallels, it also documents, as far as myth can document, certain characteristics of Tartessian society, especially the divine, powerful, and perhaps, as Caro Baroja suggests, Pharaoh-like monarchy, indicative of a stratified and passive society which would receive without alarm all its successive invaders, be they Celts, Phoenicians, Greeks, Carthaginians, or Romans. Arganthonius's offer to the Phocaeans is a perfect historical example of what the myth demonstrates.

Taken together the mythic, the historical, and the archaeological materials give us a well-defined sense of life in Andalucía in the first millennium B.C., the most striking phenomenon of which is precisely the extent to which life then resembled life in Andalucía up to our time. The relationship of rulers to the people, the division of the land, mining, fishing, farming, class structure, religion, law, trading and commerce, art, practically every facet of Andalusian life, were already determined to a large extent before the Romans arrived.

Schulten understood this when he wrote that Tartessos was a wise and ancient culture, which witnessed the flourishing in its own midst of mining, industry, and agriculture; which understood how to draw together the southern tribes; which was ruled by laws and kings; which had art and literature; which took strangers in hospitably. Yet Tartessos was in no condition to resist invaders. Schulten sagely contrasted the Turdetani with the Iberian tribesmen, finding the latter isolated; anarchic; lacking in commerce, industry, art, or literature; xenophobic; brave; fanatical; and very able in war. Instead of a peaceful culture, he found a bellicose lack thereof (*Tartessos* pp. 241–42). While he may have exaggerated the Iberians' faults, he did not describe anything in his praise of the culture of Tartessos that has not been substantially documented. Although some of his contentions, especially regarding the part played by the Etruscans, and the destruction of Tartessos by the Carthaginians, are not now generally accepted, none of these general conclusions on the nature of Tartessos has been effectively challenged.

On the contrary, Maluquer concludes that Tartessos was the result of a millenary Occidental process combining Mediterranean and indigenous continental elements, the proof of the brilliance of which is the Tartessians' rapid and efficacious assimilation of Oriental influences. "Not even the silence of the sources, the result of historical circumstances," he writes, "can close off the process which created the first great Occidental civilization. To recover it in all its aspects," he concludes, echoing and updating Schulten's words, "is the splendid task archaeological research has before it" (*Tartessos* pp. 165–66).

Our task in the ensuing chapters is also a splendid one: to examine Andalucía — ancient, passive, absorptive, conservative, and syncretistic — in the light of her storied past and to attempt to understand certain mysteries of Andalucía's timeless culture, so much of which has come down virtually unscathed from antiquity, before it vanishes into the future.

THE SPAWNING MIGRATION of giant bluefin tuna into the Straits of Gibraltar was vital to the commerce of ancient Cádiz. The Phoenician settlers, who founded the city-state around 1100 B.C., portrayed the powerful fish on their coins. The inscription of this bronze "as" reads: "The city or citizens of Agadir (Cádiz)." Three thousand years after the city's founding, Andalusian fishermen still catch the giant tuna by virtually the same methods employed in antiquity. *Courtesy Museo Provincial de Cádiz.*

CHAPTER THREE
PIGS OF THE SEA

The bluefin tuna fishery off the Atlantic coast of Spain near the Straits of Gibraltar extends so far into ancient times that we do not know whether it was established by native Tartessian fishermen or by the intrepid Phoenician sailors who were rounding the Pillars of Hercules before 1000 B.C. Neolithic men somehow sporadically trapped some of these horse mackerel, to judge from tuna bones found in caves near Tangier, and at some undetermined time early fishermen began to work together to catch the giant fish in an organized fashion. The method for trapping these migrating bluefins as they enter the Mediterranean — known today as the *almadraba* from an Arabic word meaning circle or enclosure — has remained virtually identical since that time, and the frenzied spectacle of the round-up, which was undoubtedly just as blood stirring in antiquity as it is today, offers us an unparalleled example of the changeless character of Andalusian customs.

The torpedo-shaped bluefins, which frequently weigh over five-hundred pounds and occasionally exceed one thousand, swarmed through the Straits of Gibraltar on their annual spawning run, or as Oppian, who wrote a treatise on fishing in the second century, explained it, "The breed of Tunnies comes from the spacious Ocean, and they travel into the regions of our sea when they lust after the frenzy of mating in spring."[1] The bluefins' passage took them to the Black Sea where they spawned and then returned to the Atlantic. During the full moon of May the heaviest concentrations entered the region of the Pillars of Hercules. Oppian wrote the first description of the method employed in catching the tuna:

> First the Iberians who plume themselves upon their might capture them within the Iberian brine. . . . Abundant and won-

drous is the spoil for fishermen when the host of Tunnies set forth in spring. First of all the fishers mark a place in the sea which is neither too straitened under beetling banks nor too open to the winds. . . . There first a skillful Tunny-watcher ascends a steep high hill, who remarks the various shoals, their kind and size, and informs his comrades. Then straightaway all the nets are set forth in the waves like a city, and the net has its gate-warders and gates withal and inner courts. And swiftly the Tunnies speed on in line, like ranks of men marching tribe by tribe — these younger, those older, those in the mid season of their age. Without end they pour within the nets, so long as they desire and as the net can receive the throng of them; and rich and excellent is the spoil. [3.623–48]

The essential difference between Oppian's description and the *almadraba* today is that the contamination of *Mare nostrum* has greatly reduced the throng and consequently the spoil, but the method of capture — directing the schools into the nets, and hand-gaffing the thrashing tuna — has remained virtually identical.

What we know about the earliest contacts between the Phoenicians and the Tartessians does not clear up the origins of the *almadraba*. Professor Antonio García y Bellido of the University of Madrid, who has studied the question in depth, believes that the Tartessians were fishing all along the Atlantic coast including the Canary Islands before the Phoenicians arrived. The Phoenicians, he reasons, went to Tartessos and established their factory at Gadir because of the mineral wealth, including the tin of Galicia and possibly Cornwall. We are aware of the "tin route" because tin, which was necessary for the making of bronze, was scarce and thus much sought after for the profit it produced. In contrast we hear little about the fishing then because of its more common and less spectacularly profitable nature. The Tartessians, he calculates, would have often provided the native crews and guides for Phoenician voyages from Gadir once that city became established. Thus he believes quite plausibly that any mariners capable of sailing to the "tin islands" could certainly have established fisheries in their own territory and the adjoining coast of North Africa. Since we think the Tartessians carried on this tin trade — Avienus's early source states plainly ". . . Tartessians were accustomed to carry on business to the ends of the Oestrymnides [Brittany]" (lines 113–114) — García y Bellido's contentions seem logical enough.[2]

On the other hand, Phoenician, and specifically Tyrian, salted fish was famous and well known in the ancient world. It may have begun not as a delicacy but as a necessary staple on the lengthy voyages Tyre's distant commerce required. Also the Tyrians were traditionally believed to be the inventors of fishing tackle. And it is quite possible that the early long distance sailors were following the migration paths of the tuna, whose return route would have led directly to southern Spain.

While I am inclined to believe García y Bellido, at least to the extent that the Tartessians were fishing and sailing the Atlantic coasts of Europe and Africa before the arrival of the Phoenicians, it is not unreasonable to suspect that both the Tartessians and the Phoenicians were independently adept at tuna fishing, and that precisely a combination of their efforts at exactly the spot where the big tuna, fresh from the Atlantic, made their plunge into the Mediterranean's gateway, was what produced such a famous fishery. By the time we have any reliable historical information on that fishery, the Phoenician and Carthaginian elements were thoroughly mixed with the indigenous population, and the fishery is identified with Andalucía in general and the city of Gadir in particular.

Tuna became famous in antiquity because the process of preserving the flesh by curing it with salt allowed the fish to be transported to areas beyond the immediate coastline. The Phoenicians began this process, at least to any systematic extent, and constructed the first salinas in Andalucía. The Carthaginians expanded the process and exported the *salsamentum* on a large scale. The Romans took advantage of this flourishing commerce, built their own salting factories on top of the Punic establishments, and expanded the *salazón* into one of their major industries. *Garum,* which was a paste made from the organs and the flesh too soft to salt, was considered a delicacy, surely an acquired taste, perhaps something like anchovy paste, and it fetched very high prices.

Athenian playwrights were the first to record the fame of these products of Cádiz. They allude often enough to the salted fish to indicate that it was very much in vogue—sometimes it was even described as contraband—in fifth- and fourth-century Athens. Carthaginian merchants cured and shipped it to Athens and other ports after the fishermen from Gadir had procured the fish, which were described as tuna so long and so fat they were frightening (*Fontes* 2:221). Such tuna could only be the giant bluefins, which the people of Gadir judged important enough to make emblematic of their city by putting them on their coins.

In time Gadir became the logical and wealthy center of Atlantic maritime activity. Strabo described Gades, the Roman name for the city, as never crowded in spite of its small size since "only a few stay at home in the city, because in general they are all at sea . . . " (3.5.3). The prosperity of the seaport resulted from the superimposition of Phoenician and Carthaginian commercial acumen and navigational daring on the already established Tartessian trading and fishing routes. While we must infer much about the Tartessians, a few of the exploits of the Phoenicians and the Carthaginians have been preserved. The sixth-century Egyptian Pharaoh Necho, for example, hired Phoenician sailors to circumnavigate Africa. In the fifth century the Carthaginian suffete, Hanno, sailed at least as far south as the Senegal River, founding Punic colonies as he went — the elder Pliny claimed he began in Gades and went all the way around (*N.H.* 2.169) — and Himilco, another Carthaginian, explored the far coasts of Europe and the British Isles. It is quite probable that these Carthaginian adventurers were sailing the routes already explored to some extent by Tartessian sailors and fishermen.

Finally there is the strange tale of a certain Eudoxus of Cyzicus (near the Bosporus on the Sea of Marmara), told by Poseidonius — who had spent perhaps a month in Gades — and recounted by Strabo. Eudoxus made two unsuccessful attempts to sail around Africa from Egypt. On his second attempt, however, he found on the east coast of Africa "to the south of Ethiopia . . . an end of a wooden prow that had come from a wrecked ship." Eudoxus brought it back with him and showed it to the shipmasters in Egypt who told him it came from Gades:

> . . . he was told that whereas the merchants of Gades fit out large ships, the poor men fit out small ships which they call "horses" [*hippoi*] from the devices on the prows of their ships, and that they sail with these small ships on fishing voyages around the coast of Maurusia as far as the river Lixus [Wadi Draa, near Agadir in southern Morocco]; but some of the shipmasters, indeed, recognized the figure-head as having belonged to one of the ships that had sailed too far beyond the Lixus River and had not returned home safely.

According to Poseidonius, Eudoxus then made his way to Gades where he outfitted a ship and attempted to sail around to India. He failed, returned to Gades, outfitted yet another ship, sailed off, and was apparently never heard from again (2.3.4).

Regardless how the veracity of these stories may strike us, they unquestionably reflect the eminence in the pre-Roman and early Roman world of the sailors of Gades, of whom perhaps the most noteworthy were those humble fishermen in their *hippoi* who seem almost routinely to have sailed the north coast of Africa as far as the fish-rich banks off the Canaries. The most remarkable aspect of these accounts is neither the fearlessness of these Phoenician and Andalusian sailors and fishermen nor the degree of verisimilitude with which we may choose to credit the stories told about them, which in general are believed true by scholars who have studied them. What is unusual is that they exist at all. In general the Phoenicians from Tyre, from Carthage, or from Gadir left no records of any kind, and, in fact, did their utmost to discourage any followers, often inventing nightmarish tales about the seas they sailed.

Strabo had read in Eratosthenes that the Carthaginians threw any stranger near the Columns of Hercules into the sea (17.1.19) and told the story of how a Phoenician captain from Gades kept secret the route to the "tin islands" by purposely running his ship aground when a Roman ship followed. The Roman vessel also went aground and was lost, but the Phoenician captain survived and was reimbursed by his government for his sacrifice (3.5.11). Pindar, the early Greek poet who was a contemporary of Hanno and Himilco, seems to have believed the tales these sailors told to discourage competition. He made the point that no wise man passes the Columns, nor one who is unwise either, since the sea is full of tricky shoals and sea monsters (*Fontes* 2:201). As it turns out, we are probably quite fortunate to have any extant accounts of these Atlantic voyages. The Punic and Tartessian sailors, we can conclude, may have sailed the Atlantic a great deal more than we had suspected, but it will take archaeological discoveries to demonstrate precisely to what extent.

In any case, by Roman times Gades had prospered mightily. Strabo explained that "here live the men who fit out the most and largest merchant-vessels, both for Our Sea and the outer sea" and that despite the small size of the city, "In population . . . Gades does not fall short, it would seem, of any of the cities except Rome; at any rate I have heard that in one of the censuses of our own time [the Augustan era] there were five hundred men assessed as Gaditanian knights — a number not equalled even in the case of the Italian cities except Patavium [Padua]" (3.5.3). Many of those fortunes were due to the trading that the descendants of the original Phoenician colonizers of Gades carried on throughout the Roman world. Thus it was that Strabo remarked that Gades, "because of the daring of its inhabitants as sailors, and because of their friendship for the Romans, has made such advances in every kind of prosperity that although situated at the extremity of the earth, it is the most famous of them all" (3.1.8). When Strabo recorded such prosperity, this Andalusian commerce had a tradition a millennium long.

Gades was headquarters for both the fishing and the shipping of *salsamentum* and *garum,* but many other towns along the Andalusian coast from Portugal to Cartagena owed their living to these products of the sea. Other famous fishing ports, to judge from the classical texts, were Baelo (Bolonia) which was also the port of departure for Tingis (Tangier), Malaca (Málaga), Sexi (Alumuñécar) and Carthago Nova (Cartagena). Archaeological remains show evidence of some twenty-five establishments along the greater Andalusian coast as well as several on the North African side. The most complete yet examined was Baelo with four separate salting factories, a town apparently dedicated almost exclusively to fishing, salt curing, and related activities.

These North Atlantic waters from off Cádiz to the Straits were considered so favorable that odd stories grew up to explain their productivity. Polybius, who spent a good deal of time in Spain in 148 B.C. and again around 133, and who is considered the father of Spanish historiography, is the source for one such tale which Athenaeus and Strabo both recount. In Athenaeus's version Polybius "says that there are acorn-bearing trees planted deep in the adjacent sea, on the fruit of which tunnies feed and grow fat. Wherefore one would not make a mistake if he said that tunnies were sea-swine. For the tunnies are like swine if they grow fat on acorns" (7.302). Strabo's version is somewhat embellished:

> Again, large numbers of plump, fat tunny-fish congregate hither from the other coast, namely, that outside the Pillars. And they feed on the acorns of a certain very stunted oak that grows at the bottom of the sea and produces very large fruit. This oak also grows in abundance on the dry land, in Iberia; and although its roots are large like those of a full-grown oak, yet it does not grow as high as a bush. But the sea-oak brings forth so much fruit that, after the ripening, the seacoast, both inside and outside the Pillars, is covered with the acorns, for they are cast ashore by the tides. . . . This creature [the tuna], says Polybius,

is therefore a sea-hog, for it is fond of the acorn and gets ex-
ceedingly fat on it; and whenever the sea-oak has produced a
large crop of acorns, there is also a large crop of tunny-
fish.[3.2.7]

Obviously, though, Polybius told such a story. No one seems to know
for certain where he got it, but, knowing the ways of fishermen the
world over and knowing that Polybius had the reputation of being
somewhat pompous, I do not find it too difficult to imagine some
son of Gades going on at length about the succulent acorns of the
sea-oaks so greedily devoured by those pigs of the sea.

Horse mackerel, as the Greeks called them, or pigs of the sea,
these giant bluefins caught off the Atlantic coast of Andalucía were
the most sought after fish in antiquity. First they were gutted and
cut into slabs that were then slashed so salt could penetrate. After
soaking in brine for three weeks, they were sealed in *amphorae* to
be shipped to distant parts. The *garum* was made from belly meat,
the intestines, throats, gullets, and any other part not suitable for
salting, as well as from small whole fish. The mixture was brined
and left in the sun for a couple of months to evaporate into a paste
that was said to have a piquant flavor. *Garum,* which was considered
an appetite stimulant as well as a delicacy, remained popular into
Christian times and was generally considered healthful as well as
tasty. Galen among other physicians of antiquity recommended it.[3]

Garum became such a part of Roman life that Martial, who
seems not to have been very fond of it, occasionally joked and made
puns about its odor. Martial was from northeastern Spain and often
bragged of his homeland, including the riches of the Atlantic, but
he failed to expound the virtues of *garum,* which he made
synonymous with foul breath (11.27). Seneca, the stoic philosopher
from Córdoba, considered a taste for *garum* revolting and jaded.
He called it "the costly extract of poisonous fish" and "salted putrefac-
tion" (Epistle 45).

The elder Pliny believed that *garum* had curative powers,
especially for dog and crocodile bites (31.44). In Pliny's time the
costliest *garum,* made from mackerel at Cartagena, had come into
vogue, a gallon and a half of which fetched a price of a thousand
silver coins (31.43). Perhaps more to our taste, crocodiles notwithstanding, was the tuna steak the classical gourmet Archestratus
described in his treatise *High Living.* "Slice it and roast it all rightly, sprinkling just a little salt, and buttering it with oil. Eat the slices

hot, dipping them into a *sauce piquant;* they are nice even if you want to eat them plain, like the deathless gods in form and stature" (Athenaeus 7.303).

Although the popularity of *garum* probably did not much outlive the Roman Empire, the tuna fishery and the *salazones* continued as always. Fernand Braudel in his intriguing study *The Mediterranean and the Mediterranean World in the Age of Philip II* discussed the ways in which the historian can become confused untangling all the threads that make up the Mediterranean world. Thus he wrote that the historian might have "thought of tunny fishing perhaps as a specific activity of Genoese seamen, of the fishermen of Naples, Marseilles or Cape Corse; in fact it was already practiced by the Arabs who passed on the skill in the tenth century."[4] With all due respect for M. Braudel's monumental work, we might rephrase that idea just slightly by saying that the "Arabs," many of whom were Berbers from just across the Straits, continued a skill already at least fifteen hundred years old and that the Arabs, those from the coastal Levant, continued the fishery from which their Phoenician predecessors had prospered. In any case, Andalusian fishermen, whatever their ethnology, carried on their timeless pursuit of the pigs of the sea.

When the Christians conquered al-Andalus they continued the *almadraba.* In 1294, Sancho the Brave granted the royal privilege of setting the *almadrabas* to one of his most loyal knights, the hero of Tarifa, Alonso Pérez de Guzmán, known as *el Bueno,* because he had watched his son sacrificed rather than surrender. His descendants, the dukes of Medina Sidonia, held the privileges for most of the *almadrabas* for centuries to come, including the most famous one at Zahara, a pueblo a few kilometers up the beach from the Roman ruins of Baelo.

In time the concession of the *almadrabas* brought the dukes great wealth, and the spectacle of the tuna harvest became famous as a diversion for the nobility. Even Enrique IV of Castilla, the sad, gangling half-brother of Isabel, spent three days observing the carnage. With his withdrawn nature and his love of animals, I wonder what diversion he found. Perhaps it was the growing army of thieves, beggars, and *pícaros* in general that began gathering every year for the *almadraba* that attracted his curiosity.

Columbus, nearly becalmed in the Sargasso Sea on his first return voyage, encountered large schools of tuna on the surface and duly recorded it in his journal, believing that the tuna probably headed for "the *almadrabas* of the Duke at Conil and Cádiz."[5] Samuel Eliot Morison, perhaps hoping to animate the wooden admiral, supposed that Columbus joked with his men about hooking a line to the speedy fish.[6] But the joke probably would have been on Columbus, since the migratory paths of the tuna tend to run straight away from Conil and Cádiz. Morison was surely correct, however, in supposing that Columbus's crew would have preferred to be at the *almadraba*.

In 1541 at Zahara (the full name is Zahara de los Atunes) the duke entertained the count of Olivares and other nobles and magnates with all their attendant vassals and servants. The records indicate they took 140,000 tuna that year at Conil and Zahara, put one thousand men to work at 3 to 10 *reales* a day, and cleared a profit of 80,000 *pesos*.[7] Pedro de Medina in his *Libro de Grandezas* published in 1548, wrote that the *almadraba* at Conil landed fifty to sixty thousand tuna in the months of May and June.[8] A source of Braudel's reported that in 1584 the dukes of Medina Sidonia took in seventy thousand ducats from tuna fishing (1:138). Other records show that around 1750 the duke of Medina Sidonia grossed "90,000 *ducados* from the sale of tuna" (Sole p. 27). Given such hefty sums, we have little difficulty understanding the attraction of the *hampa,* the Spanish underworld, to such an enterprise.

Cervantes, who knew so well the picaresque underside of Spanish life from direct experience in the streets and jails of his time, undoubtedly witnessed an *almadraba*. His young "hero" Carriazo, in his story "The Illustrious Kitchenmaid," went through every step of becoming a *pícaro* "until he graduated as a *maestro* in the *almadrabas* of Zahara, which is the land's end of the *picaresca* [knavery, the underworld]." Among dozens of colorful phrases regarding that underworld, Cervantes warned, "don't call yourselves *pícaros* unless you've done two full courses in the academy of tuna fishing." "There," he wrote, "you will find idleness and work, and clean dirt; fat, hunger, and undisguised gluttony; gambling always, quarreling at times, death now and again, oaths at every step, dancing as though at weddings, poetry, romance, singing, swearing, fighting, betting, and everywhere thieving" (pp. 921–47).

Foreign danger lurked as well, as the dull glitter of Tangier on the southern horizon reminded the fishermen each night. Cervantes knew only too well the fear of being shanghaied by the Barbary pirates. He had spent five years in slavery in Algeria. Sentinels stood watch every night to keep the men, as Cervantes put it, from going to sleep in Spain and getting up in Tetúan. The danger must have been real enough. In 1612, an estimated four hundred fifty Turks made an attack on the *almadraba* at Zahara, and in 1574 Turkish galleons attacked the *almadraba* at Cádiz. Playing on the danger and the fishing, the *pícaros* referred to their high adventure as the "Conquest of Tunisia."

The conditions at the *almadraba* in the sixteenth century were such that the Jesuits sent missions for the redemption of souls. Cádiz was very much a free port, in every sense of the word, in those days, and every kind of criminal and fugitive was drawn there, especially those who were fleeing to the New World. The subcultures and underworld of Cádiz and Sevilla and the surrounding towns must have been as bizarre as those anywhere. The inhabitants of Conil, to cite one example, reputedly lit torches on their beaches in imitation of other ships in order to lure passing vessels into the nearby shoals, all the while imploring the *Santísima Virgen* to run the vessels aground so they could collect the booty, which they considered rightly their own. As late as 1850 they still continued this practice.

In 1557 a Jesuit missionary to the *almadrabas* held that many of the inhabitants of those lands around Tarifa, Vejer, Gibraltar, and Medina Sidonia roamed the adjacent hills "like savages" and that, were it not for the Jesuits, these people, as they themselves admitted, "would live in every way as the beasts of the field" (Sole p. 78). Whether our personal belief inclines us toward the missionary's ecclesiastical point of view or toward Cervantes's idealization of the *pícaro,* the spectacle, both picaresque and piscatory, was quite obviously unforgettable. In its mixture of nobility and underworld, *pícaro* and priest, man and beast, and in its outdoor setting resembling a *feria* complete with music, dancing, whoring, and gaming, it was also archetypically Andalusian. As a certain Fray Gerónimo de la Concepción expressed it in 1690, "there is no *fiesta de toros* that can match it" (Sole p. 31).

The most precise details of the fishing itself come from Pedro de Medina's description of 1548. The tuna came in "herds like pigs," a thousand or two at a time. "When they come through they are fat and very good and later when they have spawned and returned, so skinny they are not fit to eat." In those days the tuna came in closer to shore and could be netted by encircling them with the boats and then by pulling the net to shore:

> . . . more than 200 men pull the final net; as the tuna come close to the beach many men go naked with no clothes at all into the sea and they carry great iron hooks fastened to wooden handles half a fathom long: these hooks are called *cloques* "gaffs": each *cloque* has a piece of rope by which, after sinking the gaff in the tuna, the men pull. Three or four men sink their gaffs into the head of a tuna: then with their lines they haul it ashore, and sometimes a tuna will drag a man under water if he is merely wounded and the man has the rope tied to his arm. Some of the tuna require ten men to drag them out and ashore; it is a sight to see the blows these tuna give with their tails and their heads on land until they die and to see the sea run red with blood. These tuna commonly reach eight or ten feet in length. Some will not fit whole into a cart. Here they catch in these two months fifty or sixty thousand tuna. [P. 59]

The sixteenth century may well have been the heyday of the *almadraba*. Antonio Ponz, in his well-known and erudite account of his travels through Spain, recorded in 1794 that "in the old days they regularly caught 60,000 tuna a year." But nowadays, he wrote, "said fishery is in much decline."[9]

Richard Ford gave one of the reasons for the decline in his description of the country south of Cádiz, which he rode through in the early 1830s: "The *almadraba,* or catching, used to be a season of festivity. Formerly 70,000 were taken, now scarcely 4000; the Lisbon earthquake of 1755 having thrown up sands on the coast, by which the fish are driven into deeper water" (p. 335).

For whatever reasons, the horse mackerel's migration pattern changed just enough that the *almadraba* could no longer easily be set and then hauled ashore to remove the fish. But the fishery was far from over, and gradually the fishermen evolved a system to net the fish in deeper water. The nets were set in much the same way except that instead of encircling the fish, the tuna were directed by blocking nets into a series of chambers. Once the fish were in the final chamber, this "death chamber" could be hauled up by the circle of boats above, bringing the "bottom," as it were, to the surface where the tuna could be gaffed in the same old fashion. The same nets were "set forth in the waves like a city" and the same "gate-warders and gates withal and inner courts," in Oppian's phrases of two millenniums ago, were employed, only now they were used in deeper water.

Another change had taken place as well. In 1817 the royal privilege was abolished and the fishery was turned over to the local fishermen's guilds. In time they prospered. By 1923 there were some thirty *almadrabas* that employed about ten thousand people. In spite of political changes and the Civil War, the *almadrabas* continued. In 1950 over eight thousand tons were taken, and in some years at Barbate alone the catch was said to reach fifty thousand tuna. After 1950 profits and catches began to diminish, and gradually it became apparent that the fishery was in permanent decline.

The *almadraba,* like any fishing, is cyclical. There are good years and there are bad ones. By 1971 it was clear the drop in the figures and the fish was no mere cycle. That year only one thousand tons were taken, and in 1972, barely eight hundred. Ten *almadrabas* were functioning, but the government liquidated its majority interest because of heavy losses and dissolved the existing consortium. Now only two small, private companies at Barbate and Zahara struggle to compete for the fish. A few men continue to net and gaff the horse mackerel that bunch up in the spring and nose into the waters at the Straits "when they lust after the frenzy of mating," and these men still take the cobalt-colored giants by hand much as their predecessors had for three thousand years. There is great shouting and swearing and heaving, much blood and salt spray as there has always been, but as commercial fishermen, they are barely surviving, more a curiosity in their anachronistic tenacity than an example of men making a living from the sea.

Two changes, one commercial and one ecological, have robbed them of their fishery. The floating fish factories—ships that pursue the elusive schools in any sea, catch them on mechanized longlines, and process and freeze them at once—have greatly reduced the number of fish entering the old spawning grounds. And the steadily increasing contamination of the Mediterranean by raw sewage, industrial waste, and petroleum, in particular, has further thinned the tuna migrations. Now the fish that do enter the Straits tend to stay farther offshore seeking the least polluted water, and fewer of their torpedo-shaped number swim within range of the stationary city of nets.

The origin of this unique fishery, once so typical of Andalusian life, may be lost in the remote seas of antiquity, but its demise seems rather clearly in view on a none too distant horizon. According to numerous reports, the end of *Mare Nostrum* is imminent, and soon enough the pigs of the sea may no longer penetrate the oil-dark sea at all.*

* As of the summer of 1979, the Compañía Sevillana de Electricidad was planning to construct a nuclear power plant adjacent to the Roman ruins at Bolonia, the site of the Roman *almadraba*. Even if no pollution were to ensue — a debatable issue since Bolonia lies near a fault where earthquakes occur — it seems highly inappropriate to construct such a plant next to the ruins along this as yet unspoiled strip of beach, but that sort of juxtaposition is unfortunately typical of what is happening to Andalucía in the late twentieth century.

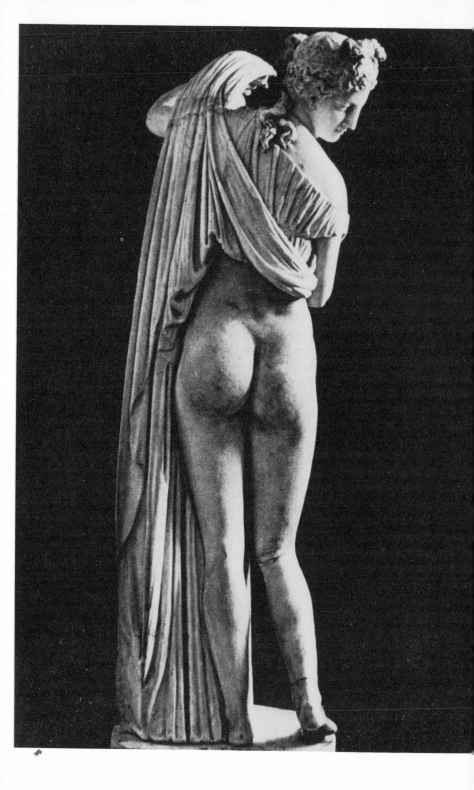

CHAPTER FOUR
DANCER OF GADES

Richard Ford, who possessed a near virtuso's ability for summing up in a few succinct words the historical essence of any place in Spain, described Gades as antiquity's Venice or Paris, "the centre of sensual civilization, the purveyor of gastronomy" (p. 315), thus adroitly juxtaposing the exports — *garum* and girls — for which the city was famous. With an uncanny knack for spooling a historical thread in a phrase, Ford informs us, "Italy imported from it those *improbae Gaditanae,* whose lascivious dances were of Oriental origin, and still exist in the *Romalis* of the Andalucian gipsies" (p. 315). Ford's intuition was sometimes as impressive as his erudition. If we follow that thread from antiquity to the present, we can begin to understand the complex and strangely beautiful world of ecstatic mime and ritual dance that Ford was attempting to concatenate in his own illuminatingly Romantic fashion.

The musically talented women of Andalucía in general, and of Cádiz — *puellae Gaditanae* — in particular, have fascinated their spectators since some indeterminate time. Already by the second century B.C., Eudoxus of Cyzicus, who outfitted a ship in Gades to sail around Africa, knew enough about their talents to sign them on for his voyage. Strabo wrote that "he built a great ship . . . and he put

---

THIS STATUE of the *Aphrodite Kallipygos* or "Callipygian Venus" (literally Venus of the Beautiful Buttocks), reminded Richard Ford of the famous dancing girls of Cádiz who were renowned in antiquity for their musical ability and sensuality. Ford believed this statue represented Martial's mistress, Telethusa, the most celebrated of the Cádiz girls. Telethusa's descendants are no less famous in our time as *flamenco* dancers. *Courtesy Museo Archaeologico Nazionale-Napoli.*

music-girls on board, and physicians, and other artisans, and finally set sail on the high sea on the way to India" (2.3.4).

No less impressed was young Lord Byron, who stormed by horse from Portugal through Extremadura and into Andalucía in the teeth of Napoleon's armies. Spain as he described it in the first canto of *Childe Harold* was a "renown'd, romantic land," whose "dark-glancing daughters" and "black-eyed maids of Heaven" were "formed for all the witching arts of love," while the most "fitting to inspire the song of love" were "Andalusia's maids," specifically those from "Fair Cádiz, rising o'er the dark blue sea." In the original manuscript the Spanish sojourn ended with the stanzas called "The Girl of Cádiz," whose "dark-eyed" subject sang to the guitar and danced "the gay Bolero."[1] Byron reserved his highest praise for a letter to Francis Hodgson (August 6, 1809): "Cadiz, sweet Cadiz! — it is the first spot in creation. The beauty of its streets and mansions is only excelled by the loveliness of its inhabitants. . . ."[2] He also described it as a "complete Cythera," the isle of origin of Aphrodite, an association with the Greek goddess of love that was hardly accidental.

Byron may have thought the *bolero* an ancient dance. Ford knew better: "The *Bolero* is not of the remote antiquity which many, confounding it with the well-known and improper dances of the Gaditanas, have imagined" (p. 285). He also seems to have known a great deal about those ancient dances "which delighted the Romans, and scandalized the fathers of the church, who compared them, and perhaps justly, to the capering performed by the daughter of Herodias" (p. 285). Ford's opinion was that "these most ancient dances, in spite of all prohibitions, have come down unchanged from remotest antiquity, their character is completely Oriental. . . .They are entirely different from the *bolero* or *fandango,* and are never performed except by the lowest class of gipsies; those curious to see an exhibition which delighted Martial, Petronius, Horace, and other ancients, may manage to have a *funcion* got up at Seville. This is the *romalis* in gipsy language and *ole* in Spanish . . ." (p. 286). The descriptions of the "*brazeo,* or balancing action of the hands," and the "*zapateado, los taconeos,* the beating with the feet, the *crissatura, meneo,* the tambourines, and castanets, *Baetica crusmata, crotala,* — the language and excitement of the spectators, — tally in the minutest points with the prurient descriptions of the ancients. . . . The sight of this unchanged pastime of antiquity, which excites the Spaniards to frenzy, will rather disgust an English spectator, possibly from some national malorganization . . ." (p. 286). But let the traveler beware, Ford admonished, for "however indecent these gipsy dances may be, yet the performers are inviolably chaste . . . "(p. 287). Ford's description may seem at first glance like some Romantic fantasy, yet Ford based his conclusions on rather specific passages from the texts of antiquity.

Martial, Juvenal, and Petronius, a puissant triumvirate, and the younger Pliny wrote the salient passages. Pliny, for example, revealed the extent of the popularity of the *puellae Gaditanae* at Roman dinners in a letter to Septicius Clarus, complaining that his friend had preferred someone else's hospitality, which included oysters, sea urchins, and *Gaditanae* (1.15).

Juvenal, a pragmatic poet like his friend Martial, and one who delighted in skewering the customs of his day, particularly if they were pompous or pretentious, described in his eleventh satire what his friend Persicus might expect at a frugal dinner. He began by telling Persicus what he would not have: "Perhaps you will wait while the Gaditanian dancer begins to feel the wanton stimulus of the loud strains of her accompanying band, and the girls, fired by the applause sink to the ground with quivering buttocks. . . ."[3] Juvenal continued indignantly that he would have none of these arts of love, nor the clattering of castanets, nor the accompanying obscenities in his home.

Martial, M. Valerius Martialis, who was from Bilbilis, today Calatayud in Aragón, is the man who left us the most complete picture of the *Gaditanae*. Pliny wrote that Martial was "a man of an acute and lively genius, and his writings abound in both wit and satire, combined with equal candor" (3.21), a description that Ford claimed turned Martial into an Andalusian: "This mixture of salt and gall is most peculiar to the satirical Sevillians, whose tongues flay their victims alive" (p. 224). Andalusian writers—the Senecas, Mela, Columella, and Lucan to name the most famous—permeated Rome's Silver Age, but it was the crusty, often obscene and explicitly candid epigrammatist from the northeastern iron-mining country who painted the most memorable scenes of these *puellae,* especially of a certain celebrated Telethusa. With good reason Martial knew these *Gaditanae* so well. Telethusa, as certain epigrams rather unflinchingly portray her, was his mistress.

Martial revealed many pertinent details about these famous performers of antiquity and their milieu. A *bellus homo* of Rome, for example, was wont to hum tunes from Egypt or from Gades (3.63). Those who trafficked in these girls—something between a dancing-master and a white slaver—were in Martial's opinion among the vilest of Rome's teeming underworld (1:41). At one of his own dinners, Martial, like Juvenal, would have no "girls from wanton Gades with endless prurience swing lascivious loins in practiced writhings," although we get the distinct impression from the epigram that lack of funds was Martial's reason (5.78). In a two-line epigram called precisely "Puella Gaditana" he bluntly expressed his unbounded admiration by telling us that her quivering movements and wanton enticements were so provocative they would drive even Hippolytus—symbolic of chastity for refusing his stepmother—to act:

> *Tam tremulum crisat, tam blandum prurit, ut ipsum*
> *masturbatorem fecerit Hippolytum.* [14.203]

That *puella* sounds like Telethusa herself. In thanking his friend Rufus, who had sent him a gift of wine, Martial wrote: "If Telethusa come, and bring her promised joys, I will keep myself for my mistress, Rufus, by drinking . . . four measures; if she be doubtful, I shall while away the time by seven; if she fail her lover, then, to throttle care, I will drink [eleven]" (8.51).

In another instance, Martial explained his relationship with her candidly:

> She who was cunning to show wanton gestures to the sound
> of Baetic castanets and to frolic to the tunes of Gades, she who
> could have roused passion in palsied Pelias, and have stirred
> Hecuba's spouse even by Hector's pyre—Telethusa burns and
> racks with love her former master. He sold her as his maid,
> now he buys her back as mistress. [6.71]

In spite of the pun on the word *mistress,* this epigram is somewhat unusual for its straightforward confessional manner, which may explain why Ford became interested in it. Were it not for Ford's curiosity about her, Telethusa might have languished in the past, one more name in Martial's long list of vocatives; but Ford, with his own mixture of salt and gall, turned Telethusa into the most interesting *andaluza* of antiquity.

To do so Ford needed to see in nineteenth-century *Gaditanae* something of which Telethusa could have been the forerunner, they the unchanged reflection. For him Cádiz was replete with echoes from Homer and Byron. He described it as "the rock-built city, sparkling like a line of ivory palaces, which rises on its headland from the dark blue sea" (p. 311). Because of the Napoleonic War and the political repression that followed under Fernando VII, Cádiz had suffered a good deal since Byron's fortnight there, and Ford found it disease-ridden and poor, conditions induced by half a century of war and revolution. It was "now a shadow of the past" and could be seen in a day (p. 318). But there was one attraction:

> This is the spot for the modern philosopher to study the descend-
> ants of those *"Gaditanae,"* who turned more ancient heads than
> even the sun. The "ladies of Cadiz," the theme of our old
> ballads, have retained all their former celebrity; they have cared
> neither for time nor tide. Observe, particularly . . . the Gadi-
> tanian walk, *El piafar,* about which everyone has heard so
> much. . . .
>   The Gaditana has no idea of *not* being admired. . . . Her
> "pace" is her boast. . . . Her *meneo* ["wiggle"] is considered by
> grave antiquarians to be the unchanged *crissatura* of Martial.
> [Pp. 321–22]

Their Oriental nature was still most apparent to Ford: "It is quite clear that Cadiz was the eldest daughter of Tyre, and her daughters have inherited the Sidonian 'stretching forth of necks, wanton eyes, walking and mincing as they go' (Isa. iii.16)" (p. 323). It is also clear that Ford was fascinated — no less so than Byron or Martial — by these *Gaditanae* and that he used every recourse of antiquity at his disposal to convey their charm. Knowing Ford's penchant and bearing in mind his richly associative erudition, it comes as no surprise to read the following assertion: "The well-known statue at Naples called the Venere Callipige is the undoubted representation of a Cadiz dancing-girl, probably of Telethusa herself (see Martial, vi. 71, and 'Ep. ad Priap.' 18; Pet. Arbiter, Varm. Ed. 1669)" (p. 286).

Ford was clearly taken at face value by some writers in Spain. Fernando Quiñones, one of the most expressive flamencologists writing today, suggested that the "statue of Telethusa" in Naples was equivalent to a Roman *flamenco* dancer.[4] The poet Rafael Alberti, from Puerto de Santa María, just across the bay from Cádiz, wrote a poem to her titled "To Telethusa, Dancer of Gades," in which the city shimmering over the Bay of Cádiz becomes indistinguishable from the naked Roman girl of Cádiz shimmering as she dances in the sunlit seascape. The vine-bound secrets of the *flamenco* songs

of Cádiz await her ancient graces, the poet tells her. At the end
Telethusa and the city fuse:

> Cádiz girds you, her waves embrace you.
> You are the sea and the spume of Cádiz.[5]

And Lorca in his superb essay on *duende,* the essential spirit
of *flamenco,* wrote that *duende* had gone from the mysterious Greeks
to the dancers of Cádiz and to the Dionysian singers of *flamenco,*
thus associating the Greek mystery religions, the wanton dances of
the *puellae Gaditanae,* and modern *flamenco* (1:1098). Ford,
Quiñones, Alberti, Lorca, and others were following the same thread
into the labyrinth the Romantics had begun re-creating as they all,
individually and collectively, sought to convey how little some things
in Andalucía had changed.

But was Ford correct, or was he merely inventing connections
that were at best coincidental? The answer is that he was doing both.
While he had plenty of reason to associate *flamenco* and the
Gaditanae, his assertion that the statue of the "Venere Callipige" was
"probably of Telethusa herself" was somewhat fanciful and proved
him to be a true Romantic.

Ford traveled in Italy in 1839 and undoubtedly saw the famous
statue. Alfonso de Franciscis, director of the National Museum of
Naples, describes her as "una delle più note sculture del nostro
Museo," but he also dates her to at least the first century B.C.[6] Clearly, the statue could not represent Telethusa who, shall we say,
flourished circa A.D. 75 or later.

In fact there is a splendid story behind this specific goddess and
her cult. Athenaeus recounts the history of this Venus — *Aphrodite
Kallipygos* in Greek — of the Beautiful Buttocks:

> A farmer had two beautiful daughters who once fell into a dis-
> pute with each other and even went out upon the highway to
> settle the question as to which of them had the more beautiful
> curves. One day a lad passed by whose father was a rich old
> man, and to him they displayed themselves; and he, after gaz-
> ing at them, decided in favour of the older girl; in fact he fell
> in love with her so passionately that when he returned to town
> he went to bed ill, and related what had happened to his brother,
> who was younger than he. So the latter also went into the coun-
> try to gaze at the girls and he too fell in love, but with the other
> girl. Now the father, at least, begged them to contract a more
> respectable marriage, but since he failed to persuade them, he

brought the girls from their country home to his sons, having got the consent of the girls' father, and joined them in marriage to them. The girls, therefore, were called "the fair-buttocked" by the townspeople [of Syracuse]. . . . It was they, therefore, who, having come into possession of splendid wealth, founded the temple of Aphrodite, calling the goddess the Fair-buttocked. . . . [12.554]

Did Ford know this story? Perhaps, since he cites Athenaeus on other occasions, but it seems unlikely he would have connected Telethusa and the Callipygian Venus over the authority of Athenaeus, however charmingly unsubstantial the latter's story may have seemed. What surely convinced Ford is what we may call the callipygian connection, the key to which is Ford's parenthetical reference to his assertion that this Venus was "probably of Telethusa herself (see Martial, vi. 71, and 'Ep. ad Priap.' 18; Pet. Arbiter, Varm. Ed. 1669)." The reference to Martial, which we have already seen, establishes who Telethusa is and what her talents are, but the 1669 Variorum Edition of Petronius was the source of Ford's epiphany. In this particular edition done in Amsterdam, there is a special section titled *Priapeia,* which is composed of unsigned epigrams dedicated to Priapus as explained in the subtitle: *Diversorvm Poetarvm in Priapvm Lvsvs.*[7] While we cannot be sure exactly who wrote Epigram 18 (Petronius himself or Martial are the most likely), we can be positive of what Ford saw in the first two lines, which begin to describe Telethusa's irresistible charms as she strolls about with no part of her *tunica* touching her *clunem,* precisely the pose of the Callipygian Venus:

> *Ecquando Telethusa circulatrix*
> *Quae clunem tunica tegente nulla.*

Without a doubt Ford considered his connection highly ingenious or he would not have included the reference to a single rare edition of Petronius. While he could only have expected the most erudite or enthusiastic of his readers to consult it, the real *aficionado* who did bother to obtain the Variorum would certainly be delighted by Ford's subtlety. And his larger assumption that this statue and the dancers of Gades must have looked alike is not awry. While the *Gaditanae* of pronounced Semitic stock were probably somewhat darker than the Callipygian Venus, it is important to bear in mind that this statue of the divinity of love is posed unequivocally as a courtesan at a classical banquet. That Telethusa and indeed all the *puellae Gaditanae* were courtesans ought to be reasonably obvious from the descriptions already examined. Telethusa herself seems to have been quite famous, as Epigram 40 from the same Variorum Edition of Petronius (not cited, incidentally, by Ford) reveals:

Nota Suburanas inter Telethusa puellas,

her meretricious charms being, of course, the reason she was so *nota.*[8]

It was the interlacing nature of meretriciousness, dancing, and the religious cults that led Ford to have his epiphany in the first place. The *puellae Gaditanae* were partly the daughters of Phoenicia, the home of the worship of the fertility goddess Astarte and of her hierodules or sacred prostitutes. That these *puellae* became celebrated in Roman times for precisely the same activity as their hierodulic counterparts in the time of Jezebel of Tyre, can only have delighted Ford's sense of the human continuum, a continuum within which he was unlikely to discriminate too severely between hierodule and courtesan. And if he could connect the callipygian charms of a famous Venus to the warmly admired charms of a celebrated dancer of Gades, then so much the better. Cádiz, if not Telethusa herself, certainly deserved as much.

Whether or not Telethusa could actually have posed for the particular statue of the Callipygian Venus becomes immaterial, since what really interested Ford, and what interests us, is that the statue of this goddess conformed perfectly to what Ford imagined from Martial's descriptions and to what he saw in Cádiz. What was important was the analogy. Here was a goddess—a nearly naked, superbly sensual, dancer-courtesan goddess—worthy of having been modeled from Telethusa herself. Ford's compliment to the *Gaditanae,* then and now, is more subtle than Byron's but not a bit less encomiastic. We cannot be sure of Ford's degree of seriousness in this matter, but giving him the benefit of the doubt, we see that intuitively—and with no coaching from a Frazer or a Jung—he was headed unerringly for the center of the labyrinth.

From time immemorial dance has been considered a magic or religious activity, as numerous prehistoric cave scenes and early Egyptian and Mesopotamian works illustrate. I have in mind, for instance, the superb horned stag dancer (much like his Yaqui counterpart in the Ballet Folklórico de México) painted and carved on the wall of the cave of Trois Frères in France during the Ice Age.

The Old Testament connects dancing and religion repeatedly. Dancing around the golden calf was precisely the activity that so infuriated Moses that he broke the tablets and had three thousand of his people killed. In the last Psalm we read of musical praise and dancing for the Lord: "Praise him with the sound of the trumpet: praise him with the psaltery and harp. / Praise him with the timbrel and dance: praise him with stringed instruments and organs. / Praise him upon the loud cymbals: praise him upon the high sounding cymbals." To celebrate the crossing of the Red Sea, Miriam the prophetess "took a timbrel in her hand; and all the women went out after her with timbrels and with dances" (Exodus 15:20). Cymbals, timbrels — those biblical *panderetas* — flutes, and drums were the favorite religious instruments of antiquity, and the natural accompaniment of sacred and profane dances.

Ecstatic dancing formed an integral part of the rites of Dionysus, originally an Eastern divinity, and of the fertility goddesses, assimilated in various guises from the Phoenician Astarte and the Babylonian Ishtar. The Syrian writer, Lucian, wrote in the second century A.D. that "dance came into being contemporaneously with the primal origin of the universe, making her appearance together with Love — the love that is age-old" (line 7). In his treatise *The Dance* (*De Saltatione*), he made a number of pronouncements that are germane, telling us that "as to the Dionysiac and Bacchic rites . . . every bit of them was dancing" (line 22), that "at Delos, indeed, even the sacrifices were not without dancing" (line 16), that "not a single ancient mystery-cult can be found that is without dancing" (line 15), and finally, for our purposes, that regarding the cults of Dionysus and Aphrodite, "the song which they sing while dancing is an invocation of Aphrodite and of the Loves, that they may join their revel and their dances" (line 20).

Since these Oriental cults came eventually into great vogue in Rome, it ought to come as no surprise that the most sought after dancer-courtesans were their original Oriental practitioners. The most celebrated dancers in Rome were precisely the descendants of the Phoenicians, from Syria as the region was called by the Romans, and from Cádiz where the rites of Astarte (Aphrodite or Venus) had already been celebrated for a thousand years.

If we keep in mind that sexuality and fertility were considered sacred in antiquity, even though fertility cults, from our Judeo-Christian vantage, may seem pretexts for orgiastic behavior, then it is not difficult to connect the dancer-courtesans of the *puellae* to the old religions. *Hierodule* and *hetaera* are but two terms — one ritual and "sacred," the other purely licentious — referring to the same activity. The Callipygian Venus, the goddess portrayed as courtesan, is a sublime example of this particular ambivalence. No mere "sex symbol," she may well be the finest embodiment we have of the baffling dichotomy — streetwalker or divine incarnation — so characteristic of our sexuality, especially in antiquity.

What Ford would have made of the dancer in the wall painting at the Villa Item in Pompeii is beyond speculation, but this virtually naked callipygian dancer is even closer to a *flamenco* dancer than Ford's statue of Telethusa. Her upraised arms, her castanets, and the unequivocal act of dancing are startlingly like the attitudes we think of as *flamenco*. Quite obviously physically analogous to the Callipygian Venus, she is a celebrant participating in a mystery rite (the central figure in the four-walled mural is none other than Dionysus himself), and her dance is clearly a ritual dance forming part of the ceremony depicted in this Villa of the Mysteries, as it is also known.

Castanets like the ones the mystery dancer holds and *tympana,* the *panderetas* of the Greeks and Romans, seem to have been equally in vogue in sacred and profane dances. Martial mentions castanets, and Andalusian ones at that, *Baetica crusmata,* in his eulogy of Telethusa: "she who was cunning to show wanton gestures to the sound of Baetic castanets and to frolic to the tunes of Gades . . . " (6.71). Juvenal, in his eleventh satire, as we have seen, would have none of the clattering — *crepitus* — associated with the *Gaditanae*. Regarding the lewd dancing he remarks, "such sights as brides behold seated beside their husbands," a phrase at first glance seemingly out of context. But if we understand that the mysteries painted on the walls of the Villa Item are interpreted as a rite of induction for a bride, as the representation of her initiation into the mystery cult, that is, into the secrets of religious sexuality, then the phrase makes better sense, and we can begin to see that the profane *puellae Gaditanae* and the dancers in the cults may have been very similar, if not in fact identical.

Martial makes precisely the same connection in an epigram that almost seems written to prove the point: "You, reader, who are too

strait-laced, can now go away from here whither you will: I wrote
these verses for the citizen of wit; now my page wantons in verse
of Lampsacus [the home of the popular, ithyphallic deity Priapus],
and beats the timbrel with the hand of a figurante of Tartessus"
(11.16). The last line in Latin, it is worth noting, *"et Tartesiaca con-
crepat aera manu,"* gives only *"Tartesiaca"* and nothing about
"figurante," the "figurante" (a female dancer from a troupe), being
Walter C. A. Ker's perfect translation for what Martial's audience
clearly understood as a literary allusion meaning dancer of Gades.
For Martial, who knew the *Gaditanae* better than any source we have,
the dancers of Gades, lewd dancing, cult dancing, and the cults
themselves with all their instruments, especially cymbals, timbrels,
and castanets, were all part and parcel of the same phenomenon. .
The use of the word *aera* — the special instrument, a cymbal or bronze
timbrel, used in the rites of the Earth Mother, Cybele — is further
proof that the lewd and sacred dancing of the *Gaditanae* amounted
to much the same thing.

The 1669 Variorum of Petronius in another epigram *Ad
Priapum* (26), provides a further example. As a courtesan strolls
about the Circus, singing and making gestures appropriate to her
profession, she plays these "arms of the itch" which are dedicated
to Priapus:

> *Cymbala cum crotalis, pruringinis arma, Priapo*
> *Ponit, et adducta tympana pulsa manu.*

In a short epigram by Martial titled precisely "Cymbala," we read:
"The brazen cymbals that mourn for the boy of Celanae [Attis], the
darling of the Great Mother [Cybele], her priest is often wont to
sell when hungry" (14.204). This epigram follows directly the one
titled "Puella Gaditana," which, as we have seen, explained in no
uncertain terms just how lewd her dances were. It is difficult to accept their propinquity as mere coincidence, given the fact that
Martial, who often intertwined his poems, wrote thousands of
epigrams collected in fourteen books.

Even so refined a writer as the aristocratic Neapolitan Statius,
in describing Domitian's Winter Carnival in the *Silvae,* wrote
knowledgeably of the *Gaditanae.* With the coming of night the dance
troupes appeared to compete for the favors and applause of the
crowd, and among the hand-clapping Lydian dancers and the raucous
troupe of Syrians we hear the jingling cymbals — *"illic cymbala*

tinnulaeque Gades" — of the girls of Cádiz (1.6). Those jingling cymbals are called *chinchines* today and they are still played in Andalucía as they were in the days of Domitian's lavish carnivals.

Cymbala, tympana, and *crotala* — castanets are still called *crótalos* in Spanish — were the instruments so cleverly wielded by the dancers of lewd and sacred dances, dancers typified by the *puellae Gaditanae.* In our time castanets are employed by the descendants of those *puellae* in certain *flamenco* dances, and the *pandereta,* that *tympanum* of our age, has become the symbol of the pseudo-folkloric and superficial side of the whole phenomenon, at least since Cervantes put one in the hands of Preciosa. Yet Lorca, in writing his famous poem "Preciosa y el aire" (in which the wind turns satyr and attempts to rape the Gypsy girl), is not reluctant to put one in her hands, nor to call it *"su luna de pergamino,"* "her moon of parchment" (1:395). But Lorca understood the ancient provenance of the instrument and undoubtedly used it intentionally. In a reading he once stated explicitly that the poem was the myth of a Tartessian shore (1:1116). Given what we now know about the *Gaditanae,* we can understand why Alberti identified Telethusa with Cádiz and why Lorca said that *duende,* the spirit of *flamenco,* had jumped from the mysterious Greeks, that is, the Greeks of the mystery cults, to the *bailarinas* (dancers) *de Cádiz,* both the *puellae Gaditanae* of antiquity and the present *bailarinas de Cádiz* as he made clear enough in his essay, and finally to the Dionysian singing of *flamenco* in our own time.

Clearly the activity we call *flamenco* today is not identical in every respect to the dances of the *puellae Gaditanae,* whatever they were like. Still, certain coincidences or correspondences can help us understand the complex phenomenon of *flamenco* which, when understood fully, becomes a key for unlocking the arcanum of Andalucía. Fernando Quiñones, the flamencologist, once asked the Spanish historian Ramón Menéndez Pidal for a concrete opinion on the connection between the *puellae Gaditanae* and *flamenco.* The eminent historian replied that he believed that some racial characteristics — we would probably say ethnic or ethnological — could last even three millenniums and that one example was the sense of rhythm of the Andalusian people, of the *puellae Gaditanae.* Quiñones adds that Menéndez Pidal had once written that although this is to associate fantastically a yesterday and a today separated by twenty centuries, all the connecting links are there, a view shared by the musicologists and ethnologists who have studied the problem in detail (p. 32).

Rhythm is not the only link between the dances of the *Gaditanae* and *flamenco*. A hieratic attitude and ecstatic mime, when not actually ecstasy, seem equally important: the beat, the cadence, the measure marked by handclaps, by castanet, tambourine, or drum; the upraised arms (Lorca held that when a *bailarina* had *duende* her arms would find expressions which are "the mothers of the dances of all times") (1:1107) in constant and sinuous motion; and the head aloof, thrown back even, always fixed between the archways of the arms. And finally there is the ecstasy — as Martial described the cult dances, "the frenzied throng raves to Phrygian strains" (11:84) — the overpowering emotion, exultation, transport, or rapture, whether the sexual frenzy of a maenad of antiquity or the magical power of *duende,* that transfigures the dancer, and that, as Lorca said, could convert with magical power a *bailarina* into a *"paralítica de la luna"* (paralytic of the moon) (1:1107), no longer under her own power but under a lunar spell. These are all interwoven parts of the same larger phenomenon, the two instances of which happen to be separated by two millenniums.

Dance, rhythmic mime, is a primal art, an original art, an ecstatic and religious art. Consider the company of prophets of 1 Samuel 10, "coming down from the high place with a psaltery, and a tablet, and a pipe, and a harp, before them," prophesying as they went, whom Samuel joined, "and the spirit of God came upon him, and he prophesied among them." Dance is frequently the subject of early painting and sculpture. From it came the measure of poetry and the mime of theater. In it were expressed happiness, hope, and fear. The earliest religious celebrations were surely dance. It was the formal expression of sexuality and fertility, life, death, and resurrection. It was, to recapitulate, rhythmic, hieratic, and ecstatic. And in the way that such activities can be analogous; in the way that the dances of the *puellae Gaditanae* and *flamenco* conform to the same primordial patterns and needs; they are much alike.

Very suggestive parts of that pattern existed long before Samuel joined the prophets, or the Greeks created tragedy as we think of it evolving into the medium of Euripides. In Crete before 1500 B.C. there were priestess-dancers who bear a quite striking resemblance to *flamenco* dancers. The upraised arms, the evident grace and movement, and the long, flounced skirts of four cult celebrants portrayed on a gold signet ring from near Knossos, remind us strongly of their modern counterparts. The famous snake priestess from Crete wears a similarly flounced skirt, holds her snake-extended arms aloft as a dancer does, and wears a transfixed expression on her face. The sinuosity of snakes and the sinuosity of the arms and hands in *flamenco* were analogous in ways that the German poet Rilke used to good effect in his poem "Spanische Tänzerin" (Spanish Dancer). Out of the conflagration of her dance the poet sees the dancer's naked arms stretching up like startled snakes, a figure so like the Cretan priestess that those who have seen her cannot fail to be reminded.

Lorca knew the connection between these priestesses and *bailarinas* as well. When he wrote his mythic ballad about the moon, he anthropomorphized her as a silvery white *flamenco* dancer whose ritual proved mortal for the little Gypsy boy who stood watching in fascination as her fatidic rite unfolded. She dances with upraised arms and her skirt is long and starched (and undoubtedly flounced as *flamenco* dresses usually are). But most important, she shows off "lubricious and pure/her breasts of hard white tin" (1:393). The detail can only be an allusion to the Cretan priestesses since it is completely out of place in modern *flamenco*. A *bailarina* in our time would never dance bare-breasted: naked, perhaps, as we shall see, but not merely bare-breasted. The peculiarly hieratic nature of that exposure, and the striking combination of long skirt and exposed breasts, can only be understood in terms of the Cretan version of the old ecstatic cults. The paradoxical adjectives "lubricious and pure" are unmistakable signs of Lorca's penchant for such an atavistic ambivalence.

By seeing how suggestively poets make use of these similarities to the practices of antiquity, we can begin to formulate the notion that *flamenco* is a modern analogue for those ancient dances. *Flamenco* is like the dances of antiquity because it is not so far removed, except temporally, from the origin of those dances. Moreover, it is most like those dances the more removed from modernity, in ambience, we find it. The more rhythmic, hieratic, and ecstatic a dance is, the more ancient or primitive it is likely to be. The distinction between primitive and ancient, or between primitive and primordial, is most important, especially if we understand *primitive* as a pejorative term meaning undeveloped and *primordial* as meaning original, essential, and ancient. *Flamenco* is not primitive, but it is primordial. And in the sense that it is primordial in spite of modernity rather than primitive by comparison with modernity, *flamenco* is the most characteristic expression of Andalucía we have.

It is the same old, or rather ancient, story. Only in a land whose collective psyche could respond to such primordial music and dance, could *flamenco* have originated. And even then the resistance to it, especially from the middle and upper classes and from "Europeanizing" intellectuals in the capital, was fierce. The French Romantic Théophile Gautier complained in his *Wanderings in Spain* that in 1840 in Madrid, whenever any *baile nacional* (national dance), whether a *jota* from Aragón or a *bolero* danced by Andalusians, was performed, all the fashionable portion of the audience rose and left the house. The only spectators left were foreigners and people of the lower class, in whom it was more difficult "to extinguish the poetic instinct."[9]

If we bear in mind the Oriental nature of Andalusian history we can trace, parallel to that history, the musicological continuum that perpetuated what Gautier thought of as the poetic instinct. The songs from Gades the Romans hummed and the dances of the *Gaditanae* should not be considered the earliest music of Andalucía. Rather they were the highly developed musical forms of the Romanized Turdetani, musically as well as ethnically the descendants of the Punico-Tartessians of Cádiz and the adjacent littoral. There is no reason to believe this music became Romanized as it developed. On the contrary the music of the Romans seems to have Gaditanianized to some indeterminate extent, the best indication of which is precisely what Strabo, Pliny, Martial, Petronius, Juvenal, Statius, and others recorded about the musical *puellae* from that region. Nor is there any reason to believe that this music of early Andalucía fell into disuse when Rome declined. It was, rather, the classical writers who had popularized it that ceased their activity and fell silent.

The Christian writers who succeeded them were far from silent. Ambrose, manipulating Theodosius, had all pagan ceremonies— except what the Church had found it useful to adopt—forbidden by law. Among the casualties were the Olympics, last celebrated in 393, sacrifices of any kind, and, of course, cult or ritual dancing, which was associated with the pagan gods and the shameless dancing performed before Herod. Ambrose's contemporary, John Chrysostom, held that where there was dance, other than "spiritual dance" such as that as performed by Angels, there was also the Devil.

Pagan dancing did not die out, as much of the folklore of Europe attests. On pagan and Christian feast days, at weddings, and at gravesides, there was feasting, singing, dancing, and behavior described as drunken orgies. The early Church fathers' writings are full of imprecations against such practices which, judging from the extent of the sermons against them, must have been quite tenaciously preserved. Isidore (560–636), who was Bishop of Sevilla, condemned activities involving carnavalesque masquerades, transvestism, and intoxicated mixed dancing. Throughout the Middle Ages, Christian Spain fulminated against nocturnal festivals and vigils involving strange practices, including dances. Dancing in honor of the Virgin, in front of the church and in the church, and the singing of songs, often obscene ones, were common, as were dancing and singing at religious processions and pilgrimages throughout Spain. To record all the singing and dancing at such festivities and occasions, which would require volumes, is not my intention. To point out the continuation all over Spain of mixed sacred and profane dancing provides, however, the necessary framework for the specifically Andalusian phenomenon.

Bearing the general phenomenon in mind, it is feasible to surmise that the *Gaditanae* stopped performing publicly in Rome and, with the decline of Rome as a city and a power, ceased being "imported" at all. At home, though, as was the case all over Europe, pagan practices did not cease altogether but were often "sublimated" by the Church. Nowhere would such sublimation have been more apparent than in Andalucía, where the early Church was often more influenced by Carthage and Byzantium than by Rome. Andalusian folk music in general, both singing and dancing, was undoubtedly preserved rather than eradicated by such a process. Thus the pre-Roman, highly Orientalized music of the *Gaditanae,* which had been so popular in Rome, survived in a modified state as the Roman Empire's ultimate legacy of the Church, rather than obliterating the indigenous "pagan" culture, ironically became the improbable agent of the preservation of some of its practices.

It is commonly held that the Arab invasion of Spain with the subsequent establishment of their high culture of al-Andalus played an important role in the development of *flamenco*. This contention is unquestionably correct, although that influence may have been less preponderant than is often assumed. The music of Andalucía has also influenced some of the music of North Africa, a fact that even the most cursory attention to the *nauba* of the Maghreb, known as the *nauba* of Andalucía or Granada, will bear out. The exact ratio of influences is probably an unsolvable conundrum and, in any case, is less important than the sympathetic aspects of pre-Islamic Andalusian and Islamic Andalusian cultures. The point is that change was so gradual and the fusion of Islamic and Andalusian cultures so complete that we have difficulty differentiating them in the study of the history of music.

On the other hand, it is highly significant that the fusion of the two produced the first literature in any Romance language. Bards such as the blind minstrel, Mocádem of Cabra, sang their bilingual verses with rhyming refrains in Mozarabic Romance in the public squares of al-Andalus as early as the first part of the tenth century. It would be possible in a different context to trace all modern lyric poetry from Mocádem and from Cordoban Jewish bilingual poets such as Judá Leví, but that is only a secondary point for our consideration.

What is important for us is that this Islamic-Jewish-Mozarabic lyric also produced, or incorporated, a primitive form of the *villancico,* a love song that is the oldest documentable form of Andalusian folk music and the direct predecessor of the pre-Gypsy side of *flamenco.* How far back into the Andalusian past these forms (usually known as *jarchas*) reach is impossible to determine, but they were prevalent enough to have emerged in Andalucía sung in three languages. Gerald Brenan suggests strongly that they may have come down directly from the songs of the *puellae Gaditanae.*[10] These love songs were known also as *canciones de habib* (songs of [Arabic] friend or lover), the macaronic expression of which speaks eloquently of the intergrated nature of Andalusian society in this brilliant and all too neglected period of European history.

Villancicos are still sung in Andalucía today, especially at the Christmas season. As Lorca pointed out, almost all of the popular ones are pagan in nature (2:1006). Many, especially the Gypsy ones, are delightful in a splendidly naïve fashion. This one, in which the child Jesus is lost and his Mother is searching for him only to find him down by the river on a binge with the Gypsies, is typical of that sense:

> *El niño Dios se ha perdío*
> *su Madre lo está buscando*
> *y está en la orilla del río*
> *de juerga con los gitanos.*[11]

One element important to the development of *flamenco,* inherited from the Moslems, is the guitar. A Persian poet-musician named Ziryab, who lived in Córdoba in the ninth century, put the fifth string on the classical cithara and created the prototype of the modern six-string *flamenco* guitar. In spite of these developments, the Moslems' active contributions to flamenco may have been less important than the adoption by the Spanish Church of the Byzantine liturgy, which continued in use up to the thirteenth century in Córdoba.

Parallel in some ways to the development of the early *villancicos* as predecessor to *flamenco* song, especially in that it seems an outgrowth of the same fusion of existing Andalusian and Islamic elements, was the popular dance called the *zambra.* Although it is still danced by that name today, we cannot be sure how exactly it resembles the original. But we can be reasonably sure that it was some combination of those dances the early Church fathers railed against, and Moslem dances. The *zambra,* however it was performed, was very popular. Not only was it dear to the caliphs of Córdoba and the people of al-Andalus, it was also most attractive to the neighboring Christians to the north, and some of the Christian kings kept Moorish performers in their retinues.

Whatever the particular order of importance we assign their components, these elements provide us with an unparalleledly Oriental background for the emergence of *flamenco.* The ancient Oriental culture of Andalucía, the songs and dances of the *puellae Gaditanae,* the Phrygian or Greek mode of the Byzantine liturgy, the music of the Hispanic Jews, the music of the cultures of the Moslems but especially those of Arabia, Syria, and Persia successively, make up the quite distinct, but all Oriental, pieces of the puzzle, what with unintentional flippancy Gautier called the poetic instinct. The only element lacking was the agglutinating genius of the Gypsies, capable of putting, and holding, the puzzle together. And before the Jews were expelled and Granada was overthrown in 1492, this newest wave of Oriental "invaders" was already looming on the frontiers of Spain. Before the Semitic and Hamito-Semitic purge was attempted by the Catholic sovereigns and their followers, before the Jews, the Arabs, and the Berbers could be got rid of or driven underground, these Hindus were settling in with them, especially in Andalucía. Meanwhile the successive waves of settlers from northern Spain, beginning from the time of Fernando *el santo* (the Holy), who took Córdoba in 1236 and Sevilla in 1248, tended more to Andalusianize themselves, as so often happened, than to Castilianize the South, as the literature and the history of the period clearly bear out. All that was needed for *flamenco* to evolve from the timeless and pervasive sediment of Andalusian folk culture was the proper interpretation.

The Gypsies seem to have been a caste of pariahs, perhaps minstrels, who for some indeterminate reason left or were expelled from their ancestral home over a millennium ago to begin a life of erratic transhumance, at best nomadic wandering, at worst purposeless itinerancy. Irredeemably truant, clannishly astute, ignorant, superstitious, and given to the occult, they were feared, often despised, frequently persecuted, and rarely treated as human beings. Their history is as pathetic as it is fascinating. Lorca characterized them as half bronze, half dream (1:394). Some of them believed themselves descendants of the Egyptian pharaohs. Historically, they were haughty and hardy, aristocratic yet primitive, thieving but fiercely loyal, salacious yet strictly chaste. Horse traders, beggars, blacksmiths, butchers, tinkers, smugglers, basket weavers, acrobats, fortune tellers, they have lived in every corner of the world. In their original Sanskrit tongue the word for farmer and the word for stranger was the same. They have been accused of causing the plague, of child stealing, of witchcraft, and of cannibalism. They were persecuted by the Inquisition and exterminated by Hitler's goons. In Spain they were legally discriminated against, especially by articles that until July 1978 allowed the *Guardia Civil* special measures of surveillance.

Since the beginning of their history Gypsies have been connected with music and dance. By the tenth century they were known in Persia as musicians and thieves. By the fifteenth they were playing citharas in Hungary, and by the nineteenth they were driving Hungarian audiences to ecstasy, as Franz Liszt made so clear. In Russia and Rumania the popular fervor was nearly equal to the Hungarian. All over Europe the Gypsies became famous for their singing, their dancing, and their playing. There are accounts, for example, of a "Moorish" Gypsy dance done at the Swiss town of Yverdon in 1459, for which the performers were paid in wine and currency, and of an early sixteenth-century tapestry in which a young Gypsy girl danced, arms up, hands open, a scarf on each wrist, her long red dress open in the front from top to bottom.[12]

Cervantes's Gypsy girl, Preciosa, who was "the most unique dancer in all of Gypsydom," and a most beautiful and witty young woman as well, won first prize at a dancing contest on the feast day of Santa Ana dancing "in front of the image of Santa Ana." She became the talk of Madrid and continued earning her living dancing in the street on the shady site of the Calle Toledo, accompanying herself with *sonajas,* a timbrel, or a *tamborín,* or *castañuelas.* She also accepted invitations to dance in private homes. But — and Cervantes makes this quite clear — all of Preciosa's songs and dances were *honestos,* rather than *descompuestos.* In fact, he says, none of the other Gypsy girls dared to sing lascivious songs in her presence (pp. 774–76). Preciosa's exceptionally chaste repertoire makes it fairly obvious that some of the other *gitanas* were performing along the lines Richard Ford had described.

Indeed timbrels, tambourines, castanets, religious dancing, lascivious dancing, the pose suggested by the tapestry, the "Moorish" dance at Yverdon, all begin to sound more than vaguely familiar. And well they should, since the Gypsies had spent some five hundred years in Persia and the Near East.

Gypsies, although it sounds paradoxical at first, were the least creative of the Eastern peoples to settle in Spain. Yet it is just that lack of creativity that allows us to disentangle the labyrinthine nature of the phenomenon leading up to the stylization of *flamenco.* That the Gypsies were doing erotic Oriental dancing typical of the areas they had come from and through at the time they entered Europe seems an acceptable assumption, especially if we bear in mind that their genius is more interpretive than creative. By Cervantes's time the Gypsies had been in Spain more than a century. Were they still doing the same erotic Eastern dances?

Not exactly. Cervantes gives us some clues because he lists precisely what Preciosa's repertoire was: *romances, seguidillas, villancicos,* and *zarabandas. Villancicos* we have already seen as the earliest European poetry and as Gypsy Christmas songs. *Seguidillas* are a Castilian verse form which eventually became the *siguiriya* in *flamenco,* the most tragic form of *cante jondo,* capable, as Lorca put it, in its *grito,* its piercing scream, of splitting the quicksilver from a mirror (1:203). *Romances,* romances or ballads, probably developed from early Castilian epic poetry. They are the epitome of Spanish popular poetry and certain ones are still sung by the Gypsies today. None of these forms could have been more Spanish. *Zarabandas* no longer exist as *zarabandas,* but in Cervantes's time they were most popular, although we could hardly include them in "honest dances." When Preciosa danced and recited a *romance,* which was never *"descompuesto,"* she drew crowds of two hundred and the coins "hailed down on her." Perhaps it is just as well she skipped the *zarabanda* in what seems to have been its usual form.

What was the real *zarabanda* like? Richard Ford knew because he had looked it up in one of the first dictionaries of the Spanish language, published in 1611 by an erudite contemporary of Cervantes, Sebastián de Covarrubias. What Covarrubias said, in fact, led Ford to make the *zarabanda*—no longer done in Ford's time— the link between the dances of Telethusa and the *romalís* of the Gypsies of his century. Covarrubias called it "happy and lascivious" because it was done with *meneos del cuerpo descompuestos* (lewd wrigglings of the body). And, said Covarrubias, "it was done in Rome in the days of Martial and the originators of it were from Cádiz and it was danced publicly in the amphitheaters." He then went on to quote Martial himself on Telethusa and to add that "although all parts of the body were moved, the arms made most gestures sounding the castanets, which is what *crusmata* in Martial's poem means. . . . " He finished by explaining that the derivation of *zarabanda* was probably from a Hebrew word meaning "to spread out, to open up, to go around, which is just what she who dances a *zarabanda* does, wiggling with the body from one place to the other and going right around the amphitheater or wherever she dances, almost causing those looking on to imitate her movements and dance along with her."[13] His description not only brings to mind a vision of the *puellae* in the Roman theaters but reminds us specifically of the verses from the Variorum we called the callipygian connection:

> *Ecquando Telethusa circulatrix*
> *Quae clunem tunica tegente nulla.*

Those verses inspired Ford to connect the girls of Cádiz, Telethusa, the statue of Venus, and the Andalusian dances he was seeing in the first place. Covarrubias's association was not as daring as Ford's, but such passages clearly put Ford on the right track. And, although Ford probably never saw the old *zarabanda,* it did not take much imagination for him to connect it to the *romalís* and the *olé* that he had seen Gypsies doing across the river in Triana.

The Gypsies' musical ability took root in two places: in eastern

Europe and western Russia, and in southern Spain. Although there are major differences between Hungarian or Russian Gypsy music and *flamenco,* the two areas where they developed had in common an already existing Oriental affinity. The Gypsies found themselves more at home in the areas where the resident populations understood Oriental traditions, areas within which the Gypsies could practice their favorite trade and where the residents were predisposed to appreciate the Gypsies' stylistic gifts. The differences between the two final developments — Russian and Hungarian Gypsy music lacks the formally hieratic dance of *flamenco* and uses the fiddle instead of the guitar for accompaniment — show how little actual creation was wrought by the Gypsies and the extent to which an indigenous musical tradition held sway in each case. Without the ancient Andalusian folk tradition, the Gypsies could have interpreted no more than they did in those non-Orientalized parts of Europe where there is nothing comparable to *flamenco.* That the Gypsies did so in spite of persecution in Spain is an indication of the cultural concentricities that the Andalusians and the Gypsies, especially certain Andalusians and certain Gypsies, had in common.

Flamenco dance, in general, is not lascivious. Yet it is primordial and powerful (and "about" sexuality and the male and female relationship), as anyone knows who has seen Carmen Amaya or Rosa Durán perform. The sinuosity and the sensuality of great *flamenco* dance evoke a timelessness and a portentousness that transcend folklore to re-create over and again out of the ashes of individual lives the collective story of humanity. What happened to the *zarabanda* and other dances to change them from lewd to transcendent dances is the ultimate secret of *flamenco.* In the final analysis it is not merely a matter of style but, as D. E. Pohren, the American flamencologist, has so aptly phrased it, "a way of life."[14]

The *zarabanda,* to judge from Covarrubias's description, was indeed like Telethusa's dances. Since the Gypsies were given to such dances long before they arrived in Spain, it comes as no surprise that we should hear of them performing this famous Spanish version. Contemporaries of Cervantes and Covarrubias confirm what the Church writings led us to suspect. In 1561 a classical scholar named Julius Caesar Scaliger wrote the following regarding the infamous dancing in the time of the Romans: *"Crissare Latini dicunt,"* and regarding the dancers, *"Omniu corruptissima Gaditana."* The Latins called it *crissare* — and the most corrupt form was from Cádiz.

Scaliger attributed the remark to Martial, leading Richard Ford to remark that the *meneo* of the *Gaditanae* of today "is considered by grave antiquarians to be the unchanged *crissatura* of Martial" (p. 322). But Scaliger made a further revealing remark: *"Apud Hispanos adhuc exercetur abominado spectaculo"* (among Spaniards this abominable spectacle is still practiced).[15]

Frederick Karl Forberg agreed with such a connection in his *De figuris Veneris,* the English translation of which, *Manual of Classical Erotology,* was privately printed in a limited edition of one hundred copies in 1844, one year before Ford's *Hand-book.* Having a decided interest in such matters, Ford quite plausibly read the following phrase: ". . . dances of the young Gaditanian girls, which were without doubt very like the dances that are still so much appreciated by the Spaniards . . . " (pp. 15, 17). Now I return to this not merely to continue unraveling Ford's sources, but to show to what extent it was perfectly clear to the students of antiquity that in these dances little or nothing had changed.

Cádiz and the surrounding ports, with their expeditions to the New World and their *almadrabas,* experienced a heyday which lasted from the fifteenth century up to the Napoleonic War. The steady stream of explorers, seamen, adventurers, soldiers of fortune, fishermen, fugitives, and swashbucklers of every ilk — the population increased tenfold with the New World trade — created a demand for *puellae Gaditanae* not equaled since Telethusa's time. When Admiral Morison supposed that Columbus joked with his crew about the *almadrabas,* he also fancied that the mere mention of Cádiz would have "caused the seamen to lick their lips in anticipation of seeing again the Cadiz girls, famous throughout Europe for their saucy beauty and salty wit."[16] As Cádiz prospered the demand for the "Cadiz girls" increased with the trade. Meanwhile the Gypsies, sifting through the ancient musical sediment of Andalucía as they arrived, flocked to the area of Sevilla, Jerez, and Cádiz and settled in as though they had known since they left India a thousand years before that this was the end of their wandering.

Even Voltaire, no friend to Gypsies and misinformed about their provenance, could easily see the figurative relationship between the ancient dancers and the Gypsies. In his *Essai sur les moeurs,* he maintained that the Gypsies were probably the descendants of the priests and priestesses of Isis and the Syrian goddess, whose castanets and tambourines derived directly from antiquity. Their race, believed

Voltaire, was disappearing now that enlightened mankind no longer believed in sorcery, talismans, and fortune telling (Vaux de Foletier pp. 25 and 238). Fortunately for our purposes no such enlightenment penetrated to Andalucía, and yet, in spite of his factual errors, Voltaire's basic intuition was close to the truth. Richard Ford, in any case, was quite positive by 1845 that the dances of antiquity and those of the Gypsies were virtually identical, and, being a Romantic, was delighted by the similarity that disturbed Voltaire.

But were they the same? It is perfectly clear that *flamenco* has become a great deal more than just erotic dancing. What happened to those dances of antiquity to metamorphose them?

Between Cervantes's age and Ford's, certain licentious dances such as the *chacona* served as a bridge between the old erotica and the newly stylized *flamenco*. The whole repertoire began gradually to change. The *seguidillas* of Cervantes's time gave us the *Sevillanas* of today, the delicately sensual folk dance performed at Andalusian *ferias* and *fiestas*. In the eighteenth century the *bolero,* which Ford knew, and the perhaps earlier *fandango,* neither licentious, were created. Undoubtedly both Gypsies and non-Gypsies danced all these forms. By Ford's time there was a double yet overlapping kind of Andalusian dancing, part of which was still quite bawdy and part of which was turning into stylized *flamenco.*

Henry Swinburne, author of *Travels Through Spain in the Years 1775 and 1776,* wrote of a certain dance practiced by the Gypsies of Cádiz called the *manguindoy,* which was considered so lascivious and indecent that it was prohibited under strictest penalty.[17] Just how indecent that was is difficult to determine, since Spanish Catholic society tended to prohibit anything different under the rubric of indecent, lewd, lascivious, or immoral. Moslem women in Granada, for instance, were forbidden as of 1511 to wear their *morisco* dresses, which the Christians called *deshonestos,* or "immoral." To our way of thinking, the Inquisition's severity may have been a greater aberration than the *manguindoy.* Yet the Gypsies did most certainly perform very provocative dances.

A description of such dancing by Gypsies in Russia declares that the bacchantes of antiquity would seem chaste alongside the possessed beauties who danced at certain fetes in some Russian country houses (Vaux de Foletier p. 146). Walter Starkie, one of the most illustrious Romany Ryes, or observers of Gypsies, in our time, made a similar comparison when he wrote of *Dukh,* the orgiastic frenzy of the South Russian Gypsies, which so possessed them that they became "like the Bacchantes of Euripides," which is to say that they resembled the maenads, the most famous of the frenzied cult dancers of antiquity.[18] There is nothing to surprise us in these descriptions, given the Oriental provenance of the Gypsies, and it is possible that some of them still preserved something of the erotic dances of Vedic tradition, although it is improbable that these dances retained their original meaning.

George Borrow, Ford's friend and one of the earliest experts on Gypsies, maintained that the Spanish *gitanas* were unrivaled in the arts of provocation:

> The Gypsy women and girls were the principal attractions to these visitors [the young Spanish noblemen]; wild and singular as these females are in their appearance, there can be no doubt, for the fact has been frequently proven, that they are capable of exciting passion of the most ardent description, particularly in the bosoms of those who are not of their race, which passion of course becomes the more violent when the almost utter impossibility of gratifying it is known. No females in the world can be more licentious in word and gesture, in dance and in song, than the Gitánas; but there they stop. . . .[19]

In 1922, Irving Brown, an American *aficionado,* wrote the following description of dances he had seen in Granada:

> The dances of the Achuchón and the Mosca recalled the primitive worship of sex, the great creative life-force. As they danced the Gypsies were no more depraved than nature itself; unconscious of any guilt in their actions as the scarlet flower of the cactus. It was a sort of barbaric religious rite, like the Dionysian revels of the Maenades. No doubt there was something of the sacred dances of India in those I saw that night, dances brought from the country of their origin, and preserved, with modifications, throughout their age-long travels. Once in America I saw a Welsh Gypsy give a similar performance, and frequently I have seen both Serbian and Russian Romanies dance in the same manner. But the Achuchón and the Mosca are older than Greece, older than ancient India and its cults in prehistoric cave temples; they are as old as man.[20]

In spite of his flourishes, Brown is, I think, on the right track in relating the maenads, the dances of India and certain forms of Gypsy dance. In any case, it is rather clear that these Gypsy dances were analogous to what their observers conceived of as the dances of antiquity.

Dancing, as we have seen, started as a religious activity, as sympathetic magic and mimesis and ritual. In time it degenerated into a profane activity. Both Andalusian and Gypsy cultures already contained this fundamental degeneration, so that what is surprising about *flamenco* is not its sexual or profane side but its hieratic side, which seems to have developed by converting sensual experience back into a kind of ritual, at once an unselfconscious homage to and appeasement of natural forces deeply rooted in the human psyche. I might be reluctant to propose this explanation were we not faced with precisely the same kind of re-creation in *toreo,* which was so intimately connected in the Andalusian mind with *flamenco. Toreo* and *flamenco* complement each other and provide us with double proof of what for the Western mind must seem an almost bizarre regression. Clearly the Gypsies continued performing lewd dances wherever they were found, but in Andalucía — and this point is worth repeating — they were also able to transcend the lascivious while still keeping in touch with the primordial Dionysian spirit we seem to have lost.

Profane dancing continues in *flamenco* circles, to be sure. James Michener tells in *Iberia* of seeing *flamenco* dancers performing nude at a private party near Barcelona (pp. 603–4), and certain elements of *flamenco* and *toreo* have always notoriously been connected with prostitution and drunkenness. Some of the foulest obscenities I have ever heard came from a famous *flamenca* on a binge one night in Morón de la Frontera, and *flamenco* is invariably steeped in alcohol. But none of these impurer elements in any way removes or interferes with the extraordinary emotional level some *flamencos* achieve. In fact, the mixture of the salacious and the transcendental only reminds us again of the very human nature of the art.

By Richard Ford's time, the more transcendental side of *flamenco* was not always evident. Ford was able to recognize the counterparts of the dances of antiquity and to agree with his friend Victor-Aimé Huber that these dances were *"die Poesie der Wollust"* (the poetry of voluptuousness) more "marked by energy than by grace" (p. 286), but was perhaps unable to understand the artistic revolution that was taking place before his eyes. In the long run Ford may be a more accurate observer precisely because he did not comprehend the larger significance of the phenomenon.

The first description we can identify as truly sounding like *flamenco* is by José Cadalso, a pre-Romantic writer from Cádiz, who in his rather autobiographical *Cartas marruecas* written sometime between 1773 and 1782, describes musical activity we can only understand as a *juerga,* a *flamenco* binge. Lost in the mountains of the province of Cádiz, precisely where we believe *flamenco* began, the narrator is taken to a *cortijo,* an isolated farm or ranch, by a young man described as wearing buckskin with many silver buttons, a cape, and a purple *pañuelo* (scarf) around his neck. He carries two handsome revolvers and rides a spirited horse. This *señorito* tells us he was educated by his grandfather, who lived to nearly one hundred and who taught him to recite *romances* and to play *polos,* an early form of *flamenco.* At the ranch a hunting party is having a *juerga,* complete with Gypsies and a certain Tío Gregorio, who beats out the rhythm for the Gypsy girls with his *palmas,* his hand-claps. The noise of Tío Gregorio's *palmas,* the castanets and the guitar, and the voices and shrieks of the Gypsies, keep the narrator awake the entire night. Although we are not told just exactly how they danced the *polo,* there is no doubt we have just attended the first literary *juerga flamenca* ever described.[21]

In Ford's time the term *flamenco* was not widely used. But Ford does mention many *flamenco* or *flamenco*-like forms: *bolero, fandango, cachucha, zapateado,* and *seguidilla,* as well as many *flamenco* terms to describe the particular ambience — *zandunga, gracia, taconeo.* Ford also knew many of the non-Gypsy forms of Andalusian folk music which would later pass into and become part of *flamenco* such as *malagueñas* and *rondeñas.* In his *Gatherings from Spain,* a rewritten and condensed version of the *Hand-book,* he describes in Triana, the Gypsy quarter of Sevilla, among the licentious wrigglings of the *romalís,* the *caña,* "The true Arabic *guania,* song, administered as a soother by some hirsute artiste without frills, studs, diamonds, or kid gloves, whose staves, sad and melancholy, always begin and end with an *ay!* a high-pitched sigh or cry. The Moorish melodies, relics of auld lang syne, are best preserved in the hill-built villages near Ronda, where there are no roads. . . ."[22] Although Ford was writing in 1846, he was remembering what he had seen in the early 1830s.

One year later, in 1847, an Andalusian, Estébanez Calderón, would supply us with splendid details in his richly evocative and definitively important sketch, "A Dance in Triana." His description, particularly of *la Perla* and her dance, is remarkably similar to *flamenco* today and is complete with "passion, delirium, frenzy," as has always been the case with Andalusian dancers, who have, he writes, since the time of the *Gaditanae* possessed "an ability and a piquancy in dancing which has been transmitted from century to century, from generation to generation, up to our time." Changed into a "passionate Terpsichore," she has in Sevilla a "workshop where the ancient dances are melted down, modified and reworked, the University in which to learn the inimitable graces, the boundless salaciousness, the sweetest attitudes, the showy whirls and the delicate movements of Andalusian dance." In Estébanez Calderón's sketch virtually all the elements of *flamenco* appear including the names of the now legendary *artistas* of the day, the singers, *el Planeta* and *el Fillo,* and the pair of dancers, *la Perla* and her escort, *el Jerezano.* *La Perla* dances "dressed in white . . . her arms raised as in ecstasy, one moment letting them fall as though in a swoon, the next agitating them as in a frenzy," while her partner follows her "less as a rival in agility than as a mortal who follows a goddess."²³ With Estébanez Calderón's article we learn definitively that *flamenco* has come into being. The wanton performances of the *puellae Gaditanae* have been transformed into a hieratic rite within the trimillenary forge of Andalusian folk culture, and the courtesan has turned back into a high priestess whose choreography, primordial but stylized, now suggests less a prostitute than a goddess. Through the stylization of certain Gypsy artists, the *baile* (dance), had been returned some share of its original purpose, a recovery impossible in most of the nineteenth-century world and perhaps only possible along the timeless corridors of Andalusian culture.

García Lorca explained the whole process of that transformation better than anyone. He called its essence *duende,* "the black sounds [which are] the mystery, the roots dug deep into the slime we all know, yet ignore, and through which all substance in art reaches us." It was not a question of talent but "of true living style, which is to say of blood, which is to say of very ancient culture, of creation in the act." It was that "mysterious power which we all feel but which no philosopher can explain"; it was, finally, "the spirit of the earth." It was Dionysian, chthonian, and immutable, the essence of Andalusian art as all Gypsies and *flamencos* knew, and without it there was no real emotion. It was most possible in *flamenco* and *toreo.* It produced unknown sensations of freshness; it was a miracle; it produced a kind of religious enthusiasm. It had to be sought in "the innermost chambers of the blood." It was the cathartic possibility still alive in art in our time, still alive in these arts of *toreo* and *flamenco* precisely because they are such atavic arts. In the dance, at the bulls, no one "enjoys himself; *duende* causes suffering through drama, through living forms, and it prepares stairways for an evasion of the reality that surrounds us" (1:1092–1109). It was, and is, a pantheistic awareness of life and death in the most primal and cathartic sense. *Duende,* like its counterpart, *tarab,* described by the poets of al-Andalus, caused a loss of all sense of self.

Duende is clearly Dionysian in the most ample sense of the word. Contrary to the Apollonian or rational, it is poetic, nonrational, intuitive, nocturnal, lunar, and probably largely a phenomenon of the right lobe of the brain. The word seems derived from a Latin form which meant house spirit, but in Andalucía it has more the sense of chthonian daimon or force. Coincidentally, the Spanish Gypsy word *duquende* has the same meaning. George Borrow wrote the earliest reference we have: in the vocabulary section of *The Zincali* (1841), he informs the reader that it means a spirit, a ghost, or, in Spanish, *duende*. It was derived from the Russian *Dook* (obviously the same as Starkie's *Dukh*) meaning a spirit, a word in turn derived from the Sanskrit term for air. A similar word, *duquendio,* meant master or principal person among the Gypsies (p. 383).

There seems to be an undeniable case of linguistic contagion involving these forms, all the more obvious if we keep in mind that *Dook* or *Dukh,* according to Starkie, meant the Dionysian spirit that produced a rare orgiastic frenzy in the Gypsies' musical *fiestas,* turning them into bacchantes. Obviously for the Gypsies this spirit was also what characterized a "principal person."

The Dionysian spirit of *duende* was, in Lorca's words, "the spirit of the earth." Juan Eduardo Cirlot, in his *Dictionary of Symbols,* has some very germane comments on what chthonian daimons, the mythological representations of "the spirit of the earth," mean:

> They are symbols of thanatic forces, of the death-wish in various guises: the subtle fascination of dreams, or the heroic thrill experienced by the man who answers the call to battle. This quest for death—extremes meet (because of the curve of the conceptual line)—is apparent in limit-situations, not only in the negative aspect but also—and principally—at the peak of the

affirmative. That is, vital optimism and perfect happiness of necessity imply the other extreme, that is, the presence of death.[24]

Duende, the chthonian spirit of inspiration of this affirmative Andalusian culture of death, never approaches, according to Lorca, "unless it sees the possibility of death" (1:1105).

The Andalusian writer and flamencologist J. M. Caballero Bonald follows these ideas of Lorca's and Cirlot's, this "logic" of Andalucía, to a poignant conclusion in the following profound passage:

> The true listener of *flamenco* expects to encounter through arriving at a presumed "limit-situation," something which, even though it does not correspond with his own life, moves him to compassion and excites him within. The truth expressed by the performer of *flamenco* is that truth intuited by the most predisposed witnesses. It is not really a *fiesta* in the usual sense so much as the biological sublimation of an anguished intimacy, even when the vehicle chosen belongs to the songs and dances appropriate to a *fiesta.* The singer or the dancer represents in a certain way the *pueblo,* the people, and it is that *pueblo* to whom the performer tells a fragment of his or her unfortunate life with the unconscious intention of purging a given affliction by having others identify with it. By virtue of a personal drama changed into a furious lament of the voice or into the fluid symbols of dance, the viewer or listener can feel himself drawn into the most esoteric zones of exaltation. Relating the ultimate meaning of this spiritual process to ancient Dionysian rites, or, at the very least, to the sacred ceremonies of certain primitive peoples, is unavoidable. The proximity to ecstasy and the appearance of delirium can obey, and in fact do obey, very similar psychological or religious reasons. The performer unexpectedly enters into a clairvoyant region or into a capacity for plenitude which is not inherent in the significance of his or her theme nor in any artistic ostentation of music or dance—much less any vocal or physical virtuosity. Rather it is inherent in that *trasfondo,* that nether world, of expression—the *duende*—from which gushes the unforseen jet of *flamenco* revelation.[25]

The Cordoban poet Ricardo Molina, with his poet's ability to synthesize, expressed the essential secret of *flamenco* as "the direct exposition of the universal anguish of death, of the mystery of sex, of the joy of being" (p. 61). Molina's threefold description of the art is brilliant. What else in Western culture combines so directly the vexing, the paradoxical, the awesome triunity — life, death, and sex — of our existence? *Flamenco* fleetingly recovers, when found in its rare purity, some of the splendor, the awe, and the mystery we have surrendered in exchange for the benefits of materialistic rationalism.

The finest interpreters of such a rare art were certain Gypsies such as Manuel *Torre,* perhaps the greatest *flamenco* singer of all time, an illiterate whom Lorca nonetheless called, "The man with the greatest culture of blood I have ever known" (1:1098). Lorca knew that some Andalusian Gypsies had identified so thoroughly with Andalucía that they had become the quintessential Andalusians. About his *Gypsy Romances* he once commented that the book was Gypsy not because it was really Gypsy but because it was Andalusian: "The gypsy is the purest and most authentic thing in Andalucía." Then he made an extremely important qualification: not the filthy beggars in rags who wandered from town to town — they were *húngaros,* that is, they were not Andalusian Gypsies. The true Gypsies were people who had never stolen and who never wore rags (1:1121–22).

Who were these mythic Gypsies of Lorca's? Did they really exist, or were they a poetic fancy of his? Indeed they did exist and Lorca knew many of them very well. In a 1933 interview he explained what he meant: "From Jerez to Cádiz, ten families of absolutely pure blood are guarding the glorious tradition of *flamenco.*" From Jerez to Cádiz is a stone's throw, but in the Gypsy quarters known as the *barrio de Santiago* and the *barrio de Santa María* of those towns, and in the mountain towns above Jerez as far as Ronda, and in Triana, the Gypsy quarter across the river from Sevilla, almost all *flamenco* was elaborated. Ten families is a sizable number of people since Gypsy families tend to be large. Ten clans he might have said, and, of course, the number ten is merely emblematic — we might say a dozen or so.

Lorca went on to tell of a small boy dancing barefoot, whose rhythmic sense of balance and proportion were so superb as to bring tears to Lorca's eyes, who possessed "the heroic rhythm of my whole people, of our whole history," who was the incarnation of the "hot ashes" of the Andalusian past. Then he said, but "let not the intellectuals tire themselves out searching for it in the old trunks of erudition," because *flamenco* was "something alive with its feet buried in the hot mud of the street and its head in the cool fleece of the driven clouds."[26]

D. E. Pohren, the American flamencologist whose study *The Art of Flamenco* won the coveted Spanish National Flamenco Award, published a family tree of the Ortega family, Gypsies of Cádiz, that graphically bears out Lorca's contention. At the top is the legendary *el Planeta,* whom we met in "A Dance in Triana," and the enigmatic singer known only as *Curro Dulce,* his stage name. There are seven or eight generations on the chart dating from about 1800, including many of the most famous *toreros* and *flamenco* performers in the history of either art. As Pohren remarks, the Ortegas are typical "of the *flamenco* dynasties of the past, when everyone in the family, from grandma to grandchildren, was steeped in *flamenco*" (p. 55). The Ortega family is also married into other *flamenco* and *toreo* clans: the Espeleta, the Jiménez, the Pavón, the Gómez, and includes such famous performers as Ignacio Sánchez Mejías, the *torero* of Lorca's "Lament"; the brothers Joselito and Rafael *el Gallo,* the most famous Gypsy *toreros* in the twentieth century (in the case of Joselito, perhaps the greatest of all time); and Manolo *Caracol,* one of the most famous singers of the twentieth century and the winner, as a boy, of the *flamenco* festival put on by Lorca and Manuel de Falla in Granada in 1922. There are many others worthy of mention, but this brief examination of one family gives an inkling of what Lorca meant by ten families.

These ten families have provided the singular guiding geniuses of these rare and beautiful art forms, as esoteric as they are complex and misunderstood. These ten families of Gypsies, more Gypsy in sensibility than in ethnic purity, these ten families of interpreters of Andalucía, represent the tip of the iceberg — or the rim of the volcano — of Andalusian art, and they were the source and substance of much of Lorca's poetry. He made some of them into the mythic heroes of that poetry as he re-created in his *Gypsy Romances* a pristine and timeless Andalucía that ran unbroken from the early part of this century back to the time of David's children, Thamar and Amnon, the subjects, at once biblical and Andalusian, of one of his finest poems (1:391–442). That time span seems figuratively shorter, especially in Andalucía, than the one that stretches forward from the turn of the century to the present. Lorca's "City of the Gypsies," as he called his visionary *barrio* of moonlight and sand, was the final ephemeral flicker of a campfire built three thousand years ago.

Skeptics who doubt that any place can remain so essentially the same for such a length of time should examine the fine, round, bronze *crótalos* on exhibit at the Museo Arqueológico in Huelva. They were unearthed at Ríotinto where some remote grandmother of Telethusa played them as she danced in the firelight centuries before the Romans set foot in Andalucía. Her dance may not have been exactly *flamenco* as we know it, but she surely raised from the watching chorus of Phoenician and Tartessian silver miners the same kind of enthusiasm that the granddaughter of Telethusa did at that *baile* in Triana.

THE RELIGIOUS CELEBRATION, actually a pilgrimage, known as the Romería del Rocío is a unique Andalusian *fiesta,* which provides an unsuspected window on the religious practices of antiquity. At the climax of the *fiesta,* the men of the town of Almonte parade La Virgen del Rocío through the streets on her palanquin and attempt to keep anyone else from touching her. *Photograph by Allen Josephs.*

CHAPTER FIVE
GODDESS

The oldest settlement on the Iberian peninsula, the oldest town we can identify as at least a collection of huts, probably dates from the fifth millennium B.C. Yet, in spite of its extreme age, El Gárcel, as the low rise is known, contained many of the characteristic elements of Andalusian life. The excavations on that hill in Almería turned up wheat and rye grains, olive pits, and grape seeds. Some six thousand years ago the traditional life of the Mediterranean had already taken shape at El Gárcel.

Bread and wine and oil, as essential and typical as they are, do not tell the whole story. At El Gárcel and at Carmona (still a thriving town near Sevilla, and almost as old as El Gárcel) there were pits used for burial. At Los Millares, a fortified town near Almería with walls eight feet thick whose inhabitants worked copper and silver and grew wheat, barley, and beans, there was an extraordinary cemetery with some hundred passage graves of the "beehive" type. Inside the huts and the tombs were a vast quantity of female figurines. Some were stone or schist plaques, others were bone, alabaster, or ivory; some had round "owl eyes," while others were more stylized. Even at El Gárcel there was a fiddle-shaped female figure. To anyone remotely familiar with her cult, these figurines can only signify the existence of the religion of the Great Mother-goddess.*

The Mother-goddess in one form or another has been venerated since the Ice Age when primitive sculptors carved numerous Paleolithic Venus figures to celebrate the miracle of fertility and birth. By the time the worship of the Goddess reached Iberia, it had become

---

*Mother-goddess and Goddess, used as proper names in this chapter, are captialized throughout.

a stylized religion, as the enormous quantity of figurines indicates. Soon the cult spread westward over all of Andalucía and southern Portugal, and the worshipers of the Goddess built the great megalithic tombs, La Cueva de Menga and La Cueva de Romeral near Antequera. They built others as well—in Sevilla, Huelva, and southern Portugal—as southern Iberia, or greater Andalucía, from Almería to the Tagus became the earliest and most important center in the West of the oldest religion we know.

The recent revisions of the carbon dating process have thrown the dates of early Spanish cultures into a state of confusion. Nothing is definite so far, but the traditional dates for El Gárcel and Los Millares, for Carmona and the megalithic graves, in fact for all the early archaeological finds in Andalucía, have to be pushed back. We can safely say that the culture that developed the passage graves and the megaliths dates from at least the fourth millennium, a development that invalidates the usual theory that the graves and megaliths stemmed originally from Minoan Crete. The new dates do not destroy the diffusionist theory that this culture came from the East, but they do suggest looking for an earlier source than Minoan civilization.

The dates of the neolithic of the Near East have been pushed back dizzyingly in recent years, and archaeologists now almost routinely begin discussing Jericho in the ninth millennium and sites in Anatolia in the seventh. Two of the Anatolian sites, Çatal Hüyük and Hacilar, provide some very interesting early parallels or analogues for Andalucía. Not only does a reconstruction of the town of Çatal Hüyük bring to mind immediately an Andalusian *pueblo,* especially one from the Alpujarra region in Granada, but certain designs and motifs are virtually identical with those found at Los Millares and other sites, especially the spiral so often associated with the Mother-goddess. Also quite suggestive are the bull worship at Çatal Hüyük and the baked clay figurine of the Goddess riding on two felines. This figurine anticipates a famous Phoenician figurine found at Galera, near Granada, and it also prefigures the usual representation of Cybele, the adopted Anatolian Goddess of the Romans, drawn by lions, the most dramatic example of which in Spain is the neoclassical statue of her in one of Madrid's central *plazas.* However tenuous the connection may seem, some of the main motifs of the Mother-goddess, which appear endlessly in Andalucía from El Gárcel to the present, were present in Anatolia at an extremely early date.

Whether the Goddess came in an early Semitic or Cycladic ship, or overland from Anatolia and the Balkans, or whether she developed over and over, slowly and individually from the cultures of the stag-dancers and the Venus-carvers, or whether, in fact, she sprang full-blown in some primeval epiphany into the mind of a Neolithic Andalusian on the low hill of El Gárcel, is not our main concern. What is important is that by the time the mining and farming settle-ment was established at Los Millares, by the early fourth millennium B.C., another constant of Andalusian life was in place: the worship of and belief in fertility, sexuality, birth, death, and regeneration, all the natural and chthonic processes understood as stemming from Mother Earth. Andalucía had joined at a very early date the wor-ship of Inanna, Ishtar, Asherah, Ashtart, Ashtoreth, Astarte, Isis, Aphrodite, Atargatis, Anath, Artemis, Cybele, the Dea Syria, Demeter, the Magna Mater, Venus, Diana, Tanit, and Salammbo, to name a few of those who were but different avatars—earth, moon, Venus, "high place," mountaintop, cave, or spring—of the same pan-theistic belief in the natural process of life. In spite of all the aber-rant modifications that succeeding civilizations have imposed on this fundamental belief, it has continued to exist in Andalucía in one form or another up to the present.

At some as yet undetermined time the culture of the megalith builders and the related dynamic culture centered around Carmona and famous for its Bell Beaker ware, gave way to cultures we usual-ly refer to as Iberian and Tartessian. The ethnological problems of the second millennium and the extent of influence from Anatolia and the Cyclades, Crete and Mycenae, Lebanon and Syria, Europe and North Africa are far from settled. Most of Iberia underwent a great deal of flux as trade routes were expanded and populations shifted, yet Andalucía and southern Portugal remained relatively stable, already absorbing and incorporating outside elements. And, aside from the possible exception of the Bronze Age culture of El Argar in Almería, the Mother-goddess remained ascendant.

As we approach historical times, we hear from the ancient sources of such cults. Avienus's uncertain description of the coast of Andalucía, drawing on very early sources, contains notices of a cave sanctuary and a temple sacred to an "infernal goddess," possibly a local cult to the Earth-mother as the goddess of death and the underworld, and of a temple complete with inner sanctuary and oracle dedicated to a "Venus of the Sea." There is also mention of an island of the Moon, and another island sacred to "Noctilucae," near Málaga and under the sway of the Tartessians (lines 241, 315, 367, 429). And Strabo echoed the reports of a sanctuary to the planet Venus by the mouth of the Guadalquivir (3.1.9). Given the many forms the Mother-goddess assumed and the close association of Andalusians and Phoenicians and other Eastern peoples, none of these versions of the Goddess should surprise us. Whether they appear as the result of contact from the East, whether they are autochthonous deities, or whether they are the result of a combination is less our concern than her multifaceted pervasiveness.

Schulten thought the Minoans were the primary outside influence on the early Tartessians. Certainly their maritime supremacy and their undivided devotion to the Goddess encourage us to accept strong Minoan influence in Andalucía. The ritual cult dances and the bull sacrifices of Crete are also powerfully suggestive and hauntingly similar to later practices in Spain. Though the Minoans do not seem to be the first traders from the East, the common occurrence of passage graves and megaliths, the common motifs of horns and spirals and similar pottery, as well as similar daggers, pendants, and jewelry, indicate more than highly analogous ways of life, although much conclusive archaeological evidence is so far lacking.

By the first millennium, when Phoenician thalassocracy replaced Minoan dominance of the Mediterranean and the Phoenicians took over the trade with southern Spain, we have some remarkable archaeological evidence substantiating continued worship of the Goddess. One of the most striking pieces is certainly the *bronce de Carriazo,* very probably, as we have seen earlier, the representation of Astarte, the Goddess of the Phoenicians, as interpreted by some Tartessian bronze-smith.

Another remarkable piece is the bronze sculpture of the seated nude figure of Astarte in the Archaeological Museum in Sevilla. Excavated nearby and sometimes called *La Diosa de Sevilla,* "the Goddess of Sevilla," she is actually Phoenician, as the language on her plinth reveals. The image, which dates from the eighth century B.C., was a votive offering by a certain B'lytn, given as grateful acknowledgement to Astarte because, as the inscription reveals, she had heard his voice in prayer.[1]

Equally of interest is the alabaster Astarte sitting on a throne between two sphinxes in the precise attitude of the Goddess from Çatal Hüyük, holding a ritual vessel of libation. This Phoenician fertility Goddess, one of the most important Phoenician pieces in the National Archaeological Museum in Madrid, has a hollowed head and holes bored through her breasts to allow the libation to flow out. Known as the Dama de Galera, she was found in a tomb near Galera in the province of Granada and is dated from the seventh century. Another Astarte—nude, standing and touching her breasts—corresponding to types from the previous millennium is also reported in a private collection in Granada.[2]

Countless other representations of the Goddess (especially winged female figures on pieces of pottery) indicate that as the first millennium moved toward our era, her cult spread eastward and northward along the Mediterranean coast, first as the Phoenician Astarte, then as her Carthaginian avatar, Tanit, and to a lesser extent, her Greek version, Aphrodite. Especially after the Carthaginians established their capital in Iberia at Carthago Nova (now Cartagena), we notice a preponderance of Oriental elements in the jewelry, pottery, and sculpture of eastern Andalucía and the adjoining province of Murcia. The Archaeological Museum in Madrid comprises a storehouse of these pieces, virtually every one of which bears the characteristic iconography of the Goddess in one form or another.

The most impressive pieces are the life-size sculptures in stone known as the Dama de Baza and the Dama de Elche. The former is a full-length seated funerary Goddess, which was excavated from a tomb near Baza in Granada in 1971 after twenty-four centuries in the earth. In her left hand she cradles a dove and within her is an urn with the ashes of the deceased. La Dama de Elche, whose precise dates and archaeological details are uncertain (she is estimated at around the fourth century also), is nothing less than the single most stunning piece of ancient art from Spain. Luxuriously Oriental in costume, she possesses a quite striking facial perfection, the enigmatic quality of which seems due to a perfect mixture of realism and stylization. Originally she was probably also full-length, and the hollow in her back strongly suggests that she too was a funerary Goddess. In all probability La Dama de Elche, like La Dama de Baza, was a native representation of the Carthaginian Goddess, Tanit. In any case, she is ancient Spain's most exquisite realization of the feminine principle. To be appreciated fully she should be seen presiding over her two rooms of pre-Roman antiquities in the Archaeological Museum in Madrid, rooms that offer an incontrovertibly sumptuous tribute to her veneration.

Many native, probably Celtic or pre-Celtic, gods were worshiped in Iberia, but virtually all the indigenous cults developed north of Andalucía. From southern Portugal across Andalucía to Valencia and the Balearic Islands the cults were almost exclusively Oriental. Phoenicians, Carthaginians, Syrians, Jews, Greeks, Cypriots, and Egyptians brought their own deities with them when they came to Spain, and these imported Eastern religions took root and flourished as though they were at home in the East. For at least fifteen centuries, from the founding of Cádiz down to Avienus's reporting of the yearly rites of Hercules in the fifth century A.D. (lines 274, 275), they formed the basis of spiritual life in southern Spain. Astarte in one of her many guises was the most widely venerated of these divinities, and she was especially popular in Andalucía, where the largest numbers of Semites were, and at Elche where she also had a temple.

By the time the Romans turned the Mediterranean into Mare Nostrum, many Eastern religions, originally from Egypt, Phoenicia, Anatolia, Syria, and Mesopotamia, had spread over the Roman Empire. In the process of flux, reflux, dissolution, redefinition, and assimilation we call religious syncretism, they had largely replaced the official religions, the pantheon of well-known Greek and Roman mythological figures, which had come to hold little significance, especially for the general populace. These syncretistic cults, usually known as mystery religions, sought some promise of individual salvation of the soul. The vast majority of them were dedicated to the Goddess in one of her many guises, so many of which existed that Plutarch was led to call her the Goddess of ten thousand names. (*Isis and Osiris* 53).

Usually the Goddess was linked to a partner—son, husband, or consort—who complemented her, often died for her, and whose redemption or resurrection became a central concern of the mysteries. Melkart, the Baal, or "lord," of Tyre, was just such a figure, and an annual feast of resurrection was celebrated in his honor. Hiram of Tyre built a temple for him, and probably for Astarte as well, which may well have been the model for Solomon's temple. When the Tyrians founded Gadir they took their deity with them and built one of the most famous temples of antiquity to him. In time Melkart became the Gaditanian Hercules, assimilating the Greek hero in the process, and his temple became known as the temple of Hercules.

Although the descriptions of the temple are somewhat conflicting, they are also extraordinarily suggestive. It probably had columns of bronze (Strabo 3.5.5), which would make them like the pillars of Solomon's temple, Jachin and Boaz, which the same Hiram had a famous Tyrian bronze-smith make. Logically enough, these columns were sometimes said to be the actual "Pillars of Hercules." One source even claimed they were made of an alloy of gold and silver (Philostratus *Vita Apoll.* 5.5), which makes them sound suspiciously like Plato's fabulous metal, *orichalcum*—but then Plato also spoke in the same breath of an island near the Pillars of Hercules called Gadeira or Gadeirus, a reference that has aroused a good deal of speculation and caused more than one writer, then and now, to believe that Andalucía and Atlantis are closely related (*Critias* 114).

The temples of Hercules were famous indeed, and Herodotus reported that the temple at Tyre, which he saw himself, had two magnificent pillars, one of gold and the other of emerald, which glowed in the night (2.44). We may have a sketch of such a temple in an Assyrian relief showing part of the city of Tyre, including a high building with two columns topped with spiraled capitals like Jachin and Boaz (1 Kings 7:21, 22). Precisely such a Phoenician capital, thought to be from the temple of Astarte, was excavated at Cádiz.[3]

The temple of Hercules was located on what is today the island called Farallón Grande, just off the coast from the town of Sancti Petri and a few miles south of Cádiz. Legend has it that Santiago destroyed the temple and dedicated it to Saint Peter. In fact, the temple seems to have lasted remarkably—the timbers were said by Silius Italicus to be imperishable (*Punica* 3)—and it was not destroyed until A.D. 1145 when an Almoravid chieftain, Ibn Maymun, demolished it searching for the treasures it was supposed to hold. Ford said the foundations were visible, owing to the earthquake of Lisbon in 1755 (p. 329). As do so many sites in Andalucía, it awaits further study.

Hannibal visited the famous temple to consult with the bald, linen-clad priests just before his famous elephant-march on Italy, and on the beach at Gadir he parted with his Andalusian wife, Imilce, and his infant son, neither of whom he would see for the next fifteen years, during which he systematically ravaged Italy (*Punica* 3). "Joy of Baal," fiercest of the lion's brood as his father called him and his brothers, Hannibal so terrified the Romans that in 204 B.C., when he was "at the gates of Rome," they brought the Phrygian Mother-goddess, Cybele, from Asia to Rome in order to save themselves. There is no little irony in the fact the Romans thus institutionalized the deities of their archenemies the Carthaginians more effectively for the rest of Roman history than if Hannibal had succeeded in taking Rome. (Cybele and Astarte or Tanit are but examples of the ten thousand names of the same Goddess.) Transporting the stone image of the Goddess from Pessinus in Asia Minor to Rome brought the Oriental Goddess to a new home in the capital of the West and ensured her syncretistic triumph from Persia to Portugal for the next five hundred years.

Hannibal was not the only famous warrior to come to the temple of Hercules. Julius Caesar saw a statue of Alexander there — a singular honor bestowed on the Macedonian "he goat," as the prophet Daniel called him (8:5, 21), for not having destroyed the temple at Tyre — and sighed or groaned aloud, as if to express his impatience at not having yet achieved the same glory as Alexander. But the interpreters of dreams from the oracle soothed the impetuous quaestor by interpreting an incestuous dream with his mother as a sign that he was to rule the world, since his mother was symbolic of the earth, an interpretation that makes us wonder if the oneiromancers of the temple of Hercules were really devotees of the Goddess (Suetonius *De Vita Caesarum* 1.7).

It was, in any case, a favorite son of Andalucía, Trajan, born at nearby Itálica, who most clearly emulated Alexander by pushing the frontiers of the Empire to the Persian Gulf. Although he spent most of his time fighting in the East, Trajan and his appointed heir, Hadrian, were reputedly members of a political and literary "clan" from Baetica. During their reigns a great number of building projects were undertaken, which began a kind of Golden Age in Baetica lasting off and on into the fourth century. Many of the Roman ruins so visible throughout Andalucía today, for example the theaters of Mérida, Itálica, Acinipo (Ronda la vieja), and the amphitheater at Itálica, were built or remodeled during this period. Fittingly enough, Hadrian minted coins, in the tradition of Punic coins that bore a likeness of Hercules, with the inscription "Hercules Gaditans."

By the time of Trajan, the late syncretistic cults with their emphasis on salvation had permeated Andalucía as they did the rest of the Empire. Perhaps it would be more accurate to say repermeated in the case of Andalucía, since the cult dedicated in Roman times to Adonis and Salammbo, for example, was essentially the same as the cult of Adonis and Astarte which paralleled that of Astarte and Melkart-Hercules already celebrated at Cádiz for over a thousand years. Whether the cults were the original Oriental versions, the later somewhat Hellenized versions, or the late Roman versions, nearly all of them were devoted to fundamentally the same Goddess and her consort. Whether we are considering, in the case of Andalucía, a Neolithic cult to the Earth Mother; the Goddess of the Phoenicians, Astarte, who was paired with Melkart-Hercules; any of the Venus-Aphrodite-Astarte-Tanit-Salammbo figures from Syria, Phoenicia, and Carthage often paired with a dying and resurrecting deity called Adonis; or the Phrygian Goddess, Cybele, paired with the dying and resurrecting Attis, we are always dealing with essentially the same figure. Her rites differed somewhat and her name may have changed ten thousand times, but she was the same essential archetype of the feminine principle. To put it another way, the syncretistic cults of the Goddess which became so popular throughout the Roman Empire, whatever her name or whatever her country of origin, were as familiar in Andalucía, where the Goddess had already been worshiped from time out of mind, as they were in Egypt, Canaan, Syria, or Anatolia. And when these cults, derived from the myths and rites of the Near East long before Roman times, evolved into the so-called mystery religions, that evolution took place in Andalucía as well.

The archaeological evidence for these cults is not nearly as great as it might have been, partly because not enough excavation has been undertaken, but mainly because the Christians ransacked the shrines and destroyed the images. The statues representing the emperors and "official" deities tended to survive because they were considered harmless, but the icons of the rival mystery cults were mutilated and destroyed whenever possible. As the Christians began to take over the reins of power of the Empire, they went about systematically and sometimes brutally eradicating any traces of their rivals.

Vandalism was probably the case, for example, at the "Tomb of the Elephant," a shrine of Attis and Cybele unearthed at the necropolis in Carmona, where the mutilated stone image of an African elephant, its tusks pulled out and its legs and trunk broken off, was found thrown into a well along with the baetyl, or sacred stone image, of Cybele. Although it is located at the necropolis at Carmo, as the Romans called this commanding bluff where the Bell Beaker culture had begun, "tomb" is probably a misnomer for a main sanctuary used by a great many of the inhabitants of Carmo from about the reign of Claudius, who made the cult of Attis and Cybele part of the state religion, in the first century A.D. down to the time of its destruction. Here the faithful came to worship the generative principle of life in the Goddess believed to have created herself. Protectress of animals, sailors, and travelers, Goddess of mountains and water, she was an all powerful Goddess who rode upon a throne in a lion-drawn chariot. And here they came to worship her sharer in omnipotence, Attis, her virgin-born lover or her son, whose death was ritualized in the immolation of a pine tree, the auto-castrator whose resurrection to life and to divinity by the Goddess theoretically ensured the change of seasons, the fertility of the fields, and, for the initiate, immortality. This ritual of burning the god may be much older in Andalucía than the Roman cult of Attis and Cybele, and it is quite possible that the "man of the sea" once observed burning away on the beach at Cádiz, as Pausanias tells the story (10.4.6), was actually the burning effigy of Hercules-Melkart in a similar but much older Phoenician rite.

In Rome, after the cult of Attis and Cybele became official, the *galli* or priests, may have forgone their original rite of castration and substituted the equivalent parts from a bull slain in the *taurobolium,* a ritual sacrifice long connected to the worship of the Goddess. Rites, games, sacrifices, theatrical performances, ecstatic dancing accompanied by the music of flutes, tambourines, drums, and cymbals, and processions with the divine attributes and images, were all part of the celebration.

The main feast days were from the fifteenth to the twenty-seventh of March. On the twenty-fourth funerals for Attis were celebrated, accompanied by wild dancing and music, lamentation and ritual wailing, and auto-flagellation with ritual instruments. First light of the twenty-fifth symbolized the resurrection and the beginning of Carnival or the Hilaria, a celebration echoing the *hieros gamos* or sacred union, celebrated by an orgiastic masquerade and banquet. The twenty-seventh was a day of ablutions and probably of initiations and baptism by water and blood, followed by a ritual banquet symbolizing union with the family of divinities.

Regardless how these practices strike us, the mystery cults made up the main religious activity of the times. Although they were much maligned by Christians, writers such as Plutarch, Lucian, and Apuleius indicate that some of the cults became highly spiritual or transcendental. Many people were initiated into more than one cult. Constantine was both a Christian and a Mithraic, and Augustine was a Manichean before he became a Christian. The value or importance of the mystery religions is probably best measured by the extent to which the early Church preserved and subsumed, whether intentionally or not, different facets, rituals, beliefs, and customs of these cults.

It is interesting, for example, that precisely nine months after the celebration of the *hieros gamos,* an ancient celebration common to many of the mystery cults, the faithful of Attis and Cybele would return to the sanctuary to celebrate the birth of the sun, *Natalis invicti,* the winter solstice sacred to Mithra, and assimilated by Attis, on the twenty-fifth of December. In Carmona on that day, the sun's rays would come directly through a special window cut in the triclinium, or sacred banquet room at the santuary, to illuminate the figure of the elephant, an animal of symbolic importance to solar cults, particularly in Africa.[4]

The elephant had been sacred to Tanit in Carthage and was also sacred to Helios in North Africa. It was probably natural to the process of syncretism that the animal sacred both to an African version of the Goddess and to an African solar deity should later be incorporated to the veneration of Cybele and Attis at Carmona, especially if the veneration of Cybele and Attis had been brought into Spain, as that of Tanit had been, and as Christianity later would be, not directly from Rome, but by way of North Africa. If that is true as seems likely, since the cult of Attis and Cybele was quite strong in Africa, the elephant of Carmona may be a very apt symbol of Andalusian syncretism, especially since his presence in Europe cannot fail to remind us once again of Hannibal, who first caused the adoption of the cult in Rome. Restored to his original pedestal in the triclinium, this numinous elephant keeps us from forgetting just how long-lived and intertwined some aspects of Andalusian life can be.

Just as pagan practice recorded by pagan writers sometimes inadvertently provides us with insight into early Christian practices, so the early Christian accounts of the martyrs can provide insights into the rites of the rival cults. Thus it is with a fascinating account from the obscure hagiographic material relating to the martyrdom of two Christian girls from Triana, the suburb across the river from Sevilla, in the year 287.

Justa and Rufina, the daughters of a Triana potter, were selling their father's wares in the market of Hispalis, Roman Sevilla, when they were surprised by a procession of devotees of Salammbo and Adonis. The brilliantly costumed cultists were parading the stone image of the Goddess on her palanquin through the streets as they performed ritual dances to the beat of noisy music. These cousins of Telethusa were collecting funds as entitled by Roman law for the maintenance of their cult by soliciting *stipes* (change) from those who watched the performance. This practice is completely in keeping with what we know about these rites. In all the famous temples of Phoenicia and Syria dancers performed in honor of the Goddess, and these women were surely dancing to collect money to celebrate their yearly festival in the proper fashion. These local ladies, *"matronae oppidanae,"* asked the girls (according to the very important sixteenth-century Portuguese text, the *Breviarium Eborense*) not merely for money, but specifically for *"vas aliquod in dei Salabovis [sic] usum,"* that is, for some piece of pottery to be used in the ceremony of Salammbo. When the girls refused, the indignant *matronae* broke up their pottery. In return Justa and Rufina, resentful or pious or both, smashed the image of the Goddess and were promptly arrested by Diogenianus, the governor of Hispalis, who put them straight into prison. Later the manuscript relates that the governor made these iconoclasts walk barefoot to a place nearby, after which Justa died in prison and her body was thrown into a deep well, while Rufina was executed in prison and then burned in the amphitheater.[5]

To understand what has happened we must examine briefly the belief behind this cult of Adonis and Salammbo, another name for Astarte. Adonis, which the Greeks evidently thought a name, was *adon* in Phoenician, a generic term much like *baal*. They were not names: *adon* meant "master" or "young lord" and *baal* meant "lord" or "ruler." Astarte and Adonis represented in Byblos, the most ancient Phoenician city, the Goddess and her dying and resurrecting consort, celebrated by all the Semitic peoples and later assimilated by the Greeks and the Romans. Adonis, Attis, to some extent Tammuz, and sometimes Osiris, are all basically the same sacrificed *adon;* in later cults Dionysus and others take on some of his attributes.

Originally Adonis and Astarte had temples at Byblos, and at

Akfa at the source of the tumultuous Adonis River, today called Nahr Ibrahim. Every year, according to the rituals, Adonis was believed killed by a wild boar in this river gorge, which is still venerated in the popular mind. The waters are considered to have healing properties, and childless women continue to bring offerings in hopes of the miracle of fertility. From time immemorial (Byblos goes back to 5000 B.C.) the plaints of the women of Phoenicia and Syria sounded in the spring for the beloved of Astarte. The red anemone — blood-red like a pomegranate's pulp — was believed to bloom from Adonis's blood (Ovid *Met.* 10.735), and the river itself turned red and ran into the sea spreading a bloodlike stain into the Mediterranean, an occurrence that still takes place when spring storms mix the red earth of Lebanon into the waters of the river.[6] As is often the case in early agricultural societies, mythic or ritual belief was used to explain and to help ensure the annual repetition of natural phenomena. When the rites of Adonis were first taken to Andalucía, the ritual mourners may have been somewhat reassured: the Guadalquivir runs more brown than red, but the fields of Andalucía glisten so intensely with poppies in the spring that the comparison with drops of blood is almost inevitable.

The rites of Adonis and Astarte varied widely, and at some indeterminate moment the festival, or one of the festivals, moved from spring to summer. Some of the rites, however, remained unchanged, especially lamentation for the death of Adonis and ritual offerings to the deities. Unfortunately we know too little about these rites whose practitioners were often bound to secrecy, but the Old Testament provides enough here and there to begin to construct a composite picture of them. Without that picture we cannot understand what happened in Andalucía since such rites were taken at an early date from Tyre to Cádiz, and in Roman times to every town in Andalucía.

Ezekiel saw the women of Jerusalem weeping for Tammuz (the Babylonian version of Adonis) at the north gate of the Temple (8:14). And Jeremiah tells us, "The children gather wood, and the fathers kindle the fire, and the women knead their dough, to make cakes to the queen of heaven" (7:18). The Jews of Egypt explain to Jeremiah in no uncertain terms that they shall continue "to burn incense unto the queen of heaven, and to pour out drink offerings unto her, as we have done, we, and our fathers, our kings, and our princes, in the cities of Judah, and in the streets of Jerusalem: for then we had plenty of victuals, and were well, and saw no evil" (44:17). The "queen of heaven" is, of course, Astarte identified with the planet Venus. The cakes for the "queen of heaven" were probably in the form of the Goddess herself. At the palace kitchen at Mari on the Euphrates just such a mold, a nude seated figure touching her breasts, for making cakes in the image of the "queen of heaven" has been discovered.[7] Hosea, who seems to have married a hierodule, a ritual prostitute sacred to the Goddess, also mentions these cakes: "Then said the Lord unto me, Go yet, love a women beloved of her friend, yet an adulteress, according to the love of the Lord toward the children of Israel, who look to other gods, and love flagons of wine" (3:1). There is no doubt that both the Canaanites and the Israelites loved wine, but the King James translation is incorrect. It should read "cakes of raisins," instead of "flagons of wine."[8]

An important description of the ritual occurs in the beautiful and enigmatic book of lyric poetry usually known as the Song of Solomon. Many biblical scholars now believe that the Song of Solomon echoes the rites of Astarte and Adonis, or at least very similar practices. In any case, the raisin-cakes show up again in 2:5 in a verse which reads in the King James, "Stay me with flagons," and which should read, "Comfort me with raisin-cakes."[9] Another important part of the ritual appears in 4:16; we read: "Awake, O north wind; and come thou south; blow upon my garden, that the spices thereof may flow out. Let my beloved come into his garden and eat his pleasant fruits." The "garden" was an Adonis-garden, a pot filled with earth and sown with seeds that sprouted quickly. These gardens of Adonis were an integral part of the Adonis ritual and were known to the Hebrews as Isaiah made clear, "and ye shall be confounded for the gardens that ye have chosen" (1:29), a practice he connected with backsliding into that old-time religion of the Canaanites. Both the cakes and the Adonis-gardens were used at Alexandria, where the marriage of Astarte and Adonis was celebrated one day and the death of Adonis mourned the next. The cry "Return, return," in 6:13 of the Song of Solomon, echoes the cry of bare-breasted mourning women who at Alexandria carried images of Adonis in a procession and threw them into the sea. At the temple of Akfa the pilgrims threw their images into a sacred cistern which is still visible.

If we keep in mind several elements of the rituals of Astarte and Adonis, especially the gardens of Adonis, the images of the deities, and the processions to the water, we can understand what happened to Justa and Rufina in Hispalis. The piece of pottery solicited by the chorus of Salammbo was not merely a request for merchandise but a specific petition for a *vas* to use as the container for a garden of Adonis. Thus the Christian girls' refusal may have amounted in the minds of the chorus to a kind of sacrilege, which probably explains why they became incensed enough to break all the pieces of pottery. The Christian girls' martyrdom took place in midsummer, when the women of the chorus were just about to celebrate their rites, which had by this time generally become a midsummer festival throughout the Empire.

Diogenianus's odd punishment is now clearer. The barefoot walk to the place nearby was veiled language for his forcing Justa and Rufina to march in the pilgrimage to the water source where the ritual took place, but the expiatory details of this pagan ritual, no doubt distasteful to a Christian hagiographer, were omitted.

Diogenianus himself led the procession to the sacred well where the ceremonies took place. It was here that, as in the ceremonies in the East, the images and the gardens of Adonis would have been thrown. And it was here at this well, which still exists beneath the Colegio Salesiano de la Santísima Trinidad, now well within the confines of Sevilla, that the body of Justa was thrown, according to the hagiographer. But what Roman governor would have risked poisoning a water source with a body, particularly when the well was sacred? The governor would hardly have polluted it with the decomposing corpse of an iconoclast. What surely happened was that the "body," that is, the image, of Adonis was thrown in, and since the waters would have kept their sacred character into Christian times, the hagiographer merely substituted the martyr's body for the deity's image, a kind of procedure that was followed widely as Christianity subsumed pagan ritual.

One final detail helps assure that such a substitution was the case. In Imperial times the rites of Adonis were celebrated on the rising of the dog star Sirius, at the beginning of the Canicula, which we call the "dog days." The rites lasted three days, the seventeenth, eighteenth, and nineteenth of July, precisely the days the martyrdom of Justa and Rufina is celebrated. Some churches in Spain celebrate the seventeenth of July as the day of their martyrdom, while others celebrate the nineteenth (in Sevilla it is the seventeenth). It is possible that the girls perished successively on those days, but in any case, the celebration on the seventeenth and the nineteenth would have been a clever way for the Christians to have obviated the rites of Adonis and Salammbo as the early Church began trying to stamp out tenacious old pagan festivals.

Gerald Brenan has explained how gardens of Adonis have survived in the Alpujarra region on the south flank of the Sierra Nevada as a courtship ritual in which village girls plant and grow herbs in pots and on Midsummer Day present the pots to the young men of their choice. In discussing such rituals Brenan made the observation a generation ago that one of the things the English have lost, or perhaps never had, is the sense that all the most important acts of life, especially courtship, have their specific rituals (*South from Granada* pp. 123–24). What was true of the English then has become infinitely more true of America in the waning twentieth century, and, to a lesser or greater extent, true of all the rootless, technological, urban societies of the West.

Even more poignant is the extent to which it is also true that the more "backward" and "primitive" a society is, the greater the urge to "modernize," which is to say, to suppress and to erase all the customs, rituals, and beliefs that constitute the collective personality of that culture. Richard Ford predicted such a loss when he remarked:

> They are every day diminishing, for in Spain as in the East, where foreign civilization is at work, the transition state interferes with painters and authors of "sketches," since the march of intellect and the exposure of popular fallacies is at least paring away something from religious and national festivities. . . . Many a picturesque custom and popular usage will pass away, to the triumph of the utilitarian and political economist, to the sorrow of the poet, the artist, and antiquarian. Now the *Progreso* with merciless harrow is tearing up many a wild flower of Spanish nature. . . . [P. 186]

The value of ritual, pageant, and spectacle, especially in Andalucía, made a deep impression on Ford. Speaking of the people of Sevilla and their love for these activities, he observed by way of contrast, that "they are not liable to bore, which haunts the most mis-named, most ennuyed people on earth, *our* gay world . . ." (p. 367).

Since he lived in Sevilla, Ford knew the accounts of the martyr-dom of Justa and Rufina, yet when it came to matters of religion, Ford was unable to preserve his characteristic equanimity. Fortunate-ly for us, his unsympathetic and anti-Catholic bias led him to bring into sharp focus one of the central questions regarding the unusual religious practices of Andalucía:

The holy week is the chief period; when we behold these [pro-cessions] and read the classics, time and space are annihilated. We are carried back. . . . The images are moved on platforms, *Andas,* and pushed on by men concealed under draperies. The *Pasos* are just as heavy to the weary as were Bel and Nebo (Isaiah xlvi.1). Among the ancients, not only the images of the gods, but the sacred boat of Osiris, the shrine of Isis, the ark of the Jews, were borne on staves as are some of the smaller *custodia* in Spain. Those who wish to compare analogies be-tween ancient and modern superstition, are referred to the sixth chapter of Baruch, wherein he describes the Babylonian *Pasos,* — their dresses, the gilding, the lights, etc., or to Athenaeus (v.7) and Apuleius ('Met.' ii.241), who have fore-stalled much of what takes place in Spain, especially as regards the *Pasos* of the Virgin. Thus the Syrian Venus was carried by an inferior order of priests: Apuleius calls them Pastofori, the Spaniards might fairly term theirs *Pasofori; Paso,* strictly speak-ing, means the figure of the Saviour during his passion. The *Paso,* however, of the Virgin is the most popular, and her gold-embroidered and lace pocket handkerchief sets the fashion for the season to the Andalucian dandyzettes. This is the exact *Megalesia* in honour of the mother of the gods, the great god-dess [a spring festival celebrated for Megale, "the Great One," the Magna Mater, Cybele], which took place in April . . .; the *Paso* of Salambo, the Babylonian Astarte Aphrodite . . . was carried through Seville with all the Phoenician rites even down to the third century. Santas Rufina and Justina, the present patronesses of the cathedral tower, were torn to pieces by the populace for insulting the image; which would infallibly be the case should any one presume to do the same to the *Sagrada imagen de la Virgen del mayor dolor y traspaso,* which is now carried at about the same time through the same streets and almost precisely in the same manner; indeed, Florez admits ('E.S.' [*España Sagrada*] ix.3) that the *Paso* of Salambo represented the *grief and agony* felt by Venus for the death of Adonis. A female goddess always has been popular among all Southrons. Thus Venus, when carried in *Pompa,* on an ivory *Andas,* round the circus, was hailed with the same deafening applause, tu Dea *major* eris! (Ovid, 'Art. Am.' i.147) as the god-dess Doorga, when borne on her gorgeous throne, draws from the admiring Hindoos at this day, and the *Santisima* does from Spaniards. There is little new under the sun, and still less in human devices. Every superb superstition has been anticipated by Paganism, and every grovelling vagary of dissent by the fanatics and impostors of the early ages of the church; these things of the present day have not even the poor merit of originality. [Pp. 174–75]

It is perhaps amusing and certainly intriguing to watch the lengths to which Ford will go in order to be critical of the Church. Suddenly our Romantic guide reverses himself and instead of telling us that these ancient practices are preserved, he claims that we are dealing with anticipated superstition and forestalled and unoriginal beliefs. Whether through the ungainly patrimony of denominationalism or the false common denominator of patriotism or some peculiar Puritan admixture of the two, Ford could not or would not understand that the religious practice he seemed so to despise was in fact part and parcel of the whole way of life which, in his words, otherwise permitted the traveler to "fly from the dull uniformity, the polished monotony of Europe, to the racy freshness of an original, unchanged country . . ." (p. 119).

Although Ford was clearly intrigued by such affairs, his aversion to the Virgin was so intense that he once claimed in a letter that his children were being raised by heathens (when he returned to England he placed them under the care of his Reverend brother for a while to "eradicate Santa Maria").[10] Ford believed there were minute correspondences between the ancient pagan rituals and the ones practiced in Sevilla, and often he equated the Virgin with the pagan Goddess: "The place of honour [on the altar] is usually assigned to *La Santisima,* the Virgin, the 'Queen of heaven'. . . . She is the Astarte, Isis, and great Diana, the focus of light and adoration . . ." (p. 193).

The mass at the cathedral of Sevilla, as a chosen spot for lovers' rendezvous was identical to "going to the mass of Isis [as] an excuse to meet their lovers" (p. 388). He compared the devotion to the Virgin with the pagan enthusiasm for the Goddess: the Spaniard's "worship of an Astarte is almost sexual" (p. 399). Regarding the doctrine of Immaculate Conception he explained that the declaration "of that mysterious event . . . diffused joy over all Spain. Seville went religiously mad. Zuñiga and Valderama enter into all the details of the bull-fights which were celebrated on the occasion" (p. 401). The *romerías* or pilgrimages, especially of Andalucía, were for Ford identical to those of antiquity:

These *Romerías* and *Ferías,* the fairs, offer the only amusement
and relaxation to their hard and continued life of labour: *Fería,*
as the word implies, is both a *holy* day and a fair. . . . On the
recurrence of certain days devoted to these excursions, men and
women, and children desert their homes and occupations, their
ploughs and spindles. The cell, hermitage, or whatever be the
place of worship, is visited, and the day and night given up to
song and dance, to drinking and wassail. . . . Indeed, if ob-
servance of rites formed any test, these festivals would appear
especially devoted to Bacchus and Venus; the ulterior results
are brought to light some nine months later: hence the proverb
considers a pilgrimage to be quite as attractive to *all* weak
women as a marriage, *a Romerias y bodas, van las locas todas*
[the wild women all go to pilgrimages and weddings]. The at-
tendance of female devotees at these alfresco expeditions,
whether to *Missas de Madrugada,* masses of peep of day, or
to *Virgenes del Rocio,* Dew-Virgins, of course attracts all the
young men, who come in saints' clothing to make love. Both
sexes remain for days and nights together in the woods and
thickets, not *sub Jove frigido,* but amid the bursting, life-
pregnant vegetation of the South. Accordingly, many a fair
pilgrim *sale Romera y vuelve Ramera* [starts out a pilgrim,
comes back a whore]; the deplorable consequences have passed
into national truisms, *detras de la cruz, está el diablo* [behind
the cross, there is the devil]. Those who chiefly follow these love-
meetings are, unfortunately, those whose enthusiasm is the most
inflammable. In vain do they bear the cross on their bosoms,
which cannot scare Satan from their hearts. *La cruz en los
pechos, el diablo en los hechos* [the cross on their chests, the
devil in their deeds]. This is the old story: "After the feast of
Bel, the people rose up to play". . . . However, the sight is so
curious that *the traveller, during this time of year, should make
inquiries at the principal towns what and when are the most
remarkable Fiestas and Romerias of the immediate
neighbourhood* [emphasis Ford's]. [Pp. 185–86]

The question is: Is Ford right? Are these practices similar to
those of antiquity?

The answer is not simple. To begin, we may dispense with Ford's
implicit *roman à clef,* in which the Andalusians are the Canaanites,
the English the Chosen People, and Ford Isaiah. Despite Ford's
politico-religious superciliousness, much of what he said, though
marred with exaggeration, confusion, and misleading statements
(there is only one Virgen del Rocío, for example), has a basis in
observable reality. Ford slanted his rhetoric to suit his own purposes,
but he did not invent anything. In the long run, Ford's fascination
with these things, regardless of his negative attitude, made him an

invaluable source. Once we get around his rhetoric, we can see that Ford has again led us to practices which do indeed resemble those of antiquity.

Romerías or pilgrimages take place all over Spain. Countless pilgrims still wend their way through the northern passes to Santiago de Compostela, where legend has it St. James was buried, or to the shrine of the little black Virgin (La Moreneta) of Montserrat in the jagged pinnacles above Barcelona. But the most extraordinary *romería* for our purposes, the most "pagan," is without doubt the pilgrimage to the edge of the great marsh of the Guadalquivir delta at the Pentecost festival celebrating La Blanca Paloma, La Reina de las Marismas, the White Dove, Queen of the Marshes, la Virgen del Rocío, the Virgin of the Dew.

Over half a million *rocieros* come seven weeks after Easter to celebrate this festival of la Reina y Madre de Andalucía, the Queen and Mother of Andalucía. The pilgrims come in every conceivable conveyance: in the traditional procession of ox-drawn wagons (or lacking oxen, tractor-drawn), on horses, on mules, on burros, on foot, on motorcycles, in cars, in trucks, and in convoys of buses. Many wear the traditional *flamenco* dress, the women and girls in long flounced skirts, the men and boys in the short jackets, leather chaps, and boots that gave rise to American cowboy dress.

For three days and nights *flamenco* music, dancing, and wine never cease: the big drums, the *tamboriles,* are the heartbeat of the *fiesta,* the arrhythmic and staccato hand-clapping and the smaller drums its nervous pulse. Horses everywhere, sometimes skittish from the crowds, raise the thick dust of the dirt streets. Fires burn in the field beyond, glowing a dim red in dusty halos. In years when Easter comes late and there is little rain, clouds of mosquitoes swarm off the marshes in the moist night air, and the full moon, looming large and melon-yellow, rises with an eerie nimbus in the dust-laden air. Over the music of flutes and guitars, castanets and tambourines, and the chanting of the *rosario,* the sudden rush of roman candles startles even the accustomed. Under the glare of the fireworks and amid torches and candles, clouds of incense billow up, and the wide dark eyes of Andalusian children mirror an ageless sense of awe.

It is the apogee of Andalucía, seasonal and sensual, rhythmic and timeless, mysterious and natural. And it is the most authentic celebration of popular culture, that peculiarly fixated, rough-country, backward-looking, ancient-seeming creation of the Spanish, and especially the Andalusian, people that we have. Religion, wine, heat, dust, the mass pressing of flesh, the heavy saline air of the marsh, the incessant throbbing of drums, the piercing uluation of pipes, the ceaseless movement of *flamenco* skirts in an unending whirl of *sevillanas,* make a sleepless spectacle in the collective vertigo of which you can only immerse yourself, surrendering your identity to the river of humanity come 'to pay homage to the Blanca Paloma.

When we read in the ancient texts of the Egyptian *romerías* to Isis in the delta of the Nile; or of the pilgrimage to Artemis upriver at Bubastis, when more wine was drunk than at any other time, with a great number of people going in each boat, some of the women playing flutes and rattles, others dancing, the men keeping time by clapping (Herodotus 2.59–60); or when we read of the pilgrimages to Artemis-Diana at Ephesus (Strabo, 14.1.23) or to Astarte at Hierapolis with the faithful working themselves into an ecstatic frenzy by dancing to the music of flutes and drums (Lucian *De Dea Syria* 50); or when we read about the meticulous dressing of Isis and of her procession with crowds of men, women, and children marching at night with candles and torches to the accompaniment of flutes and drums and timbrels (Apuleius *The Golden Ass* 11.8–10); or even at Rome when we read of the festival of the Moon-Goddess, Anna Perenna, out along the Tiber where the common people went to celebrate by dancing, by singing their songs and beating out the rhythm with handclaps, by drinking vast quantities of wine and camping out under the open sky (Ovid *Fasti* 3.523–42) — we cannot help being reminded of the Romería del Rocío. Ford's anti-Catholicism notwithstanding, we are dealing with similar practices.

And yet we cannot establish an unbroken concatenation of Goddess-worship from Los Millares to the Mariolatry of modern times. Questions of faith aside, a break, a missing link, is perhaps more apparent in Andalucía than anywhere in Europe. From Los Millares down to the martyrdom of Justa and Rufina, or the destruction of the Tomb of the Elephant, or even down to Avienus's sighting of the rites of Hercules, we can trace such an unbroken chain. And we could argue convincingly for "survivals" in remote areas up to the Islamic invasion. But unlike the slowly and reluctantly Christianizing north of Europe, in Andalucía we cannot very well argue for the continuance of Goddess cults in the face of centuries of Islam.

The cult of the Virgin was a relatively late development in Christianity. Mary was not declared *Theotokos* (mother of God) until 431, nor did her cult spread to the West in force until Eastern monks, escaping the Moslem invasion of the Holy Land, fled to the West. Even if we admit that the Eastern cult may have had some "pagan" elements (the declaration of *Theotokos* occurred precisely at Ephesus) and even if we concede that contact beween Andalucía and Byzantium was strong, it remains difficult to believe that pagan practice survived centuries of Moslem occupation. Although legends bear out the pre-Moslem existence of Virgin worship, there is a more plausible, if less tempting, explanation. A brief history of the Virgen del Rocío will help bear this out.

Some say, although the only evidence for it is legendary, that there was a Roman shrine on the edge of the *marismas* and that the Roman shrine was built, as was so often the case, on top of an earlier, perhaps even Tartessian, sanctuary. While we have no concrete proof for such a supposition, it requires little imagination to understand its origin. Schulten spent years digging for Tartessos just a few kilometers away, where the waters of the *marisma* and the Guadalquivir (the Tartessos) empty into the Atlantic. Be that as it may, the whole area belonged to the Moslems from 711 until 1262, that is, for five and a half centuries. After the Christians took it, the area was noted for its extreme poverty, although it was visited frequently by the Spanish crown and by the Guzmán family, who hunted the rich *marisma*. Alfonso X (the Wise) declared the area a royal reserve and built the first shrine to Santa María de las Rocinas in the late thirteenth century. The carved Gothic image of the Virgin (in legend she appeared from heaven one morning to become the Queen and Mother of Andalucía) dates from the reign of Alfonso, a great admirer of the Virgin, to whom he wrote lovely early lyrics called *cantigas*.

The legend originated much later. The first written version of it is dated 1758, although it may have begun in the sixteenth century. Almonte, the town nearest the shrine (fifteen kilometers away), made Santa María de las Rocinas their *patrona* by the seventeenth century. The first document to refer to her as such dates from 1653 and names her "Nuestra Señora del Rocío," a significant name change from her toponym, Rocina (which connotes "nag," as did Don Quixote's Rocinante), to Rocío, "Dew," a symbolic allusion to the Holy Spirit. The Virgin was probably brought to Almonte on numerous occasions in those drought- and hunger-ridden years. In 1653, in any case, her patronage of Almonte and her immaculate conception were celebrated with *toros* and fireworks and a jubilant procession of the entire population of the town.

Years of drought, hunger, and epidemic succeeded each other in Andalucía as the seventeenth century closed on the bleakest period of Spanish history. Carlos II, *el hechizado,* "The Bewitched," the final inbred and impotent issue of the Hapsburgs, gibbered on the throne for twenty-five years, bringing the House of Austria to its abysmal and long overdue demise. Floods and drought alternated, the plague broke out, and the economy collapsed as the aristocracy picked clean the bones of the moribund Empire. Words cannot describe, wrote Ortega, how low the aristocracy had sunk ("Goya" p. 114). The misery in Castilla was unparalleled. In Andalucía it was worse: the towns filled up with sick, unemployed, and starving beggars. Small wonder people turned to the Virgin for relief, to the Virgin and to their own inextinguishable sense of life.

If the last half of the seventeenth century marks the eclipse of Spanish grandeur and the nadir of their history, the new century seems to have brought some sense of hope. The Andalusian people, Phoenix-like, almost Lazarus-like, slowly re-created themselves. One of the main sources of strength was the Virgin, as the records of Almonte plainly indicate. At every period of joy or stress, the Virgin was carried from her shrine to Almonte: in 1713 to celebrate the peace at the end of the War of Succession; in 1729 when Felipe V visited; in 1730 because of crop deterioration; and in 1734 because of drought. In 1738 she was brought in three times to bring rain, in 1744 once again for drought, and thus over and again for the rest of the century. When the French army of Napoleon marched through Andalucía, she was carried to the town, which had no *afrancesados* (French sympathizers), to intercede to protect it. What happened is not clear, but somehow Almonte was spared destruction or damage.[11]

The custom of celebrating *fiestas* and *romerías* to different Virgins in Andalucía gained prominence in the sixteenth and seventeenth centuries, and the *fiesta* celebrated in honor of Santa María de las Rocinas was no exception. Toward the end of the seventeenth century, in the worst years, the first *hermandades* (brotherhoods) grew up in the neighboring towns beyond Almonte. It was precisely at this crucial time at the turn of the eighteenth century that the style and the particular practices of the *fiesta* and the pilgrimage took shape.

Religious festivals in Spain had long combined secular feast and religious celebration. As the Rocío grew in popularity in the eighteenth century, the different *hermandades* brought in their own dances for celebrating the secular part of the *fiesta,* some of which are preserved today in regional *flamenco* dances. And as the seventeenth-century dances, the *chacona,* the *zarabanda,* the *seguidilla* and others, evolved into the *flamenco* of the eighteenth century, the Rocío took on the decidedly *flamenco* style that has become its hallmark. The Rocío and *flamenco* evolved simultaneously, inextricably bound together, part and parcel of the same specifically Andalusian style that is the source of *flamenco, toreo,* and religious celebrations such as El Rocío.

It is difficult, perhaps impossible, to establish exactly when the fusion of religion and *flamenco* or proto-*flamenco* began. Gypsies were dancing in Corpus Christi processions as early as 1632, and *saetas* (literally arrows or darts), the piercing *flamenco* songs sung at Easter processions, date back in Granada as far as 1678.[12] Slowly and gradually in that hybrid and obscure culture, *flamenco* and popular religious celebration in Andalucía fused. They remain inseparable today, especially at the Rocío, which has become the maximum expression of that fusion.

Flamenco, as we have already seen, is primordial music. Lorca said it produced an unknown sense of freshness, something of a miracle, a kind of religious enthusiasm (1:1102). The Andalusian sense of religion is equally primordial: it is based on dramatic representation and spectacle. Tableaux, pageants, processions, candles, incense, wine, song, and dance, the trappings of religion in antiquity, are the trappings of religion in Andalucía. This sense of living spectacle exists throughout Spain and in other "Latin" countries, but nowhere does it have the vitality or the originality of Andalucía because nowhere else was that sense of spectacle revitalized and enriched by *flamenco*. Critics call the spectacle irreligious and pagan. *Aficionados* speak of devotion and fervor. But no one who has spent Easter in Sevilla or been to the Rocío doubts the originality or the extraordinary vitality of these occasions.

The primordial sense of *flamenco* and the primordial sense of spectacle in the religious practices of Andalucía are clearly analogous. And just as some *flamenco* dancing was analogous to, but not exactly the same as, the dances of the *puellae Gaditanae* which, as we have seen, were both sacred and profane, so the Rocío is analogous, but not identical, to the ancient veneration of the Goddess.

Seen in their broadest context, the Rocío and *flamenco* conserve the primordial sense of celebration, of ritual, of Dionysian spirituality that has gradually been purged from the Western way of life. *Flamenco* at the Rocío celebrates the Virgin. The veneration of the Virgin at the Rocío spiritualizes *flamenco*. Together they form a unique kind of *fiesta* that provides an unsuspected window on antiquity. El Rocío is not a direct religious survival of antiquity, but it is as close as we can come in the Western world. That it is also a Catholic festival within the orthodox Church speaks more for the syncretistic nature of Catholicism than it does for the orthodoxy of the Rocío. Yet matters of faith aside—and I am purposely being as eclectic as possible—one point must be made. Both Holy Week in Sevilla and La Romería del Rocío are supremely *religious* festivals. To be sure, much goes on that in modern thinking does not seem orthodoxly, or even unorthodoxly, religious, but no one witnessing either celebration could remain unaware of the passionate devotion and the ecstatic abandon of many of the participants.

Listen, for example, to Curro Camacho, a young *torero* from Sevilla whose sentiments have been poignantly recorded by Robert Vavra. Curro has explained that the first time he went, it was only for the festive part, but while there he heard an old man describe what it was like to make the whole journey by oxcart. The following year Curro went on foot with the brotherhood from Triana:

> We left Sevilla at seven in the morning, and I counted fifty-seven ox carts and I don't know how many carriages and horsemen carrying behind them beautiful girls in flamenco dresses. From the moment we left the city, everyone was full of joy—singing and clapping. At midday we stopped to eat, and then continued on our way until the sun set. . . . Every group had its own campfire, which we visited with our guitars, and each of us sang what we knew. And in this way we passed the night, drinking, singing and dancing flamenco, and going from fire to fire. . . . And in this way we followed the pilgrim route until Saturday afternoon, when we arrived at El Rocío. All in all it's about ninety miles from Sevilla to the Virgin's shrine. Not only the Triana group makes the pilgrimage. There are brotherhoods in cities and pueblos all over Andalucía, and each one takes the most direct route to the shrine. The Jerez brotherhood has to cross the Coto de Doñana Reserve, which

is a lovely trip, for as they ride along they see all the deer, wild boar and other animals and birds that live there. . . . When Sunday arrives, I don't know where all the thousands of pilgrims come from. . . . Everyone waits excitedly for Monday, which is the most important day of the fiesta. Early in the morning the Virgin's float is carried from her shrine into the streets, where thousands of people try to get close to her as she is circled and carried by fifty or sixty strong men. It's dangerous to get too near to her, because the men who guard and carry her are from the nearby pueblo of Almonte, and they say she belongs to them, and that only their shoulders shall feel her weight. Because of the rough crowds moving from side to side like the strong currents of a river, it's very difficult to get close enough to touch the float, and you can get hurt trying to do so.

Once I tried to push through those men so full of strength and wine to touch the Virgin. I wanted to ask her to let me triumph with the bulls that year. . . . By the time I had touched her skirts and pushed my way out of the crowd, my shirt was ripped, my shoulder was bruised from having been slugged and I had a big scratch on my face. But none of this makes any difference [when you feel] such devotion to the Virgin. The shouts of thousands of voices ring across the marshes: "¡Viva la Virgen del Rocío! ¡Viva la Blanca Paloma! ¡Viva la Reina de los Cielos!"[13]

Curro Camacho's description of the Rocío is as ingenuous, in the best sense of that word, as it is accurate. It catches unintentionally an ambivalence that existed in the religious practices of antiquity, an ambivalence on which Ortega commented brilliantly, pointing out that the cult of Dionysus in antiquity was both "devotion" and "diversion." Such an ambivalence appeared strange to the literal-minded Romans, who were unsure whether the cult represented a religion or some kind of farce and occasion for license. They were unable to understand that it was devotion precisely because it was diversion, literally a turning aside into another, a wine- and dance-induced state, an ecstasy, that is, an ex-stasis, a journey into another state, an *other*—hence, so it was believed, divine—dimension (7:490).

By and large in the West, from the Romans on down, we have refined away and purged as "pagan" that ability to journey smoothly into other dimensions of our minds, but the frantic searching among so-called "cults" by alienated souls in the West reveals the crippling price our rationality has paid for that refinement and purgation. In Andalucía, however, the old way, the ecstatic wine-dance of antiquity, is still practiced as religious ritual, incorporated now into the worship of the Virgin, but unchanged as dramatic ritual and devotion-diversion. Ortega never applied his own theory, which he worked out with his friend, Johan Huizinga, to celebrations in Andalucía—no doubt due to what he thought of as the *"quincalla meridional"* (the southern frippery) (6:112), of *flamenco*—and it is a shame he did not. Had he given up his fierce Castilian bias and done so, he would have seen how perfectly his theory of antiquity fit actual practice, alive and vibrant in the marshes of the Guadalquivir, which the Andalusian people had created or re-created in their communal wisdom.

In Andalucía, ancient, passive, syncretistic, absorptive, things have not changed, have not evolved, have not progressed, partly through oppression and partly, I think, because the Andalusians sensed that evolution or progress as it developed in the West was not suitable to them. The eighteenth century is the turning point. Some collective instinct meshed perfectly with the vagaries of history, and the Andalusians "revolved" rather than "evolved." We in the West moved "forward." They moved "backward," especially by comparison. The continuum of history did not stop in Andalucía, but the absorptive, syncretistic nature of the culture tended to neutralize any sense of motion. All the survivals of antiquity are both the results and the proof of the process.

Agrarian Andalucía has always been matriarchal without ever being a literal matriarchy; that is, the veneration of fertility and fecundity and the cyclical and seasonal sense of birth-life-death always has been the spiritual basis of life. It was only natural (what we would call perfectly "logical") that worship of the Goddess in Andalucía should become worship of the Virgin, and that that worship should therefore resemble in so many ways the previous practices. In Andalucía as in antiquity, theater, spectacle, ritual, religion, costume, dance, song, wine, devotion as diversion, diversion as devotion, and the spiritual sense of life itself in nature are all intertwined. They are all con-fused, as Ortega would say (7:494), that is fused together in a natural synthesis that is difficult for us in the rational, logical, Western world only because we have relinquished, evolved beyond, lost perhaps irreparably the ability to confuse. The con-fusion of Andalucía confuses us because we are blind to relationships they still see.

The modern rationalist will perhaps see Holy Week in Sevilla as "barbaric" or "pagan." He may not understand that he is watching religious spectacle, street theater at its most poignant, a reenactment of the passion of Christ, the Virgin's lamentation for a crucified, dying, and resurrecting God, and the final, inexplicable, and urgent mystery of restoration in all its ancient seasonal glory. He probably will not realize that the raw and perfect emotion of the *saeta* he hears rending the night is an echo of the ululation of wailing women, or that the whole spectacle harks back thousands of years, not merely two thousand years, but beyond to the rituals from which Greek tragedy developed and beyond that, to the Canaanite and Babylonian rituals that are the earliest theater we have. He will see the wine flowing and watch with amazement as, for example, the *paso* of the Virgen de los Rosarios inches down the narrow Calle de Cuna out of the Plaza del Salvador, her *costaleros* (bearers) beneath making her "dance" so that her rosaries swing from side to side creating a delicate tintinnabulation on the balconies on either side. The wine and the dancing Virgin will seem inappropriate to him because he does not know what Ortega knew, that for all humanity, up to and including some of the Greeks and Romans, feasts were religious and religions ended with a feast, a *fiesta* feast, a wine-drinking, dancing *fiesta*. Our *fiestas,* wrote Ortega, by which he meant those of the modern Western world, have been *"desdiosadas"* (ungodded) and *"profanadas"* (profaned). Apart from Carnival, he thought Spaniards conserved the only real relic of an authentic *fiesta* in the *corrida de toros*. Christianity, he wrote, "by taking the quality out of human life as a consequence of having discovered a God more authentically God than the pagans, which is to say more radically transcendent, killed forever the festival sense of life" (7:487).

Ortega was certainly correct about the *corrida,* but he was only partially right about the *fiesta* sense of life. In Andalucía the festival sense still pervades the springtime. The streets of Sevilla pullulate with what Lorca called strange unicorns and fantastic wizards from a mythic woods, and the Virgins float on ships of lights along the high tide of the city, down the rivers of the streets (1:182–83). A crush of people surrounds each Virgin chanting "Guapa y guapa, y guapa guapa guapa," while certain individuals make more direct remarks: "¡Que esto e divino! ¡Olé! ¡Viva! ¡Qué guapa ere, de verdá! ¡Qué guapa ere, hija! ¡Joé, qué guapa e!"[14]

If our rationalist spoke *andaluz* he would have caught the incongruous obscenity, but would he have known that at ancient festivals obscenity was common as well? If he went to the pilgrimage of the Gypsies at the "high place" of the Santuario de la Virgen de la Sierra (1,223 meters high), known as the Balcony of Andalucía, he would hear stranger things still. He would hear the constant arrhythmic beating of hands, the *palmas,* and the singing of the *bulerías* so dear to the Gypsies. He would crowd into the little chapel, if he did not mind heat and intense physical contact, to hear the exquisite, chill-producing *santa misa flamenca,* that remarkable mass which "con-fuses" religious ritual and *flamenco* in a plaintive, wailing liturgy of lamentation. There among *fiesta*-clad *gitanas* with the huge black eyes and the thick black hair of tourist-posters, he would hear the old familiar phrases, ". . . ahora y en la hora de nuestra muerte . . . ," sung to the rhythm of *bulerías.* Afterwards, when the little Virgin was taken out of the chapel on her palanquin he would hear the *vivas* and the guitars starting up again so the *gitanas* could dance for the Virgin. Amid the shouting, the dancing, and the *palmas,* he would hear clearly enthusiastic voices shouting out "¡Viva nuestra mare!" then "¡Viva el divino consuelo!" and then "¡Viva la má guapa de Andalucía!" and finally the incomprehensible adoration "¡Viva tu puta mare!"[15]

If he went to the town of Moclín outside Granada he would hear the pilgrims called "¡Cabrones!" (he-goats and by extension cuckolds). And someone would explain to him that the pilgrimage was famous for its powers of fertility, but that what really went on was no miracle at all. In Lorca's time ten thousand came in carts and wagons to this pilgrimage for whatever the "miracle" was, and Lorca, sensing the deeply Dionysian nature of the whole affair, turned the *cabrones* into something more poetic in *Yerma,* his tragedy of barrenness.

Amid the wild and remote mountain setting of the hermitage the throngs have gathered at dark around campfires, drinking wine and singing to the accompaniment of an occasional guitar. Suddenly there is a rattling of bells and the masked *macho* and the *hembra* (the male and the female), the male brandishing a bull's horn, burst on the scene to perform a phallic ritual dance while children scatter screaming, "The devil and his wife! The devil and his wife!" (2:734).

It was not the devil, to be sure, but Lorca's genius for staging ritual had not failed him, and he captured in one brief scene the complex Dionysian substrata so pervasive in Andalucía. He struck a chord that echoed into the Andalusian past along the lines we have been tracing for time beyond memory or beyond words, but not beyond record. Nearby in the province of Almería, not far from Los Millares, in a cave called La Cueva de los Letreros (The Cave of the Inscriptions), from prehistoric inscriptions that date back to the time of Los Millares or El Gárcel or perhaps beyond, there is an extraordinary figure of a he-goat-man with two long goatlike horns. He may be dancing, and he is certainly performing a ritual. In one hand he has a kind of sickle with which he is about to cut a gourd or plant, in the other he holds what looks like a bull's horn. Undoubtedly his rite is to ensure fertility, fecundation, the changing of seasons, the bounty of crops. Dionysian figure, goat-man, *macho,* whatever else he may be, he is also the direct agrarian forefather (and priest of the same chthonian Goddess) of Lorca's ritual dancer. Lorca may have had this strange figure in mind, but whether he did or not, their resemblance reveals again the strikingly changeless continuum of life in Andalucía.

Richard Ford, whose "rational" Anglican side sometimes got the best of his Romantic instincts, may not have gotten to see the question of these religious practices clearly in his time, but about one thing he seemed to be quite right. These religious practices are fast disappearing, and although uncountable multitudes now attend Holy Week and El Rocío, many people already lament the passing of older, meaningful ways. If those customs and rituals are eradicated, we will have lost a great deal more than quaint and rustic practice extending into a distant past. We will have lost the whole festival sense of life so deeply rooted in the Andalusian earth.

If the marshes of Doñana are not filled and urbanized as some have already thought mindlessly to do, we can still observe in the natural beauty of the *marismas* the perennial rites of Spring in honor of La Blanca Paloma. And if in Sevilla they do not destroy the exquisitely beautiful inner city, we can observe in the night air thick with incense and orange blossoms, candlewax and torch smoke, the celebration of Easter with all its diversions and intense devotions so much closer than our own to the spirit of that palm-waving multitude rejoicing, praising God in a loud voice, and singing Hosannas as they trooped into Jerusalem.

Richard Ford found this festival sense of life too similar to the practices of antiquity for comfort, and in that regard he anticipated the rational observer's modern sense of incredulity. Ford's Anglican values prevented him from seeing the vital beauty and the theatrical truth these celebrations contained. Of course Ford shared the optimism of his age, and, having no inkling of just where our fine powers of reasoning might eventually lead us, he saw none of the value inherent in an extant Dionysian sense of celebration. He was certainly correct about one thing, though. If during the processions of Holy Week anyone laid an injurious hand on one of the images of the Virgin, or if at the Rocío anyone attempted to damage the image of the *patrona* of Almonte, the aspirant iconoclast would not be arrested by the current Diogenianus. He would surely be, as Ford charmingly worded it," "torn to pieces by the mariolatrous mob" (p. 376).

CHAPTER SIX
MATADOR

Agadir-Gadir-Gadeira-Gades-Cádiz, or Cai as the Andalusians call it now, and the surrounding territory of Andalucía *la baja* (lower Andalucía), fairly glitters with myths and mythic concentricities. Here, as we have seen, was reputedly the edge of Atlantis, here the Western Troy of Tartessos, here far Tarshish with some of Solomon's mines. Here came Tyrian Hercules to his immolation and final rest (Justinus 44.5) and here came Greek Hercules to pierce triple-bodied Geryon with a single arrow and to steal his herd of red bulls. These were said to be the Elysian fields and the abode of fair-haired Rhadamanthys (*Od.* 4.563–65). Here came Nestor's peer, sagacious Menestheus, after the fall of Troy,[1] following the intrepid Phoenicians, those greedy men in black ships full of trading beads (*Od.* 15.415). Here to the oldest city of the West, Jonah would have fled the Lord because this was the other end of the known world, the *finis terrae,* beyond which lay the great Exterior Sea, the Abyss, and the Palace of Night (Alberti *Ora Marítima* p. 29). Vague and frightening stories of mud shoals, sea monsters, exotic islands, and flaming seas were told by the early Andalusians.[2] Even Seneca, that stoic son of Córdoba, wrote that one day the Ocean would open up and a great land would be discovered (*Medea* lines 375–79).

Of all the myths and tales woven about Andalucía, the story of Hercules' rustling of Geryon's red bulls sticks most in the mind. When Perseus lopped off Medusa's head, out sprang winged Pegasus,

---

THE MATADOR PEDRO ROMERO is one of Goya's most splendid portraits. Romero, the quintessential Andalusian hero, was quite probably the greatest *matador* of all time. *Courtesy Kimbell Art Museum, Fort Worth, Texas.*

whose name meant born at the springs of Ocean, and Chrysaor, who held a golden sword in his hands (Hesiod *Theogony* 270–94). While Pegasus, the delight of poets and the kindler of imaginations, may be more interesting intrinsically, it is Geryon — Chrysaor's monstrous offspring by his union with Callirrhoë, daughter of Ocean — or rather Geryon's red cattle, that vie for our attention, for they are the mythic forebears of the Spanish fighting bull, and their very real descendants still graze in Andalucía.

You cannot travel from Cádiz to Tarifa along that windy headland that overlooks the "springs of Ocean" where the Mediterranean enters the Exterior Sea without the red cattle's bringing the myth to mind, and it requires little euhemeristic bent to understand why the Greeks placed the myth there. Literal Strabo reported that the milk of these cattle was so rich water had to be mixed with it to make cheese and the grain was so fattening the cattle had to be bled every fifty days so they would not suffocate, the obvious reasons, he deduced, for the fame of Geryon's celebrated herds (3.5.4). Classical Andalusians, we may conclude, were as given to hyperbole as those of our day, especially regarding the riches of their *patria chica*. Yet, hyperbole and myth aside, many herds of red cattle pasture on that coast today, and along the Guadalquivir graze the finest fighting bulls in the world, mostly black, but some red and a few white.

The bull is, of course, the most revered animal. It was sacred to virtually all early civilizations. The stone carving of the paleolithic "Venus of Laussel" holds a bull's horn as a symbol of fertility and power in her right hand while her left points to her rounded belly. The caves of Altamira and Lascaux are underground temples dedicated to the bull. At Çatal Hüyük, eight thousand years ago, numerous bulls were depicted in wall paintings and in sculpture within the sanctuaries dedicated to the Mother-goddess of fertility. In Crete the bulls and the Goddess reached their apogee in the splendid bull rituals and sacrifices represented in some of the finest ancient art we have. The highly religious Etruscans graphically connected the bull with fertility. A wall painting in a tomb at Tarquinia shows a standing couple copulating in the path of a charging bull.

Enlil, the great Mesopotamian god, was a bull, and Osiris was frequently depicted as a bull. Zeus could turn into a bull at will, and Dionysus was often represented as a bull. The father of gods in Phoenicia and Syria, El, and his son Baal, were also bull-gods, as was Yahweh for the early Hebrews. In the ancient mind no animal could compare in strength and power with the bull, so it was natural to identify the animal with the gods. As a result of this identification, the bull became one of the first subjects of art and of literature and the first animal of ritual veneration in all the ancient societies of the eastern Mediterranean.

But the bull, like the god or the king or the consort of the Goddess for whom he was an analogue, had to die. In the bull rituals of Crete the bull was sacrificed, as the famous sarcophagas at Hagia Triada so clearly shows. The Babylonian hero Gilgamesh killed a "bull-of-heaven," and Mithra, the great Persian hero-god, also slew a white "bull-of-heaven." The story of the ritual was told many ways but the ending was always the same: the bull had to suffer a sacrificial death to ensure the life of the community. The sacrifice of the holy animal, of the god-animal, and the eating of his flesh brought about a state of grace. The sacrifice of the sacred animal, which some scholars believe reflected an earlier ritual sacrifice of the king or his surrogate, seems to have been a nearly permanent concept in the mind of early man, and it no doubt prefigured, and in some instances accompanied, the concept of the dying god.

The tauromorph, bull-man, bull-god, god-bull, or heavenly bull, is evident in all the early mythologies. But nowhere was he celebrated so ritually or elegantly as in Crete, where a pantheistic worship of the Mother-goddess, ritual fertility dances, and bull spectacles and sacrifices formed an inseparable hierology that was unique in antiquity and that prefigured much of Greek thought, including the development of theater, especially tragedy.

Bull rituals and sacrifices were also observed in Egypt, where sacred bulls were mourned and mummified. Even in Atlantis, Plato tells us, bull rituals were observed (*Critias* 19). Bull symbolism, especially the bull's horns, became an integral part of the fertility rites of virtually all the ancient religions, and horns were represented on coins, gems, and rings, and in painting, sculpture, and altars known as the "horns of consecration." Priests and priestesses often dressed as bulls, either wearing horns or bull-masks or bull hides. The masked figures that developed into the actors of Greek theater evolved under the aegis of the bull-god Dionysus from just such practices.

The extravagant worshipers of Cybele and Attis sometimes had a bull sacrificed over a grate so they could stand below to receive a baptism in its blood. When Mithraism spread over the late Roman Empire, rivaling Christianity, the Mithraic cult, which admitted only men, became identified to some extent with the worship of Cybele and Attis with its many female devotees. Mithra's slaying of the heavenly white bull, from whose body came grains and plants and from whose blood came wine, found a sympathetic echo in the *taurobolium,* as the bull sacrifice sacred to Attis and Cybele was known.

In Spain, and especially in Andalucía, bull cults, including the ritual of the *taurobolium,* were common. At Mérida, to cite a curious example, the modern bull ring was built precisely where the Mithraeum had been. Roman inscriptions show that *taurobolia* were celebrated all over Andalucía, and shrines to Attis and Cybele and Mithra have been recorded at Mérida, Cádiz, Lebrija, Itálica, Carmona, Ronda (Acinipo), Málaga, Lucena, Cabra, Córdoba, and Elche among others.

Bull cults in Iberia were far more ancient, of course, than these late Roman practices. One version of the myth of Hercules recounts how Hercules crossed from Africa at the Straits of Gibraltar, subdued the armies of the three sons of Chrysaor, and drove off the herds. After honorable treatment by a native, which is to say Tartessian or Iberian, king, Hercules returned a portion of the cattle, and the grateful king thereafter sacrificed the finest bull each year to Hercules, a sacred practice continued down to Roman times (Diodorus Siculus 4.18.2–3).

Spanish ethnologists believe this kind of myth had some counterpart in Spanish prehistory. Given the early Oriental contact we know existed and the evident profusion of native cattle, there is no reason to doubt the existence of quite early bull cults. In any case, archaeological testimony is abundant. A cave painting at Despeñaperros pictures two human figures interpreted as wearing bull masks in the fashion of similar ceremonies known from Cyprus and Syria. Stone bulls such as the famous *toros de Guisando* in Ávila, or the enigmatically humanesque bull known as the *bicha de Balazote,* or the stone bulls of Porcuna, Écija, and Osuna, provide eloquent testimony of reverence of the bull. The splendid bronze Iberian bull found in a temple and known as the *toro de Azaila* has a rosette on its forehead, indicating its sacred nature, like the rosettes so characteristic of Minoan design and very similar to the rosette on the forehead of a type of Mithraic bull. Any student of ancient art who sees the long, upswept horns of the Mallorcan *toro de Costitx,* also found in a temple, in the Archaeological Museum in Madrid will be reminded of the famous Cretan bull rhyton from Knossos. The lost stele of Clunia, of which we have drawings, showed a man about to kill a bull with a sword, and the excavations of the Celtiberian town of Termes have revealed a kind of primitive semicircular amphitheater in which some kind of public bull sacrifice took place in pre-Roman times. The horns were discovered along with swords and hachets. Numerous votive offerings in the form of a bull or a bull's head have been found in Iberian sanctuaries, indicating this powerful animal was clearly held in reverence.

After the imposition of Christianity, animal sacrifices were forbidden and Theodosius piously threatened offenders with the death penalty. The American *matador* and artist John Fulton ironically explains how the Church effectively stifled opposition: "The first theological definition of the devil, issued in 447 A.D. by the Council of Toledo, came right to the point: The devil is 'a large, black, monstrous apparition with horns on his head, cloven hoofs, hair, fiery-eyes, terrible teeth, an immense phallus, and a sulphurous smell.' So it was that the bull-god of Mithraism, the prince of light and giver of life, became the Christian symbol of darkness and evil."[3]

The Spaniards seem not to have taken such tactics completely to heart, and ethnologists, working with folklore and legend, have demonstrated a continuing belief in the bull's magical and fertilizing powers. Bull rituals, including dressing in the bull's hide and horns, a practice reminding us at once of Lorca's ritual fertility dance in *Yerma,* and the sacrifice of a bull, especially at weddings, are customs that never really ceased in many rural areas. Isidore of Sevilla railed against dressing in bull or stag disguises, but the custom lasted long enough to be taken to the New World. Even the Catholic King Fernando seems to have been susceptible to the bull's magic. On the advice of two of his royal chambermaids he attempted to fructify his union with his niece Germaine de Foix by eating bull's testicles. Unfortunately, though, the cure seems to have been too potent for him and he died. General Primo de Rivera must have had a stronger constitution, as he regularly had the testicles of the first bull of the afternoon served to him in the Madrid bull ring during the fight of the fifth. The blood of the bull has always been considered potent as well, and the Spanish writers Solana and Eugenio Noel have both described tubercular old women coming around the slaughterhouse in Madrid to drink the blood as a cure. Hemingway had heard about this custom as well. In discussing the odor of death, Pilar, the wily Gypsy heroine of *For Whom the Bell Tolls,* tells Robert Jordan that part of that odor smells like the breath of the moribund old women who go before dawn to the slaughterhouse to drink the blood of the animals slaughtered there.[4]

It would be very convenient if at this juncture we could say that myth and history in Spain provide us with a perfect analogue for the modern bullfight, but I do not believe that would give us an altogether accurate idea of what really took place. What did take place is more complex and far more interesting. The development of the art of *toreo,* which we shall call *toreo* since the term *bullfighting* is inaccurate, is the final piece of our puzzle and, in some ways, the proof of the whole anomalous Andalusian phenomenon.

We cannot conclude that the treatment of the bull in Spain always amounted to *toreo.* We must limit the analogy somewhat and understand that in antiquity the bull was sacred and was therefore sacrificed, a practice which never entirely died out, although it degenerated from a formally religious act to a folkloric rite. Parallel to that degeneration the sport of hunting wild bulls developed. In neither case, however, are we dealing with art.

The sine qua non of the bull sacrifices, the bull sports, and *toreo,* the bull art, is, of course, the bull. And what has survived in relatively unchanged form from the days of Geryon to our time is the very special, the unique animal known as the *toro bravo.* That Spanish bull, *Bos taurus Africanus,* is the direct descendant, and probably the only direct descendant, of the *Bos primigenius,* the aurochs or urus of antiquity, which Julius Caesar claimed looked nearly as big as an elephant (*De Bello Gallico* 6.28).

The bulls at Lascaux and at Çatal Hüyük and at Knossos were probably some form of aurochs. No one knows exactly where or how the *toros* of Andalucía got there or where they came from. They may have been brought in from Egypt or Carthage, a theory that gave rise to the *Africanus* connected to the *Bos taurus.* Angus Macnab, a naturalized Spaniard and authority on bulls, theorized that the bulls were taken from Crete to Tartessos long before the Carthaginians went to Spain.[5] However they arrived, the *toros bravos* of Andalucía, the descendants of the mythical herds of Geryon, have pastured in the rich delta of the Guadalquivir, much as the Egyptian bulls hunted by the Pharoahs in the delta of the Nile, from the remotest past. And, what is more important, only by way of Andalucía has the *toro bravo* survived up to our time.

In the earliest days of *toreo* there were at least two types of *toro bravo* in Spain, the Pyrenean bull and the Andalusian bull, but now the former is virtually extinct. All *toros bravos,* whether they are found in Mexico, in Peru, or in Castilla are descended from Andalusian stock, and the best bulls all come directly from Andalucía.

To turn that around, without Andalucía there would be no *toro bravo,* and with no *toro bravo,* no *toreo.* I cannot stress to those unfamiliar with the animal how important the *toro bravo* is to the *fiesta de los toros.* Hemingway aptly said they compared to other bulls the way a wolf compares to a dog.[6] Without the *toros bravos,* which have consistently killed lions, tigers, and bears and have even vanquished elephants, there is no spectacle, no ritual, no sacrifice, no art, and no emotion.

The combination of spectacle, ritual, sacrifice, art, and emotion brings us to the real problem of continuity. That striking combination so characteristic of *toreo* is missing in the past. The Roman circus lacked the important aesthetic dimension, as well as the vitally important element of ritual sacrifice. When a gladiator and a bull met in the arena it was a contest, a true bull *fight,* which either might "win." The *taurobolium* was no spectacle and had none of the emotion, none of the unleashed danger, of *toreo.* The bull hunts of the Pharaohs, the Caesars, and the Moslem and Christian nobles were exciting sports, but they lacked the ritual and the plastic beauty of *toreo.* The folkloric bull games at weddings preserved a kind of fertility rite, as do the *encierros* or the runnings at Pamplona, but had none of the theatrically controlled, perfectly executed nature of *toreo.* Only *toreo* itself is the combination of all of them and nowhere in antiquity do we find the entire combination except possibly in Crete.

The tantalizing, mysterious, and, judging from their art, evidently exquisite, Minoan sense of life *seems* to have combined spectacle, beauty, ritual, emotion, and sacrifice in their tauromachy, about which we know unfortunately very little. Yet even if we accept the similarity between the two tauromachies, the most we can say is that despite the spread of three or four thousand years, they seem to be analogous. Macnab's theory that the Cretans brought the bulls to Tartessos, Schulten's firm belief in their cultural contact, archaeological evidence, and other similarities notwithstanding, we can hardly derive the existence of *toreo* in Andalucía from a Minoan precedent when *toreo* as we know it did not develop until the eighteenth century.

Any direct connection is obviously out of the question, and the only possible explanation is that, given the presence of the *toro bravo,* the Spaniards, and especially the Andalusians, in the eighteenth century re-created a tauromachy; that is, they reinvented a ritual and aesthetic spectacle of the sacrifice of the bull. It is precisely the lack of direct connections or precedents that is important. *Toreo,* then, was not exactly passed down as a material legacy or a traceable heritage. On the contrary, it was an invention all the more original for its archaic bent or its atavistic qualities. The only true heritage we can speak of, the only real direct survival from antiquity, is the bull itself, *Bos taurus Africanus,* the grandson of Geryon's kine.

Ortega best understood what happened and his insight was the fundamental one that leads to all the rest. Ortega, who was no *aficionado,* who by his own admission never went to more than the minimally requisite number of *corridas;* who was so uncongenial to the demimonde of *toreo* that he paradoxically claimed to be the only one to understand what it was about since his distance gave him an objectivity no *aficionado* possessed; Ortega, the self-styled "analyzer of humanities" (7:27–28), posited the fundamental consideration when he wrote in no uncertain terms that anyone who did not understand *"with complete clarity"* (Ortega's emphasis throughout), the historical importance of *toreo,* could not understand Spanish history from 1650 to the present. To understand what a *torero* is, Ortega modestly affirmed, you have to know many things, and unless you figure out what he is you cannot comprehend "certain *fundamental* secrets of our modern history." *Toreo* did nothing less than "to change profoundly, or rather, to invert the social structure of Spain, an inversion that has lasted more than two centuries, giving the Spanish collective body characteristics opposite to those other European nations have had" (9:123). He reiterated this importance, maintaining that *corridas* were a spectacle "which has no similarity to any other, which has resounded throughout the world, and which, within the dimensions of the last two centuries of Spanish history, signifies a reality of the first order" (7:28).

No one had realized this before, Ortega correctly surmised, because *aficionados* and critics lacked the objectivity of the "analyzer of humanities." If an *aficionado* made the claims Ortega did, he would at once be written off as a foolish exaggerator. On the other hand, no historian or philosopher or "analyzer of humanities" worth his salt would bother to deal with such an "embarrassing" topic. No one, that is, but Ortega, whose genial antipathy garnered him some sympathy within the metier: the famous *flamenco* performer *La Argentinita* once told Salvador de Madariaga that Ortega reminded her of a *torero* from Málaga, and the celebrated *matador* Ignacio Sánchez Mejías devised an ironic theory explaining how in reality Ortega was a Gypsy. Yet it was Ortega's Germanic training and rigor (the novelist Juan Goytisolo, playing on Carlos I of Spain who was also Charles V of the Holy Roman Empire, has called him the first philosopher of Spain and the fifth of Germany) and his fertile and open mind that allowed him to see clearly one of the most evident facts about Spanish history. He was none too modest about it: "If anybody in the world really knows what a *torero*—that bicentenary, historic, Spanish reality—is, that anybody is I" (9:122). When it came to understanding exactly what a *torero* was, "no one in Spain, and therefore in the world, knows better than I." And he was right in his own bullheaded way.

No one in Spain, wrote Ortega, had bothered to make an issue of *los toros,* no one had approached so seemingly trivial a subject with the proper "freshness of soul and mind" (8:588). No one had bothered to ask why it was that in Spain there were *corridas* as opposed to there not being *corridas,* or why they had begun when they did. And yet probably no single thing, he continued, had for generations made more Spaniards happy or given them more to talk about (9:122).

Why had the thinkers and writers left alone the one incontrovertibly unique Spanish spectacle? The answer ought not escape us. *Toreo* belongs to the *leyenda negra* (the Black Legend), the cruel and bloody Spain of the Inquisitors, the torturers of Indians in the name of a perverse faith, a sadistic society given up to the bloody sports of the *auto de fe* and the cock- and bullfight. And *toreo* belongs to the *pandereta,* the gay Spain of colorful Gypsies and quaint customs and ennobling poverty and flowerpots and *burros* and bottled sunshine and cheap shoeshines, the sun-drenched Mecca made for tourists, with Carmen rediviva on every corner. And *toreo* belongs to backward Spain, to the country that failed to progress; that lived in unenlightened despotism; that missed out on the burgeoning Industrial Revolution, the equalizing reforms of democracy, and the rise of a literate bourgeoisie. Spain failed to develop materially, and it was to that materially undeveloped country, that savage, ignorant, illiterate, ungovernable, anarchic, and, above all, backward nation that *toreo* shamefully belonged. No rational man could in good conscience admit the existence of *toreo*.

But *toreo* was not created by rational men. It was created by the Spanish *pueblo,* particularly the Andalusians. The diversion of the nobility, a kind of combination of jousting and bull hunting, became popular particularly after the conquest of Granada in 1492. During the sixteenth and seventeenth centuries, the Spanish nobility lanced bulls from horseback. These *fiestas de toros* or early *corridas* were celebrated on the occasions of royal weddings or births and on religious feast days. As they became more organized, they were brought in from the open fields and celebrated in confined areas such as the Plaza Mayor in Madrid. Here the horseman's attendants were used to distract the bull from a fallen horse or rider or to finish off a wounded bull. These attendants, who used their capes to maneuver the bulls and their swords to kill them, became popular with the crowds and in time developed into modern *toreros* as we know them today, especially after Isabel de Farnesio, wife of the first Bourbon, discouraged the participation of the Court in such affairs.

Some of these proto-*toreros* came from Navarra from the area around Pamplona where the terrain was too uneven to work with bulls in the field on horseback. In Andalucía, where the terrain was level and where the best bulls and horses were, *toreo* on horseback remained popular and took on great style, especially at Sevilla under the auspices of the Real Maestranza de Caballería, a kind of royal equestrian society that grew out of a religious brotherhood and came to promote public *corridas* as training in horsemanship as well as public benefits. When *toreo* on foot became popular, the Andalusians applied to it many of the principles of equestrian *toreo,* thereby transforming the gymnastic and chaotic exercise of dodging the bull into the structured and ritualized art of controlling him.

By the eighteenth century Andalusian *toreros* had literally taken over, and they "invaded," as Cossío, the maximum authority on *toreo* put it, all the *plazas* in Spain, creating a contagious and pervasive sense of style and ambience.[7] This new *torero* was characteristically an Andalusian of the lower classes trained in the milieu of the *matadero* (slaughterhouse) of Sevilla. As the century wore on, *toreo* flowered and the peculiar style of the *toreros* that we already know as *majismo* took the country by storm.

Ortega was the pioneer in this area, precisely in his late article on Goya (1950), certain phrases of which are germane:

> . . . in Spain during the eighteenth century, a most curious phenomenon occurred. Enthusiasm for the popular . . . seized the upper classes. To the curiosity and philanthropic concern which sustained popularism everywhere, in Spain there was added a strong tendency towards "plebeianism" . . . [which] extended . . . to the costumes, dances, songs, gestures and amusements of the common people. [It was] . . . an impassioned and exclusive enthusiasm, a veritable frenzy which makes it nothing more nor less than the greatest source of energy in Spanish life in the second half of the eighteenth century. . . . Elsewhere the normal course ran in a completely opposite direction: the lower classes admiringly contemplated the manners of life created by the aristocracy and endeavoured to imitate them. It is the inversion of this norm that has sustained Spanish life for many generations. The common people lived enthusiastically in their own style, aware of themselves and taking pleasure in their self-knowledge. For their part, the upper classes felt happy only when abandoning their own customs and saturating themselves in plebeianism. ["Goya" p. 113]

The "inversion" Ortega mentions is precisely that inversion he mentioned as the result of *toreo*. The *torero* became the *matador de toros,* the commoner risen to the level of hero, and he was venerated from above and from below.

Ortega's term *plebeianism* betrays his own sense of enlightened intelligence, but his bias does not prevent his understanding why this revolution took place:

> Words cannot describe how low the Spanish aristocracy had fallen in the second half of the seventeenth century. . . . The Spanish nobility had lost all creative powers. They showed themselves incompetent not only in matters of politics, administration and war, but also incapable of reviewing or even graciously maintaining, the forms of this daily existence. They ceased, therefore, to exercise the principal function of every aristocracy, which is the setting of an example. In consequence the people felt forsaken, without models, help or discipline from their superiors. ["Goya" p. 114]

This catastrophic vacuum extended to every sphere of society: "The dearth of scientific, literary and plastic talent in Spain from 1680 is appalling, to the point where it constitutes a pathological phenomenon demanding elucidation" ("Goya" p. 115).

The response of the lower classes was to fall back on their own resources: "From 1670, the lives of the common Spanish people began to turn in on themselves. Instead of looking outside for their manners, little by little they developed and *stylized* their own traditional ways." Thus attitudes, postures, gestures, pronunciation, dress, all were affected: living was, as Ortega notes, "living 'in style.' " This style became in time "a second nature which was shaped by aesthetic qualities." But most important of all, from that sense of popular style, from the "repertoire of constantly-used lines and rhythms," there emerged the popular arts, which therefore represent "a second, deliberate stylization performed on top of the primary style of movement, gesticulation and conversation." This stylized style was most evident in "the two greatest artistic creations of the Spanish people in that century: the bullfight and the theater" ("Goya" p. 114).

Ortega's highly lucid theory is the most cogent basis for understanding what amounts to a revolutionary inversion of values in Spanish society. The only trouble with it is that he did not develop it enough. He realized that the virtual imposition of popular style in manners and customs came from "the people of Madrid and certain Andalusian capitals" ("Goya" p. 114). And he realized just how vitally important *toreo* was:

> We could say that it was about 1740 when the fiesta took shape as a work of art. The effect it produced in Spain was devastating and addictive. Only a few years later, government ministers were perturbed by the frenzy the spectacle aroused in all social classes. Rich and poor, men and women, dedicated a large part of every day to getting ready for the *corrida,* attending it, and talking about the deeds of their heroes. It was a total obsession. And do not forget that the bullfight itself is only the outer and momentary appearance of a whole world that goes on behind the scenes, which includes everything from the pastures where the fighting bulls are bred to the wine-shops and taverns where bullfighters and *aficionados* forgather. ["Goya" p. 115]

And he connected theater with *los toros,* even to the point of asking the same kind of pertinent questions that had led him to understand the importance of *toreo.* "Why is it not recognized as a fact of common knowledge that the years between 1760 and 1800 formed the epoch in which Spaniards most enjoyed the theater?" He knew that a new kind of genre—*sainetes, jácaras,* and *tonadillas*—often employing music and dance had been invented in Spanish theater and that it was "of plebeian origin and style." He asked the fundamental question about such theater: "These new genres lacked merit; indeed they did not pretend to any. How can it be explained that, nevertheless, the Spanish theater was then experiencing its finest period?" ("Goya" p. 115).

But he could not see, judging from what he wrote, that he was in the process of describing an underground Romantic revolution. Theater and *toros* were indeed the basis for the popular culture he was attempting to see clearly, but it was not a two-legged stool at all. *Cante jondo* or *flamenco,* which Ortega had deprecated in his "Theory of Andalucía" years before (1927), formed a third very necessary leg, as Ricardo Molina, the erudite poet from Córdoba realized when he wrote, "the art of *flamenco* as well, we would add. The origins, development, and ambience of taurine art from 1740 to 1900 make up a history which is parallel to that of *flamenco.*" He went on to add that the great *matadores* of that first golden age, Pedro Romero and *Costillares,* were analogous to and contemporary with the great early *flamenco* singers we met at that *baile* in Triana, *el Planeta* and *el Fillo* (p. 165).

The short plays Ortega describes as making up "perhaps the finest period" of Spanish theater dramatize the whole affair: popular culture and the popular arts make up the subject matter of these highly self-conscious pieces. The titles alone provide ample proof as *gitanos, majos,* or *toreros* turn up literally by the hundreds: "The Jealous Gypsy," "A *Majo* and a *Maja,*" "The Gypsies and the *Payos*" (a *payo* is a non-Gypsy, that is, the "bad guy"), "The Gypsies of Cádiz," "The Poor Gypsy Girl and the Enamored *Majo,*" "A Day of Bulls in Cádiz," "The Toreador Mayor" and "The *Torero's* Apprentice" are typical examples. In many instances the dialogue was *ceceado,* that is, lisped in the most affected Andalusian Gypsy style, which can be very funny. There were even such strange developments as *mojigangas,* which were short plays of this same type or pantomimes acted out in the *plaza de toros* and followed by the release of a live bull to be killed by the actors themselves. Most of these functions were undoubtedly in the worst taste, but their very existence shows to what extent the effects of *toreo* and theater were intertwined.

Popular culture did indeed stem from Madrid and certain Andalusian capitals, notably Sevilla and Cádiz, although it might be more accurate to say *from* Andalucía *into* or *through* Madrid, where the whole phenomenon enlarged and took the capital and to some extent the rest of the country by storm. And just as the whole process had moved northward from Andalucía to Madrid, so it moved upward from the lower classes to the court, in the process effecting one of the most triumphantly Romantic spectacles of its age. There was relatively little "intellectual" Romantic movement in Spain, and there were few Byronic dandies in the nobility to set the fashion. But, as Ortega suspected, the *pueblo,* especially the old, style-conscious, syncretistic *pueblo* of Andalucía, when left to its own devices, was capable of inventing in fact what other cultures only conjured up in their imaginations. Richard Ford provides us with a fine description of going to *los toros,* which catches that whole triumphant sense of pageantry:

> The next afternoon all the world crowds to the *plaza de toros.* Nothing can exceed the gaiety and sparkle of a Spanish public going, eager and full-dressed, to the *fight.* They could not move faster were they running away from a real one. All the streets or open spaces near the outside of the arena are a spectacle. The merry mob is everything. Their excitement under a burning sun, and their thirst for the blood of bulls, is fearful. There is no sacrifice, no denial which they will not undergo to save money for the bull-fight. It is the birdlime with which the devil catches many a male and female soul. The men all go in their best costume and *majo*-finery: the distinguished ladies wear on these occasions white lace mantillas. . . . [P. 273]

Goya, whose long and fecund career spans the whole period, provides us with abundant graphic proof of the entire process. His artistic trajectory stretched from the rose-colored rococo of the illustrated reign of Carlos III through the portraits of weakness and willfulness of that utterly uncharming *ménage à trois,* Carlos IV, María Luisa, and Godoy, and finally into the post-Napoleonic bleakness and reactionary darkness reflected as dull horror in the "Disasters of War" and the "black paintings." As he documented the failing fortune of Spain, which paralleled the disintegration of the monarchy, Goya also recorded the triumph of style created by the lower classes (Ford's description dates from the reign of Fernando VII, the last and worst period, a few years after Goya's death in 1828).

It is perhaps ironic that Ortega should have elaborated his social theory of *majismo* is his essay on Goya, since he often seems to be trying, in a somewhat demythologizing vein, to get us to see the effects of the "Age of Reason" on Goya. But I for one remain unconvinced of such effects, since Goya's magical world portrays in splendid detail and at every level of society the indigenous Romanticism that we call *majismo*. Goya in fact illustrates Ortega's thesis about the popularity of *majismo* in the upper classes in some of his portraits: there is, for example, hideous María Luisa dressed up as a *maja* in precisely the full-length portrait she had Goya do as a gift for her "favorite," Godoy. Even more revealing of the appeal of *majismo* is the splendid full-length portrait Goya did in 1797 of the Duchess of Alba dressed as a *maja*. On her rings are inscribed the names "Goya" and "Alba" and below her in the sand is an inscription to which she is pointing which reads "solo Goya" (only Goya). That was the year of their split, and Goya covered over the word "solo," but he kept the portrait himself for another fifteen years. Then, too, there is the portrait of Leocadia, Goya's young mistress who moved out to the Quinta del Sordo to tend after him, now an old, deaf, and ill-tempered visionary who painted his nightmares all over the walls of that house. She was the only beautiful thing he painted on those walls and she, too, is dressed as a *maja*.

If Ortega is right about Goya, he eventually came to reject *majismo* and to see the whole national scene in a different light after his association with the "illustrated" French sympathizers in the rarer spheres of the court's social life. Yet it ought to have been perfectly obvious to Ortega that only one who loved the bulls — possessed true *afición* — could have or would have produced some fifteen years later the invaluable historical document on *toreo* known as *La Tauromaquia,* a series of etchings that trace the history and development of *toreo* from the days of *El Cid* up to the nineteenth century. Then there are the masterpieces known as *Los toros de Burdeos* and the rich oils depicting *corridas* in the *pueblos,* and finally there are the two plendid portraits of Pedro Romero and his brother José.

Given time we could work through all of Goya's art and pick out painting by painting and sketch by sketch the ones in which he documented that subtle social upheaval that amounted to the real romantic revolution in Spain. If we are willing to suspend our belief that the rationality of the Enlightenment and its consequent progressivism lead trippingly to the best of all possible worlds, we can begin to see that Goya became the solitary and fecund recorder of the popular and collective Romantic movement of Spain. His paintings and sketches of *majos* and *majas, toreros,* witches, martyrs and heroes, religious processions, superstitions, festivals and feasts, in short the whole teeming world of the *pueblo* — in all its greed, horror, arrogance, vanity, and ignorance but also in all its contagious finery, its unique stylishness, and its undying and creative vitality — constitute a visible testimony that Goya never quite heard those foreign voices of reason and listened instead to the native voices within. Where is there a finer or more unjustly executed hero of the *pueblo* than that brave *campesino* standing against the faceless rank of soldiers about to execute him in *The Third of May?*

If I had to choose Goya's finest single representation of the world of the *pueblo,* I would pick without hesitation the wonderful portrait of the *matador* Pedro Romero. Joaquín Rodríguez, called *Costillares,* from Sevilla, and Pedro Romero from Ronda were the greatest of the very early *matadores.* They were the men responsible for modern *toreo,* for elevating the status of certain *toreros* — only those who actually killed the bulls — to that of *matador.* Theirs was the first golden age of *toreo* in every respect.

Costillares was a brilliantly inventive child of the *matadero* of Sevilla. He is said to have invented the basic cape pass and to have perfected the method of killing the bull still most in use today. His great rival Pedro Romero, whose grandfather reputedly invented the *muleta,* killed 5,600 bulls in his long and unmarred career. He may well have been the greatest *matador* of all time, and he was at any rate the most respected *matador* of those waning years of the eighteenth century when the men of Andalucía were creating one of the most anomalous arts of all time. Son and grandson of *toreros,* his infallible killing in the most dangerous manner — *recibiendo,* that is, "receiving" the charging bull rather than going to it — made him into a somewhat legendary figure.

Pedro Romero and *Costillares* were the first professional *matadores* to achieve real fame, and their competition became a matter of great importance and passion in Cádiz, in Sevilla, and especially in Madrid. *Costillares,* more inventive and more flamboyant, came to be the favorite of the upper classes. Romero, serious, dignified, and known for his upright character and bravery, appealed more to the popular classes. Their fifteen-year competition, which was to divide the capital, was just beginning in 1775, the year a twenty-nine-year-old painter named Goya arrived at court. Some twenty years later, after *Costillares* had been forced to retire with an arm injury and a painful carbuncle on the palm of his sword hand, Goya painted the portrait of his favorite in the prime of his maturity.

Romero retired at the end of the century and returned to his mountain town of Ronda. He was later made the *Maestro* of the newly founded school of Tauromachy in Sevilla, and at sixty-six offered to kill a bull in Madrid for the benefit of the court. When he died at eighty-four there was not a scar from the bulls on his body, and not one drop of his blood had been spilled in the *plaza de toros.*

Goya's exquisite portrait reflects the genius of the man with no exaggeration or flourishes. His dress is that of the *majo,* the whole spirit of which Ford captured so well when he described the *majos* of Andalucía as those "who in the other provinces become stars, patterns, models, the observed of all observers, and the envy and admiration of their applauding countrymen" (p. 223). When we see Goya's portrait of Romero—the assured grace, the understated elegance, the paradoxical delicacy of that prominently displayed right hand that dispatched 5,600 bulls—we can only conclude that in Romero we have a prototype of the *majo* and of the *matador* as the Spanish Romantic artist and popular hero.

Spanish Romanticism produced two truly great artists: Goya's portrait of Romero preserves for us the one rendered by the other, and Goya's tribute is eloquent. John Fulton, the first American to have reached the full rank of *matador* in Spain (he took his *alternativa* or ceremonial promotion in Sevilla), is the only American to have written knowledgeably about the killing of the bull from the unique vantage of a professional life dedicated to the bulls. He writes succinctly that "Romero is the most impressive matador in bullfight history" (p. 14). When Hemingway wrote *The Sun Also Rises,* his splendid novel of manners revolving around a brilliant young *matador,* he used Cayetano Ordóñez, *Niño de la Palma,* who was brilliant for a season or so and who was from Ronda, as his model. The fictional name Hemingway chose for his young hero—the most admirable main character in the novel and the one against whom the modern misfits of the "Lost Generation" are measured—was Pedro Romero.

Toreo is above all an art. It is, as Hemingway pointed out, a performing art, and therefore it is impermanent. But it is nonetheless an art. Like ballet or the opera or the theater it is an art of spectacle, but the medium is not movement or words or music or even their combination, although all three are present. The medium—the raw material of the art, the block of stone, the blank canvas, the sheets of paper, that which is to be choreographed, orchestrated, staged—is the awesome and powerful *toro bravo,* whose presence in the *plaza de toros* may bring with it the presence of death and always brings the presence of pain. That fact, and the ritual nature of the orderly and carefully ordered sacrifice of that noble and totemic animal, have led to many interpretations of the meaning of *toreo.*

John McCormick in his richly erudite study, *The Complete Aficionado,* has done a quite provocative sociohistorical analysis of *toreo* by comparing it to the English novel and showing how *toreo* and the novel served the same ends: "Denied its human rights, deprived by a peculiar history of the possibility of seizing those rights through revolution, the Spanish people took the only way open to it, rejection of the aristocracy through symbolic action. It elevated its own, the new matador who had been *peón* to the status of folk hero; *toreo* offered apolitical politics, satisfying a need which was as urgent as it was below the level of consciousness."[8] In Spain *toreo* allowed the common man to project himself to the level of hero and nobleman in much the same way that the novel did for the bourgeoisie in England. Instead of the Englishman's vicarious identification on the printed page, the Spaniard had visual identification in spectacle. The two arts are as different as the two cultures but their effects, even their respective *raisons d'être,* are curiously alike.

McCormick also compared *toreo* to Greek tragedy, a comparison which at this point will only seem unlikely to our hardened rationalist. His point is not so much that tragedy and *toreo* are exactly alike but that they grew out of similar origins in the sacrifice of bulls: "We are not suggesting that because the ritual of the dithyramb grew out of a primitive association between bulls and fertility, and that because the dithyramb developed into tragedy, the modern art of *toreo* is therefore to be directly equated with Greek tragedy. Rather, what we are attempting to establish is a certain coincidence of effect between tragedy and *toreo,* a coincidence which can be accounted for in the ritual origins of the two disparate arts" (p. 24).

McCormick's point is well taken: in actual fact *toreo* is "less developed" than classical tragedy since it never evolved beyond the stage of the sacrifice and became fixed on the sacrifice itself. Tragedy may echo sacrifice but in tragedy all is mime and symbolic action. The *corrida* on the other hand is quite real; it is, as Ortega knew, the only spectacle that is really spectacle and yet is reality too. To make this point Ortega told how a certain famous actor was once heckling the *matador Cúchares,* who was having trouble killing a difficult bull. At a certain point when *Cúchares* had had enough, he looked up at the actor, safe in his seat, and said with his best Andalusian scorn: "¡Zeñó Míquez o zeñó Maíquez, que aquí no ze muere de mentirijilla como en er teatro!" ("Mister Míquez or Mr. Maíquez, down here you don't just die a make-believe death like you do in the theater!" (7:465).

In his wonderful essay on theater "Idea del teatro," in which Ortega developed his notion of the *fiesta* sense of life, he explained how the mystic and visionary cult of Dionysus, which gave rise to "Carnival" and to tragedy, combined in its primitive stage mimetic dance, sacred orgy, and feast, that is, *fiesta.* All that was left of this in Europe was "Carnival" and eventually that too atrophied. The only authentic surviving *fiesta,* which is in a state of agony, he went on, is the *corrida de toros,* "in a certain sense—which I will not develop here—also Dionysiac, Bacchic and orgiastic" (7:487). Ortega never did go on to develop that Dionysiac side of the *corrida,* just as he never wrote his long promised treatise on *toreo, Paquiro,* but it is not difficult to see that he was thinking along the same lines we have been following. The *corrida* is no primitive orgy in any sense, but it does not take much of a Jungian leap of faith to see the analogy between the Greek god who as bull was sacrificed in Spring rites to ensure the order of nature and the unconscious (remember McCormick's phrase "below the level of consciousness") fear of nature projected onto the sacrificial surrogate of the bull that is safely, from the spectator's point of view, killed by the cultural hero. Many classical scholars believe the Greeks developed the symbolic action of tragedy out of such a process, but the Andalusians, who never evolved and were never allowed to evolve into as keenly *conscious* a society as Socratic Athens, did not get that far. To satisfy their subliminal or unconscious or irrational or Dionysian need, they created the *corrida* and turned the killing of the scape-bull into an art that is closer to the origin of art than any we know.

My description sounds complex because the phenomenon is complex. But all the necessary elements of the collective mental substrata were there, and they were just the elements we find in archaic Greece and the ancient Near East. The society was agrarian, often impoverished, dependent, and desperately uneducated except in its own profound folkways. Logic or rational thought, what eventually elevated classical tragedy out of ritual, was absent. The society was matriarchal to the extent that it depended on Mother Earth and the Virgin Mother for everything (Gypsies are still at least matrilineal to the extent that they are often known, as indeed many non-Gypsies in the *pueblos* of Andalucía are, by their mother's name, as for example the erratic but brilliant *torero, Rafael de Paula*). The spiritual or religious sense of life was still dramatic and founded in spectacle. Even the accompanying ecstatic dance existed and was intimately connected with religious celebration. Finally, the bull, the *only* bull that could have been used for such a ritual art, was there. Everything we have looked at, the whole surviving archaic and conservative bent of the people of Andalucía, led almost inevitably to the spontaneous creation of *toreo.* Indeed, *toreo, flamenco,* and religious spectacle were as interwoven in the unchanged unconscious of the Andalusian people as similar related phenomena had been in the Mediterranean cultures of antiquity.

It should come as no surprise that Lorca knew this perfectly. He wrote with utter clarity about the religious spectacles, about dance, and about the bulls; and he related them in no uncertain fashion. For him, greatest of the Andalusian seers though not a fervent *aficionado, duende,* the Dionysian and chthonian inspiration of Andalusian art, was found in *toreo* just as it was in *flamenco.* And it was an unmistakably "religious" experience. He called *toreo* "the liturgy of the bulls, an authentic religious drama, in which, just as in the Mass, there is adoration and sacrifice of a God" (1:1107).

The "god" sacrificed in *toreo* is clearly an allusion to the pre-Christian rituals we have already discussed, rituals that in so many ways prefigured or foreshadowed the rituals the Church would later employ. For Lorca there was no getting around the "classical," that is, "pagan" or pre-Christian, nature of *toreo:* "it is as though all the *duende* of the classical world had come together in this perfect *fiesta*" (1:1107). In New York in 1930 he introduced his close friend, the *matador* Ignacio Sánchez Mejías, with these words: "The only serious thing left on earth is *toreo,* the only living spectacle of antiquity in which we find all the classical essences of the most artistic peoples in the world." *Toreo* was "sacred rhythm of the purest mathematics . . . discipline and perfection. In it everything is measured, even anguish and death itself." The *matador* was a hero fixed within time, a "hero within the strict norms of art and within a norm stricter yet in its forgiveness."[9] That stricter norm would claim Ignacio Sánchez Mejías's life a few years later in the *plaza de toros* at Manzanares, and Lorca would write his finest poem, "Llanto por Ignacio Sánchez Mejías," one of the greatest of our century, on the occurrence of that tragic moment, that fatal "five in the afternoon."

Death—the awareness of death, the possibility of death, the certainty of death—is the essential element in the *fiesta* sense of life, a sense of life that amounts to what we identified in the beginning as "the culture of death." In spite of the death of his friend Sánchez Mejías, Lorca was able to affirm in one of his last public interviews that *toreo* was probably the greatest poetic and vital resource in Spanish life. He was unequivocal about it: "I believe that *los toros* is the most cultured *fiesta* in the world today; it is pure drama . . . the only place you can go with the assurance of seeing the most enlightening beauty" (2:1087). The play of death and geometry formed the coordinates for this unique *fiesta,* the most Spanish and the most Andalusian of creations. As Lorca had written in his essay on *duende,* "Spain is the only country in the world where death is the national spectacle, where death trumpets long blasts to announce the arrival of each spring . . ." (1:1108). It was precisely for that reason that the young Ernest Hemingway would spend so much time in Spain seeking a purity of emotion in the atavistic spectacle of death in the afternoon, a purity he could find nowhere else.

The culture of death, that is, the entire cultural history we have traced, reached its apogee in the popular creation of *flamenco* and *toreo* in the modern age. Yet in spite of their relative modernity, both are primordial arts, still very close to the threshold of artistic creation. As such, as we have seen with *flamenco,* they provide the possibility of catharsis, especially if we understand catharsis not merely as Aristotelian "purgation," but as the sense of ex-stasis, that is, a temporary state of unselfawareness or unselfconsciousness, a removal from self, an ecstatic identification with, or vicarious participation in, the ritual of the performance itself. We have already seen this phenomenon in the intimate theater of *flamenco.* The same effect is no less possible in *toreo* when on that rare occasion the *matador* is able to unleash through his art, through his *duende,* the collective response of the whole resonant *público* of a *plaza de toros.* I have no doubt that this irrepressible collective response (the word *olé* derives from the Arabic word for God) was what Ortega had in mind when he wrote of *toreo* as the only authentic surviving *fiesta* and, more specifically, as "Dionysiac, Bacchic and orgiastic" (7:487), allusive language suggesting that the mixture of the effects of *duende* and wine within the charged ambience of the *plaza* can turn the spectacle of a ritual sacrifice into a collective ecstasy.

Hemingway understood exactly and described precisely the nature of that collective ecstasy in this, perhaps the most profound, passage from *Death in the Afternoon:*

> If the spectators know the matador is capable of executing a complete, consecutive series of passes with the muleta in which there will be valor, art, understanding and, above all, beauty and great emotion, they will put up with mediocre work, cowardly work, disastrous work because they have the hope sooner or later of seeing the complete faena; the faena that takes a man out of himself and makes him feel immortal while it is proceeding, that gives him an ecstasy, that is, while momentary, as profound as any religious ecstasy; moving all the people in the ring together and increasing in emotional intensity as it proceeds, carrying the bullfighter with it, he playing on the crowd through the bull and being moved as it responds in a growing ecstasy of ordered, formal, passionate, increasing disregard for death that leaves you, when it is over, and the death administered to the animal that has made it possible, as empty, as changed and as sad as any major emotion will leave you. [Pp. 206–7]

Anyone fortunate enough to have experienced that rarest of occurrences, a complete and authentic *tarde de toros,* an "afternoon of the bulls," should understand, should, in fact, remember the peculiar uplifting, the sense of momentary transport or remove I have in mind. As Lorca expressed it in a passage worth repeating, "neither in Spanish dance [that is, *flamenco*] nor in the bulls does anyone enjoy himself; *duende* causes suffering through drama, through living forms, and it prepares stairways for an evasion of the reality which surrounds us" (1:1107).

If we couple Lorca's description of the effect of *duende* to the comment he made regarding the intimate connection between the bulls and the rites of Holy Week, we will begin to understand how for the Andalusian mind none of these elements is really independent of, or separable from, the whole cultural context, the *ambiente* of which they are all part and parcel and in which they all flourish: "The innumerable rites of Holy Friday along with the most cultured *fiesta* of the bulls form the popular triumph of Spanish death" (1:1105).

If our rationalist has managed to follow this far and still objects to such a juxtaposition, I can only answer that he is no longer able to understand something which for more primordial minds, such as Lorca's, was luminously clear. Our rationalist fails to understand that the bull could be numinous or "divine," a belief common to most of the early civilizations from the Ganges to Cádiz, but then our rationalist seems to lack much mythic bent. If we tried to explain the *matador* as a quester or a hero, as a Thesean penetrator of the labyrinth and slayer of the minotaur, as well as the modern version of the Minoan bull-leaper, which is to say taurine celebrant of the Goddess, he would no doubt object. If we were to say he is analogous to the Mithraic bull-slayer, a Prometheus-like bringer of heavenly gifts, he would surely scoff. And if we pointed out that the *matador* in his pink tights, ballet slippers, and gold-brocaded, wasp-waisted *traje de luces,* which for all its overt feminity still clearly accentuates in the skin-tight *taleguilla* those famous Spanish attributes of fertility and manhood; if we pointed out that this singular costume is thoroughly androgynous, our rationalist might laugh out loud. And yet from a certain anthropological perspective, as bull-killer and horn-toucher, the *matador* is the ensurer of fertility and the only mystagogue or Dionysiac priest remaining in the Western World.

The extent to which my elucidation seems darkly incomprehensible to our rationalist is roughly equal to the distance between the popular culture of Andalucía, in many ways fixed in a prerational or prelogical mentality, and our own culture, an assertion with which our rationalist will probably agree wholeheartedly, believing modern Western culture to be superior, advanced, and progressive, the triumph of logical thought and technology. And he will be right. But he will also be profoundly wrong, because he will be ignoring altogether what the distinguished historian of religion, Mircea Eliade, called "a continuous encounter with things that are 'wholly other' to us as modern Westerners."[10]

Indeed the mythic or anthropological or archetypal interpretation of *toreo,* especially the androgynous part, one of its most "sacred" aspects in that androgyny signifies a "whole being," would not be obvious or very acceptable to the average Spanish *aficionado.* Plato may have thought that man and woman were the split halves of a once perfect being, but that notion has long since been Judeo-Christianized out of the Western mind except at an unconscious or subconscious level. You will not therefore get much rational acceptance of this interpretation from most *aficionados* and you might even get more disagreement than you would care to have. Yet certain artists and critics, whose concerns often overlap, have seen the "sacred" side of this phenomenon clearly enough, and have understood the complex nature of *toreo* to which the *aficionado* intuitively responds, even though he may opine to the contrary.

When Joselito, the great Gypsy *matador,* who many say was the greatest of all time, was killed in the *plaza* of Talavera in 1920, all Spain mourned his death. And Lorca's friend, the poet Rafael Alberti, wrote in his memoirs: "He was twenty-five years old. Young and beautiful, he died like a god."[11] Picasso, always fascinated with bulls, has gone a step farther: in some of his work, Christ on the cross appears in the *plaza* acting literally as savior as he lures the bull away from a fallen horse and *picador.* The idea is not quite as original as it may strike some, since the depiction of divine intervention, especially by the Virgin, in *toreo* goes back at least to the thirteenth century.

I do not believe that Picasso meant to suggest, and I certainly do not, that all *matadores* ought to be seen as Christ-figures. But it is clear enough that Picasso, whose work so frequently and characteristically harked back to antiquity, saw the possibility of a "sacred" dimension in *toreo.* He recognized relationships that our rationalist fails to perceive. He recognized that *toreo* still possessed a quality which had for the most part disappeared from Western culture.

Figuratively or metaphorically or analogically speaking, in *toreo* the *matador,* the hero, the man-god, controlled and dominated and ultimately vanquished the god of nature. It is perhaps the oldest story of humanity, the most ancient myth we have. Yet only through *toreo* has the content of that powerful and timeless myth evolved into a complex ritual art without turning into symbolic reenactment: in *toreo* the bull must still die. If we can pare away most of our rational objections to such an act, we can see *toreo* in its essence as a quite unique and splendidly characteristic creation of Andalucía. To fail to grasp the significance of that creation (whether we "like" it or not is irrelevant) is to fail to understand the Andalusians' daringly divergent, we might almost say subversive, response to the modern age.

The people of Andalucía still cling to what most of the rest of our world has given up, a strong cultural identity rooted in antiquity, the core of which, primordial but not primitive, preserved but not archaic, is an unremitting sense of what religious historians would call the sacred, what Lorca would have called hieratic, and what depth psychologists would refer to as archetypal (an Andalusian would probably call it *lo andaluz,* "the Andalusian way"). The preserved sense of the sacred, what many Andalusians think of as their own kind of "pantheism," is what binds and informs Andalusian culture. It forms the common ground for all that we have examined, and it lies behind the special syncretism of Andalucía, that traceable heritage of Oriental influences constantly reshaped in a unique and synthesizing image. It has undifferentiated the passage of time, neutralized any sense of history, and ignored the notion of progress. Changeable and changeless as the sea, ordered and repetitive as the seasons, fertile and mysterious as the earth, this collective *duende* has been responsible for the creation and the re-creation of the Andalusians' diversions and devotions, their rites and rituals, their chants and litanies, their processions and pilgrimages, their feasts and sacrifices, their heroes and martyrs, their gods and goddesses. *Toreo,* in all its pristinely ordered savagery and its paradoxically exquisite beauty, has provided, as Goya, Lorca, Ortega, Picasso, and Hemingway have enabled us to fathom, the irrefutably Romantic theater for the celebration of that *duende* and for the ritual purgation of the tragic sense of life and death as the *pueblo* of Andalucía know it. In a more than figurative manner, it is what Ortega, writing on Greek tragedy, called "religion of the *pueblo,* by the *pueblo* and for the *pueblo*" (7:473).

Unfortunately the spectacle of *toreo* is corrupt, perhaps more corrupt than it has ever been. Hemingway outlined a multitude of reasons for this corruption in *Death in the Afternoon,* his still very readable classic on *toreo.* When *matador* John Fulton writes his memoirs we may well have another classic treatment of the subject by an American. My intention meanwhile has not been to discuss the seamy side of *toreo* but to try to shed some light on its social, historical, and artistic facets as a particularly Andalusian creation. In my mind at least it is a singular and truly popular Romantic art that is as significant for its revolutionary creation within the milieu we have examined as for its lack of acceptance beyond the concentricities—Spain and Hispanic America—of that milieu. Yet despite its significance, or perhaps because of it, *toreo* is in crisis.

The internal decadence of the art—graft, bribery, favoritism, abuses of the bull such as horn-shaving—concerns me less than the external pressures on it as an "anachronism" and as a *vergüenza nacional*, a "national disgrace" in the modern world. *Toreo* can probably survive internal decadence and abuse as it has always done. But it cannot survive the attitudes of the modern Western world that are being so remorselessly imposed upon and accepted by many of the Spanish people. Our materialistic rationalism is too radically opposed to the *fiesta* sense of life to allow it to endure other than as a quaint survival of once primitive Spain, a throwback, a national malfunction too much like the Inquisition or the shamefully prolonged demise of fascism's dream and lie. The association is, of course, a false one, but so is the notion that the extirpation of such a deeply rooted spectacle is indicative of "progress" or any betterment of the human condition.

If *toreo* fails to survive, it will be because the whole Andalusian sense of life as revealed in Holy Week, in the Rocío, in *flamenco,* in *toreo* itself, has succumbed, and because that sense of the sacred, that sense of the spiritual, that *duende* of Andalucía which has so affected all of Spanish life, has vanished. In the mountain *pueblos,* in the coastal villages not ruined by tourism, in certain *barrios* of Sevilla and Cádiz, of Córdoba and Granada, some of that peculiar spirit, so integral a part of the traditional way of life in Andalucía, is still precariously surviving. But I cannot believe it will continue to flourish. Modern praxis, rightly or wrongly, is mightier than the millenary and earthy *duende* of Andalucía.

Yet the extent to which we in the West so demonstrably lack and need that manifestly spiritual side is roughly indicative, I suspect, of our necessity for preserving such a sense in Andalucía. The more anomalous or incomprehensible these Andalusian vestiges of antiquity appear to us, the more we probably have to learn from them. And the less faith we have in the idea that progress and materialism are the natural products of our own collective experience, the less likely we will be to ignore the fragile environment that nurtures the *fiesta* sense of life and the culture of death.

From the late eighteenth or early nineteenth century it became increasingly apparent to the travelers from the lands of progress that here in Andalucía there still existed a way of life that the modern world had lost forever. Richard Ford, in his best Anglican-positivist vein, summed up the "plight" of the whole country: "Spain was once in the advance of Europe in many matters, but her sun has long stood still: moored by pride and prejudice, she has allowed the world to sail by and leave her far behind" (p. 228). Yet, of course, it was precisely the lack of progress that allowed the preservation of Andalucía. To some extent all of Spain, and to a much greater extent Andalucía, remained apart from that journey into modernity marked by increasing dependence on reason alone. Andalucía, once it had suffered the final invasion of the Castilians, was spared the traumas that mark modern society as we understand it. Cut off from the rest of the West, Andalucía began a Phoenix-like rebirth, creating a chimerical culture that was as anomalous as it was original. Ford was closer to the truth about that culture in his description of the typical *ventas,* the "inns," of his day: "These night-scenes at a Spanish *venta* transport the lover of antiquity into the regions of the past. The whole thing presents an almost unchanged representation of what must have occurred two thousand years ago. . . . The same may be said of the tambourines, castanets, songs and dances – in a word, everything. . . " (p. 51).

Andalucía, spared the benefits of the modern world, and also spared the peculiar anthropomorphism of the late Renaissance, the exclusive dwelling on rational consciousness as the way and the light in the Age of Reason, and the often mindless progressivism of the nineteenth century, came into our age with her antiquity still intact. The extent to which we employ certain very familiar terms to describe our own society – sterility, alienation, dehumanization, rootlessness, meaninglessness – provides us with what is, I suspect, an accurately inverse measure of what we will have lost if the culture of Andalucía ceases to exist. And the extent to which all of Western society eventually becomes aware of the pernicious side of growth, the destructive aspects of technology and the wasteful nature of consumerism will provide us, I believe, with an inverse evaluation of what that culture meant.

If we let *toreo* stand for that culture, a question Lorca once asked makes the whole matter poignant for the rest of Spain and allows the rest of us in the West to extrapolate: "What would become of the Spanish springtime," he once mused, "of our blood and of our language, if the dramatic horns of the *corrida* failed to sound?" (2:1087). The question also implies, taken into the context of all we have considered, that we must try to preserve that authentic culture, for to attempt to restore it at some future date rather than to preserve it now, would be tantamount to turning Andalucía's living museum into a house of wax.

As a result of the internal decadence of *toreo,* the lack of any consistently great *matador* at present, the high prices for tickets, and other obligations on my time and energy, I do not go to the bulls as often as once I did. Always a den of thieves, the *plaza de toros* now has more moneychangers than ever. I keep hoping things will be reversed somehow. And in the unchanging utopia of my mind's eye, *in illo tempore* of memory, I can still see—as once I actually did—a lone man, a motionless *matador,* standing in the center of an ecstatic *plaza* as a great white bull charges and charges again, and the man, the *matador,* winds him and winds him again in inconceivably slow and successively longer arcs around his waist, spinning a lair for their common minotaur, through the sunlight, through the shadow, as though possessed of some ageless thread of Ariadne.

PABLO PICASSO, *Les Demoiselles d'Avignon* (1907), oil on canvas, 8′ ×7′8″. *Les Demoiselles* was the first great revolutionary painting in which Picasso, the premier Andalusian artist, began challenging the basic assumptions of Western art. *Collection, the Museum of Modern Art, New York. Acquired through the Lillie P. Bliss Bequest.*

CODA
THE ANDALUSIAN PICASSO

... when it comes to reflecting upon art, complacently accepting the
mysterious is nearly as pointless as complacently accepting the rational.

— André Malraux, *Picasso's Mask*

THIS CODA first appeared in the *Boston Review*
(November/December 1980) as a review of the Museum of
Modern Art's exhibition, *Picasso: A Retrospective.* I have
included it, with a few minor changes, because it summarizes
much of the previous material and because it reverses the
focus of my examination. This essay looks from the vantage of Andalucía's ancient culture at one of the great artists of the modern age. This kind of reversal — the externaliza-
tion of the whole complex Andalusian phenomenon — seems
a fitting close to the book.

You went into the Garden Wing on the first floor where the early
paintings were, past images and brushstrokes reminiscent of Degas
and Gauguin and Toulouse-Lautrec, less imitations than precocious
efforts to absorb what had already been done by painting them his
own way. Past his dead friend, Casagemas, illuminated in a harsh
light and buried, like Goya's dog, up to his neck. Past paintings
signed Ruiz Picasso and P. Ruiz Picasso, and then in 1901 a self-
portrait called *Yo Picasso,* with obsessive alienated eyes of love and
hatred. Past Harlequins and children and Bohemian selves gradually turning blue — *Two Women at a Bar* is precisely the sordid and
bathetic blue of Barcelona's *barrio chino* — and later turning a nearly
morbid rose. Finally the color darkened into terra cotta and the faces,
especially his own and Gertrude Stein's, began to harden and inten-
sify into opaque icons like the ancient Iberian votive sculptures that
had inspired them. Then almost without warning you were face to
face with the painting of that holy whorehouse — *Les Demoiselles
d'Avignon,* ladies of the night in a Barcelona brothel on the *carrer
d'Avinyó.* This was Picasso's first startling revelation of divine feminity, and the painting with which he shattered the mirror of "realistic"
art and announced the Cubist revolution.

The Museum of Modern Art's retrospective is history now, and the Picassos have come down and have been shipped back to their respective museums. France celebrated his centenary with the opening of the Musée Picasso and Spain with the installation of *Guernica* in the Prado. Yet for New York, 1980 was the glorious summer of Picasso, and undoubtedly, as a good many critics rightly claimed, it was one of the most important exhibitions—perhaps even the single most important one—of the century.

But what did we learn from this nearly overwhelmingly impressive retrospective? Beyond the litany of clichés—"Show of Shows," "Artist of the Century," "Most famous artist of all time," all true enough—what do we know or have we confirmed about Picasso because of this show? And, if those epithets are correct, why are they correct? Why is Picasso—"the towering progenitor of the art of our time," as Grace Glueck wrote[1]—the greatest artist of the twentieth century?

William Rubin, who conceived the show before Picasso's death, said, "No artist invented so much in one lifetime. There is enough material in the MOMA show to make 50 other careers." And Dominique Bozo, codirector of the show and curator of the Musée Picasso (formed by taking 3,500 pieces from Picasso's personal collection in lieu of taxes), claimed that Picasso was equal to a combination of Rembrandt, Balzac, and Victor Hugo: "He links the 19th and 20th centuries in his relationship to art of the past and the culture of the present. He was the foremost painter of reality; he proposes the question 'What is reality?' and he put his own life into his work."[2]

John Ashbery, writing in *New York* magazine, gets right to the point by describing Picasso's "capital act of subversion whose liberating consequences are still being exploited by artists" as "the flattening and fragmenting of three-dimensional objects and space, the simultaneity of different viewpoints . . . , which toppled the last vestiges of traditional illusionism and in doing so cleared a foundation on which art—realistic as well as abstract—continues to build."[3] Robert Hughes caught his Protean power of creation and his Titanic originality: "If ever a man created his own historical role and was not the pawn of circumstances, it was that Nietzschean monster from Málaga."[4] Calvin Tomkins hinted at the significance of the hieratic nature of his shaman's visage: "Although he revealed himself at every turn, he remained as enigmatic, as impenetrable, as the Iberian stone carvings with which he shattered all those centuries of Western art."[5] And John Richardson, although he failed to develop the idea, recognized Picasso's revolutionary role in the turning around of modern art, when he called him the "canniest of art historians . . . the most Faustian of artists . . . determined to turn yesterdays into tomorrows."[6] Liberator from old laws, toppler of traditional values, founder of a new basis for modern art, artist as Nietzschean hero with a magician's ability to manipulate and transform style. Yes, he has all those. But there is more.

Although we all realize that Picasso was quintessentially Spanish, we have so far failed to understand exactly what that means. For Picasso was not just "Spanish," which like "Italian" can mean everything from "Germanic" and blond to pure Mediterranean. He was Andalusian on both sides of his family, the paternal branch of which, Ruiz Blasco, has been traced in Andalucía to at least the sixteenth century, the maternal to the fourteenth.

The child born on October 25, 1881, in Málaga under the sign of Scorpio and baptized in the Church of Santiago Apóstol with the names Pablo, Diego, José, Francisco de Paula, Juan Nepomuceno, María de los Remedios, Crispiano de la Santísima Trinidad Ruiz Picasso, was a prototypical Andalusian who lived in Málaga for the first ten years of his life and during subsequent summers. The story his mother told of his first word — *piz, piz* for *lápiz,* "pencil" — may be a fanciful remembrance, but there is no doubt where and when he learned to paint. His first drawings and oils, done when he was eight or nine, are of *corridas* his father took him to see in their native Málaga.

Andalucía provides us with the surest approach to Picasso's revolutionary importance. I do not mean to slight other places. His late adolescence in Barcelona and his early maturity in Paris are undeniably important, especially to his intellectual formation, but his sensibility nevertheless remained thoroughly Andalusian. And I do not mean merely his vanity, his dandy's ego, his anarchy, his love for bulls and horses, his *donjuanismo,* his energetic and fecund longevity, his obsession with death — all Andalusian to a fault. No, what I do mean is that his ability to *see* was Andalusian.

Andalucía, as we have seen, developed a relatively high civilization at a very early date — the huge dolmens just north of Málaga at Antequera, for instance, date from 4000 B.C. As a federated commercial kingdom of city-states, it had already undergone a complete cycle of development and dissolution spanning more than a millenium before the Romans ever set foot there. Tarshish as the

Hebrews called it — Jonah was headed there when the big fish got him — or Tartessos as the Greeks wrote it, was the first independent, flourishing civilization in western Europe. In time, due to its vast mineral resources, Andalucía received, traded with, and absorbed the influence of a surprising number of mostly Oriental cultures: the megalith builders, the Bell Beaker culture, Tartessos, traders from Crete, Anatolia, and Cyprus, the Phoenicians, the Carthaginians, the Hebrews (one of Solomon's thousand wives was quite possibly a remote ancestor of Picasso), Celts, Greeks, Romans, Visigoths, Vandals, Arabs, Berbers, Gypsies. Yet the most remarkable aspect of Andalusian history is how little change occurred through all those centuries. As the great Spanish ethnologist Julio Caro Baroja eloquently expressed it, an Andalusian village is a living museum stretching from the Neolithic age to the present.

Life there until very recently was always much the same. The eight centuries of Arab conquest and the cultural neglect the Castilians showed after their "Reconquest," spared the land of María Santísima, as the Andalusians call it, the rigors of the European revolutions, the "benefits" of progress and, most importantly for our consideration, much entrapment in Cartesian consciousness.

Andalucía was, in effect, frozen in time while the Western world evolved into the society of rationalistic materialism we now think of as normal. It was precisely this poverty-stricken and neglected Mediterranean archaism that so enchanted the Romantics who, rebelling against the strictures of too much Reason, flocked eagerly to such a "quaint" and "timeless" and Oriental place. We must, I believe, keep this primordial, pre-Cartesian quality in the Andalucía of Picasso's childhood in mind. Without it, his "revolution" is merely rebellion. With it, Picasso's art is visible proof that *cogito ergo sum* is only half of the equation of consciousness.

The "primordial" nature of Andalucía is an imposing and esoteric issue, yet we can approach it through several famous Andalusian institutions. In the eighteenth century, while most of Europe was going through political, social, scientific, and industrial transformations, the common people in Spain and particularly in Andalucía reinvented a ritual slaying of the bull-god and developed the cathartic testimonial of *flamenco*. Even today, Easter is celebrated in the streets of Sevilla and Málaga and in many *pueblos* of Andalucía in ways that closely resemble their counterparts in antiquity.

The *corrida de toros* is more like the bull dance of Crete four thousand years ago than it is like anything else in the Western world. Some of *flamenco* is directly traceable to the ancient music of Andalucía in which the Romans delighted —they "imported" girls from Cádiz, famous throughout the ancient world, for their fetes. And, finally, if you read the descriptions of religious pilgrimages and celebrations in antiquity and then go to Holy Week or to any number of pilgrimages, especially to the *Rocío* in the delta of the Guadalquiver, you will see that the *Virgen* and the goddess of ten thousand names are part and parcel of the same changeless phenomenon. This world of sacrificed *toros,* bejeweled *Vírgenes,* and ecstatic dance was the primordial world in which Picasso grew up and learned to see. Only by holding that anomalous world in mind can we fathom his meaning in our own.

In *Pablo Picasso, Toros y Toreros,* Luis Miguel *Dominguín,* the *matador,* asked: "Why do we fight bulls? Why do we dress in our suits of lights and put on those pink stockings . . . in the middle of the Atomic Age? More than once I have thought of the reason, and that reason is that there are women in the front row. If there were no women as spectators of the *fiesta,* there would be not *toreros* either. Not me anyway."[7]

Shortly thereafter he recounted how Picasso had once asked him why he fought bulls. Apparently forgetting that he had just answered a similar question, he wrote that this was a problem he had pondered frequently and that would always remain unanswered. Not knowing what to reply, he asked Picasso: "Why do you paint, Pablo?" (p. 17). Which, of course, was equally inexplicable.

Then, discussing *duende,* or "artistic inspiration," *Dominguín* wrote: "Much has been said and much has been written about *duende.* It was Federico García Lorca's warhorse. *Duende* is not easy to explain. It's an *escalofrío,* a "chill," some say. It's just that *something* and you have it or you don't, say others. It could be the *manantial del arte,* the wellspring of art, because I have realized that the most important things have no exact definition. When we are with a person or work of art that has *duende,* no explanations are needed, and you don't have to be an expert to know rapidly and intuitively that the person or that thing has *duende*" (p. 15).

Like *duende, Dominguín's* reason for fighting bulls—women, and he does not mean *donjuanismo*—is no "reason." It cannot be rationally explained. You either know it rapidly and intuitively or you do not know it at all. In his very perceptive essay on the Andalusian sense of art, called "Theory and Function of the *Duende*," Lorca explained the nature of that "mysterious power that everyone feels but no philosopher can explain" as "the spirit of the earth," as the Dionysian force behind the *corrida* and behind *flamenco,* as a kind of religious enthusiasm or divine inspiration which had "jumped" from ancient Greece to Andalucía (1:1098). *Duende,* demiurge, the Dionysian, call it what you will, what Lorca meant — what *duende* means in Andalucía — was the plumbing of the intuitive side of consciousness to its deepest levels.

The reason Andalusians in particular ponder such matters is that, deprived of our march into bright solar consciousness, they remained aware of this ageless chthonian force as the truest source of artistic inspiration, as what Lorca called the point where all arts join their roots, "ultimate matter, the uncontrollable and quivering common ground of wood, sound, canvas and words" (1:1109).

As an example of this openness to such nonrational expression, remember this description which Nobel poet Vicente Aleixandre (who like Picasso was from Málaga) wrote of Lorca: "[His] long and sudden silences had about them something of the silence of a river, and in the late hour, dark as a broad river, you could sense flowing, flowing, passing through him, through his body and his soul, blood, remembrances, grief, the beating of other hearts and other beings that were he himself in that instant, the way the river is all the waters that give it body but not limit" (Lorca 2:xi).

Or consider what André Malraux said at the end of the inauguration of his "Museum Without Walls," which was a cross-cultural way of understanding art as a continuum: "This afternoon we have truly heard the ageless river throb: perhaps one day, when the Museum Without Walls is thrown into the charnel house of great dreams, someone will remember these hours during which we heard the creations of mankind singing back through the centuries. . . ." After the ceremony, reflecting on Picasso's recent death, Malraux wrote, "All through my speech, especially while I was talking about the creative power, I kept thinking: There once was a Little Man from the Cyclades . . . ," which was Malraux's reminiscent way of regarding Picasso as a modern avatar of the sculptors of ancient fertility goddess figurines.[8]

What do these descriptions point to, if not to the collective unconscious as Jung explained it, to the sacred, the mythic, and the archetypal, to what Yeats called *Anima Mundi?* Is not the concept of a Museum Without Walls, which would intentionally juxtapose a prehistoric Venus, a mask from the New Hebrides, and a piece of sculpture by Picasso, based on an insight — later adopted by the structuralists — that cuts across time and space to the heart of belief itself? And is not *Les Demoiselles d'Avignon,* in fact, the first great "structuralist" painting, the work of art that, as always, prefigures the theory? And could Picasso have had his insight had he not come from a culture that had already cut through time and space, that still lived *in illo tempore,* and that had not yet lost in the withering light of objective consciousness, its belief in the sacred?

Let's go back to the exhibit, to that room containing the painting of what I called a holy whorehouse, and all the studies leading to it. What happened, what epiphanies, what revelations of the sacred and the profane, took place to transform a gouache and charcoal sketch called "Sailors in a Bordello" (winter 1906–7) into *Les Demoiselles,* into the most explosive and important painting of our time?

First we must remember his 1907 self-portrait and the portrait of Gertrude Stein, both of which show a strong Iberian influence. In the spring of 1906 the Louvre had an exhibit of Iberian votive sculptures excavated at Osuna (the ancient town of Urso, a little north of Málaga), which so fascinated Picasso that he began painting faces in his own stylized Iberian manner. He even painted out the face of Gertrude Stein, although she had sat for him some eighty or ninety times, in order to repaint her with no further sittings in that Iberian, mask-like, sculpted style, which the ancient art of his native region had inspired.

That purposely archaic quality, revolutionary enough in itself, carried over into *Les Demoiselles.* As the sketches progressed, a medical student with a skull and a sailor disappeared, leaving only the stylized Iberian nudes themselves. Sketches of the female form done that same spring of 1907 show how he was consciously exaggerating the deltas and angles of the female form, clearly seeking an idol-like, fertility-goddess effect to go with the mask-like heads.

Then in May or early June, he visited the ethnographic museum at the Palais du Trocadéro where he saw for the first time the African pieces already in vogue with artists such as Matisse. In early July he repainted the faces of the two figures on the far right and the one of the far left in an "African" style. Although he subsequently quibbled and denied that he had Africanized *Les Demoiselles,* sketches and later pieces shown in the MOMA retrospective leave absolutely no doubt that that was precisely what he had done.[9]

Listen, too, to what he told Malraux years later:

> When I went to the old Trocadéro, it was disgusting. The Flea Market. The smell. I was all alone. I wanted to get away. But I didn't leave. I stayed. I stayed. I understood that it was very important: something was happening to me, right?
>
> The masks weren't just like any other pieces of sculpture. Not at all. They were magic things. . . . They were weapons. To help people avoid coming under the influence of spirits again, to help them become independent. They're tools. If we give spirits a form, we become independent. Spirits, the unconscious (people still weren't talking about that very much), emotion — they're all the same thing. I understood why I was a painter. All alone in that awful museum, with masks, dolls made by the redskins, dusty manikins, *Les Demoiselles d'Avignon* must have come to me that very day, but not at all because of the forms; because it was my first exorcism-painting — yes absolutely! (Pp. 10–11]

It was the atavistic and un-Western obsession with art as magic that must have appeared as an overlapping, threefold vision that day in the Trocadéro. The Iberian sculptures were votive offerings to Iberian gods. The African masks were spiritual weapons, fetishes for protection from evil spirits. Picasso's painting was an exorcism-painting. That is, it too was an exorcism-painting: *I understood why I was a painter.* The ancient and anonymous Iberian sculptor, the unknown tribal mask-maker and the Little Man from the Cyclades in his Andalusian avatar had conspired through Picasso's vision to reverse the course of Western art.

But not at all because of the forms: no, because of the magic, because of the sacred, because of the numinous. Yet in order to fit the Iberian and the African masks together and in order to retain their hieratic significance as revealers of the feminine unknown, he had to explode the forms. There in the old Trocadéro, he *saw* the Iberian and the African, the ancient and the tribal, which coincided in their primordiality, but he *saw* them by looking through the formal to their sacred and *other* nature. That vision was precisely the opposite of their material or representational nature.

The painting of Gertrude Stein is important because it does not look like her. And yet it does. The women in *Les Demoiselles* are important because they do not look like what they are, and yet do. They are—like so many ancient depictions of the goddess as courtesan—ambivalent, both sacred and profane, goddesses and doormats to use Picasso's words, an exact and baffling modern rendition of the hierodules, the sacred prostitutes of antiquity.

The demoiselles are not reality or of reality. They are released from being particular women at a particular time. They are an extrapolation from reality, from time, from history, from the flux that is death. Not reality, but mystery itself. Not a semblance or a likeness, but a vision from the intuition that is revelation, that is *duende*.

The form exploded. The whole painting is an explosion. In its center, that strange window seems to lead not into a Barcelona street but into another dimension altogether. Cubism was here, in spirit if not formally, and it began destroying the complacent images of objective beauty that in turn reflected the confident notions of progress and evolution and social concern that characterized the optimism of the beginning of the century.

Picasso was present and aware when the archaeologists and curators were finding, cataloging, and storing in their own museums all the tribal and ancient artifacts, icons, masks, and totems of the *other* world—which since Abraham and Amenhotep and Aristotle we have chosen to ignore—present and aware and utterly comprehending.

The spirit of his Cubist insight—his Andalusian insight—defied our logical, linear, and progressive notion of history because it defied the reflection of that notion in our art. He understood that art was a timeless continuum and that the only way to realize that continuum—or to make us realize it—was to undo it and repaint it and resculpt it all anew. That was what Picasso's Modernism—the restoration of numinous meaning to art—was to become. He told Malraux that painting was "like a bullfight: you know, and you don't know." And he said: "The painter takes whatever it is and destroys it. At the same time he gives it another life. For himself. Later on, for other people. But he must pierce through what the others see— to the reality of it. He must destroy. He must demolish the framework itself" (p. 137).

The rest of the MOMA retrospective was dedicated to showing us chronologically how Picasso managed that strategy, how he worked his way almost systematically upstream against the main currents of Western art in order to undo what had been done (he un-painted, painted, and repainted Velázquez's masterpiece, *Las Meninas,* more than forty times) and to do what had not. "I paint against the canvases that are important to me," he told Malraux, "but I paint in accord with *everything that's still missing* from that Museum of yours" (p. 135).

One of the revelations of the show was that he never ceased—in painting or in sculpture—that struggle. Critics who thought that after Cubism Picasso's power waned, were misled into thinking that his revolution was only formal. But the retrospective made clear that above and beyond the ceaseless iteration and reiteration of styles and the formal recapitulation of the history of art, loomed an identity, a sameness, a luminous core of subject matter—bull and horse, artist and woman, minotaur and goddess in all her guises—unchanged and unchanging amid the kaleidoscope of styles.

Art before Picasso was largely a product of the same Cartesian world that produced Marx and Darwin and Freud. But Picasso revolted against that material world. He was a painter for our time and for all time, an artist against the void who was not so much dismantling the surfaces of illusionistic art as unhinging the illusions of the Western world. The intensity of his quest for the sacred places him, in my mind at any rate, more in the visionary company of the Gnostic Jesus, of Simon Magus, of Blake and Jung, than in the beau monde of Braque and Breton and the real Gertrude Stein.

As Jung wrote in his essay "Picasso": "The journey through the psychic history of mankind has as its object the restoration of the whole man, by awakening the memories in the blood. The descent to the Mothers enabled Faust to raise up the sinfully whole human being—Paris united with Helen—that *homo totus* who was forgotten when contemporary man lost himself in one-sidedness. It is he who at all times of upheaval has caused the tremor of the upper world, and always will. This man stands opposed to the man of the present, because he is the one who ever is as he was, whereas the other is what he is only for the moment."[10]

What this laudable retrospective made overwhelmingly clear is that Picasso, by the sheer volume and inventiveness of his work, came closer than any other artist of our time to staging that revolt against man's fate that Malraux described as the purpose of art.

NOTES

CHAPTER ONE **CULTURE OF DEATH**

1. José Ortega y Gasset, *Obras completas* (Madrid: Revista de Occidente, 1961), 6:111–20.

2. Richard Ford, *A Hand-book for Travellers in Spain* (Carbondale, Ill.: Southern Illinois University Press, 1966), 1:463. This edition in three volumes is a reproduction of the definitive 1845 edition. I have kept Ford's spelling and punctuation throughout, and since I cite only Volume 1, which treats Andalucía, I will use page numbers only in the text.

3. James A. Michener, *Iberia: Spanish Travels and Reflections* (New York: Random House, 1968), p. 5.

4. *Boswell's Life of Johnson,* 6 vols. ed. George Birkbeck Hill (Oxford: Clarendon Press, 1887), 1:409–10.

5. The great Spanish historian Ramón Menéndez Pidal gives Dumas the credit for formulating this grandest of commonplaces in his *The Spaniards in Their History,* trans. Walter Starkie (New York: W. W. Norton, 1966), p. 106. But it was already common in Ford's time: ". . . many contend that Africa begins even at the Pyrenees" (p. 3). W. S. Maugham, *Andalusia: The Land of the Blessed Virgin* (New York: Arno Press, 1977 reprint of the 1920 edition).

I discuss Hemingway's gaffe in "Hemingway's Poor Spanish: Chauvinism and Loss of Credibility in *For Whom the Bell Tolls,*" in *Hemingway: A Revaluation,* ed. Donald R. Noble (Troy, N.Y.: Whitston, 1983).

6. Miguel de Cervantes Saavedra, "La gitanilla," *Obras completas* (Madrid: Aguilar, 1964), p. 787.

7. Rufus Festus Avienus, *Ora Maritima,* ed. J. P. Murphy (Chicago: Ares, 1977), lines 273–74.

8. Julio Caro Baroja, *Los pueblos de España* (Madrid: Istmo, 1976). Originally published in 1946, this is clearly the most important ethnological essay on Spain to date. Especially important to me were Chapters 5 and 17.

9. Stanley G. Payne, *A History of Spain and Portugal* (Madison: University of Wisconsin Press, 1973), 1: 26.

10. Juvenal, Satire 10, 1–2. My translation.

11. Gerald Brenan, *South from Granada* (Harmondsworth, Middlesex: Penguin Books, 1963), p. 260.

12. Gerald Brenan, *St. John of the Cross* (Cambridge: Cambridge University Press, 1973). An excellent introduction to Américo Castro's work is José Rubia Barcia, ed., *Américo Castro and the Meaning of Spanish Civilization* (Berkeley and Los Angeles: University of California Press, 1976).

13. Even by Ford's time the Gypsies' tongue was deficient: "In Spain they have lost their original grammar, and have adopted that of the country; their dialect is fast disappearing" (p. 131).

14. José-Carlos de Luna, *Gitanos de la Bética* (Madrid: Ediciones y Publicaciones Españolas, 1951), pp. 13–21.

15. Ricardo Molina, *Misterios del arte flamenco* (Barcelona: Sagitario, 1967), p. 167.

16. José Ortega y Gasset, *Velázquez, Goya, and the Dehumanization of Art,* trans. Alexis Brown (New York: W. W. Norton, 1972). It is the essay on Goya (pp. 107–34, hereafter "Goya" in the text) that concerns us.

17. Julian A. Pitt-Rivers, *The People of the Sierra* (Chicago: University of Chicago Press, 1971); Alvaro Fernández Suárez, *España: Árbol vivo* (Madrid: Aguilar, 1961); Brenan, *South from Granada,* especially chapter 10.

18. In Richard Ford, *Las cosas de España* (Madrid: Turner, 1974), p. 8.

19. Federico García Lorca, *Obras completas* (Madrid: Aguilar, 1977), 1: 1107.

20. Cited in an editorial foreword to Federico García Lorca, *Granada, paraíso cerrado y otras páginas granadinas* (Granada: Miguel Sánchez, 1971).

21. This magnificent description appears in Aleixandre's prologue to volume two of Lorca's *Obras completas,* pp. ix–xi.

22. Pedro Salinas, "Lorca and the Poetry of Death," *Hopkins Review* 5 (1951): 1, 9.

CHAPTER TWO **SHIPS OF TARSHISH**

1. Adolph Schulten, *Fontes Hispaniae Antiquae* (Barcelona: Universidad de Barcelona, vol. 1, 1955 and vol. 2, 1925).

2. For the whole fascinating story, see Adolph Schulten, *Tartessos,* 2d ed. (Madrid: Espasa-Calpe, 1945).

3. Juan de Mata Carriazo, *Tartessos y el Carambolo* (Madrid: ASTYGI, 1973), pp. 32–47.

4. Juan Maluquer de Motes, *Tartessos: La ciudad sin historia* (Barcelona: Destino, 1970), p. 136.

5. For an account of the excavation, see Antonio Blanco and J. M. Luzón, "Pre-Roman Silver Miners at Riotinto," *Antiquity* 43 (1969): 124–31.

6. Marcus Junianus Justinus, *Justin's History of the World from the Assyrian Monarch down to the Time of Augustus Caesar.* . . . (London: J. Matthews, 1713), pp. 399–401 (44. 4).

CHAPTER THREE **PIGS OF THE SEA**

1. Oppian, *Halieutica* 3. 620, in *Oppian, Colluthus, Tryphiodorus,* ed. and trans. A. W. Mair (London: William Heinemann, 1928).

2. See Antonio García y Bellido's chapter "Tartessos y los comienzos de nuestra historia," in Ramón Menéndez Pidal, *Historia de España* (Madrid: Espasa-Calpe, 1975), tomo 1, volúmen 2: 281–308.

3. Cited in Antonio García y Bellido, *Fenicios y cartagineses en occidente* (Madrid: Consejo Superior de Investigaciones, 1942), pp. 85 and 88.

4. Fernand Braudel, *The Mediterranean and the Mediterranean World in the Age of Philip II* (New York: Harper & Row, 1972), 1: 763.

5. *Diario de Colón,* ed. Carlos Sanz (Madrid: Biblioteca Americana Vetustísima, 1962), p. 58.

6. Samuel Eliot Morison, *Admiral of the Ocean Sea: A Life of Christopher Columbus* (Boston: Little, Brown, 1942), p. 408.

7. Pablo Antón Sole, *Los pícaros de Conil y Zahara* (Cádiz, privately published, 1965), p. 27.

8. Pedro de Medina, *Libro de grandezas y cosas memorables de España,* in

Obras de Pedro de Medina (Madrid: Consejo Superior de Investigaciones, 1944), p. 59.
   9. Antonio Ponz, *Viage de España* (Madrid, 1794), 18: 50.

CHAPTER FOUR DANCER OF GADES

   1. *The Works of Lord Byron,* ed. Ernest Hartley Coleridge (New York: Octagon, 1966), 3: 1–3.
   2. Cited in Leslie A. Marchand, *Byron: A Portrait* (New York: Alfred A. Knopf, 1970), p. 66.
   3. I have used Forberg's translation since it is closer to the spirit of Juvenal. In Fred. Chas. (Friederich Karl) Forberg, *Manual of Classical Erotology* (De figuris Veneris), facsimile of the 1844 edition (New York: Grove Press, 1966), p. 17.
   4. Fernando Quiñones, *El flamenco: Vida y muerte* (Barcelona: Plaza y Janés, 1971), p. 29.
   5. Rafael Alberti, *Ora Marítima* (Buenos Aires: Losada, 1953), p. 46.
   6. "One of the most famous sculptures in our Museum." Alfonso de Franciscis, *Il Museo Nazionale di Napoli* (Naples: Di Mauro, 1963), p. 67. Signor Franciscis confirmed the date in a letter to me (March 3, 1978): "La statua . . . risale per lo meno al I secolo av. Cristo. . . ."
   7. Petronius Arbiter, *Titi Petronii Arbitri . . . Satyricon, cum fragmento nuper tragurii reperto . . .* (Amsterdam: Typis Ioannis Blaeu, 1669).
   8. "Telethusa, famous among the Suburana girls." Subura, a quarter northeast of the Forum, was well known for its prostitutes.
   9. Théophile Gautier, *Wanderings in Spain* (London: Ingram Cook, 1853), p. 92.
   10. Gerald Brenan, *The Literature of the Spanish People* (Cambridge: Cambridge University Press, 1976), p. 469.
   11. My transcription from the recording sung by Amós Rodríguez on Vergara's *Archivo del cante flamenco.*
   12. François de Vaux de Foletier, *Mil años de historia de los gitanos* (Barcelona: Plaza y Janés, 1974), p. 141.
   13. Sebastián de Covarrubias, *Tesoro de la lengua castellana o española,* ed. Martín de Riquer (Barcelona: Horta, 1943), pp. 394–95.
   14. D. E. Pohren, *The Art of Flamenco* (Sevilla: Society of Spanish Studies, 1972), p. 15.
   15. Julius Caesar Scaliger, *Poetices Libri Septem* (Stuttgart–Bad Cannstatt: Friedrich Frommann Verlag, 1964), p. 29.
   16. Samuel Eliot Morison, *The European Discovery of America: The Southern Voyages* (New York: Oxford University Press, 1974), p. 83.
   17. Cited in Ian Robertson, *Los curiosos impertinentes: Viajeros ingleses por España 1760–1855* (Madrid: Editora Nacional, 1976), p. 122.
   18. Walter Starkie, *Raggle-Taggle* (London: John Murray, 1947), p. 199.
   19. George Borrow, *The Zincali: An Account of the Gypsies of Spain* (London: John Murray, 1914), pp. 73–74.
   20. Irving Brown, *Nights and Days on the Gypsy Trail* (New York: Harper & Brothers, 1922), p. 198.
   21. The most accessible source is the selection from *Cartas marruecas* in Angel del Río, *Antología general de la literatura española* (New York: Holt, Rinehart & Winston, 1967), 2: 58–60.
   22. Richard Ford, *Gatherings from Spain* (London: Everyman's Library, 1970), p. 355.
   23. Again the most accessible source is the selection from *Escenas andaluzas* in del Río's anthology, 2: 235–38.
   24. Juan Eduardo Cirlot, *A Dictionary of Symbols* (New York: Philosophical Library, 1962), p. 44.

25. J. M. Caballero Bonald, *Luces y sombras del flamenco* (Barcelona: Lumen, 1975), pp. 69-70.

26. Cited in Antonina Rodrigo, *García Lorca en Cataluña* (Barcelona: Planeta, 1975), p. 320.

CHAPTER FIVE GODDESS

1. The translation from the Phoenician is by Professor J. Ferrón.

2. José María Blázquez, *Diccionario de las religiones prerromanas de Hispania* (Madrid: Ediciones Istmo, 1975), p. 32.

3. See A. Blanco, "Notas de arqueología andaluza," *Zephyrus* 2 (1960): 151-63.

4. Manuel Bendala Galán, *La necrópolis romana de Carmona* (Sevilla: Diputación Provincial de Sevilla, 1976), chapter 6, "Los cultos mistéricos en Carmona: La 'Tumba del Elefante,' " pp. 49-72, to which I am indebted, is the definitive study on this fascinating elephant.

5. The text is published in Franz Cumont, "Les Syriens en Espagne et les Adonies a Séville," *Syria* 8 (1927): 330-41. Much of my subsequent interpretation is based on this fine article.

6. Sir James Frazer, *The Golden Bough* (sec. 211) puts the whole story together, using especially Lucian's *De Dea Syria*. I used *The New Golden Bough*, ed. Theodor H. Gaster (New York: New American Library, 1964), pp. 343-44. See also Nina Jidejian, *Byblos through the Ages* (Chicago: Argonaut, 1969), pp. 119-30.

7. The Anchor Bible: *Song of Songs,* ed. and trans. Marvin H. Pope (Garden City, N.Y.: Doubleday, 1977), plate 1.

8. John Mauchline in *The Interpreter's Bible* (New York: Abingdon Press, 1956), 6: 595.

9. Theophile J. Meek in *The Interpreter's Bible,* 5: 114. Meek states that *flagons* is "quite wrong."

10. *Richard Ford in Spain,* ed. Denys Sutton and Brinsley Ford (London: Wildenstein, 1974), p. 20.

11. The only histories of the Rocío are Juan Infante-Galán, *Rocío: La devoción mariana de Andalucía* (Sevilla: Editorial Prensa Española, 1971), and Antonio Burgos, *La Romería del Rocío* (León: Editorial Everest, 1974).

12. Eduardo Molina Fajardo, *El flamenco en Granada: Teoría de sus origenes e historia* (Granada: Miguel Sánchez, 1974), pp. 41-42, and Edward F. Stanton, "The Origins of the Saeta," *Romanische Forschungen* 88 (1976): 4, 392.

13. Robert Vavra, *Curro: Reflections of a Spanish Youth* (Sevilla: Robert Vavra, 1975), pp. 220-24.

14. "This is divine! *Olé! Viva!* How beautiful you are, really! How beautiful you are, daughter! Fuck, how beautiful you are!"

15. "*Viva* our mother! *Viva* the divine consolation! *Viva* the most beautiful (Virgin) of Andalucía! *Viva* your whore mother!" On obscenity at Greek festivals see Albin Lesky, *A History of Greek Literature* (New York: Thomas Y. Crowell, 1966), pp. 234-35.

CHAPTER SIX MATADOR

1. Legend. See Alberti, *Ora Marítima,* p. 51, for all the sources. Strabo (3. 1. 9) mentions a port called Menestheus (today Puerto de Santa María) opposite Gades, but there is no textual proof it was named for the Homeric hero (*Il.* 2. 552).

2. These stories are legion. See for a start *Fontes,* 2: 200, 209, 214, 216, 222. And for one that Schulten does not quote, *The Works of Aristotle* ed. W. D. Ross (Oxford: Clarendon Press, 1913), 6. 833a: "It is said that the places outside the Pillars of Hercules burn, some constantly, others at night only, as Hanno's *Circumnavigation* relates" (*De mir. ausc.* 37).

3. John Fulton, *Bullfighting* (New York: Dial Press, 1971), p. 11.

4. Ernest Hemingway, *For Whom the Bell Tolls,* (New York: Scribner, 1940), pp. 254–55.

5. Angus Macnab, *Fighting Bulls* (New York: Harcourt, Brace, 1959), p. 6.

6. Ernest Hemingway, *Death in the Afternoon* (New York: Scribner, 1932), p. 105.

7. José María de Cossío, *Los Toros* (Madrid: Espasa-Calpe, 1960), 1: 572.

8. John McCormick (with Mario Sevilla Mascareñas), *The Complete Aficionado* (Cleveland: World, 1967), p. 193.

9. Daniel Eisenberg, "Un texto lorquiano descubierto en Nueva York (La presentación de Sánchez Mejías)," *Bulletin Hispanique* 80 (1978): 134–37.

10. Mircea Eliade, *Myths, Rites, Symbols: A Mircea Eliade Reader,* ed. Wendell C. Beane and William G. Doty (New York: Harper & Row, 1967), 1: xvii.

11. Rafael Alberti, *La arboleda perdida* (Buenos Aires: Fabril, 1959), p. 143.

CODA **THE ANDALUSIAN PICASSO**

1. *New York Times,* May 18, 1980.

2. *Ibid.*

3. *New York,* May 12, 1980.

4. *Time,* May 26, 1980.

5. *New Yorker,* June 30, 1980.

6. *New York Review of Books,* July 17, 1980.

7. Luis Miguel *Dominguín* in *Pablo Picasso: Toros y toreros* (New York: Harry N. Abrams, 1961), p. 10. My translation from the Spanish text.

8. André Malraux, *Picasso's Mask* (New York: Holt, Rinehart & Winston, 1976), p. 240.

9. All the important sketches are reproduced in *Pablo Picasso: A Retrospective,* ed. William Rubin (New York: The Museum of Modern Art, 1980).

10. C. G. Jung, *The Spirit in Man, Art, and Literature* (Princeton, N.J.: Princeton University Press, Bollingen Series 20, 1971), pp. 139–40.

INDEX

Achuchón, 91, 92
Acinipo, 108, 136
Adonis, 108–9, 112, 113, 114, 115
  garden, 114, 115, 116
  River, 113
Aegeans, 9–10, 14, 31
Aera, 77
Agadir, 52, 113. *See also* Cádiz
Akfa, 113, 114
Alalia, battle, 42, 48
Al-Andalus, 13, 14, 15, 17, 60, 83, 95
Alans, 12
Alberti, Rafael, 71, 72, 78, 156
Aleixandre, Vicente, 24, 25–26, 168
Alexander, 108
Alfonso X, 122
Aljarafe, 45
Almadraba, 53, 54. *See also* Fishing;
  Tuna
  decline, 63–64
  managed by guilds, 64
  origins, 54
  setting of, 60–61
  spectacle, 60–63
  underworld, 61–62
Almería, 10, 15, 46, 101, 103, 130
Almohads, 17
Almonte, 100, 122, 123, 126, 131
Almoravids, 17, 107
Alpujarra, 12, 20, 102, 116
Amaya, Carmen, 88
Ambrose, 82
Anacreon, 38, 39
Anatolia, 102, 103, 166
Andalucía, 3. *See also* Tarshish; Tartessos
  African influence, 8, 11, 12, 13
  ancient commerce, 32–35
  anti-Eastern bias, 9, 15–17
  antiquity of culture, 3–5, 12, 21, 23, 72, 166

archetypal culture, 157
artists, 24, 25, 163–72
atavistic culture, 4, 18, 27
Atlantis and, 41, 107, 133, 135
as Baetica, 11, 13, 49, 108
Christian times, 11, 20
chthonian culture, 5
early history summarized, 165–66
Gypsies, 11, 18–19, 20, 85, 88, 91, 94, 97, 98, 99
invasion of Germanic tribes, 12–13
matriarchal culture, 127, 152
mineral wealth, 10, 32–33, 46–47, 54
Minoan influence, 102, 104
music, 81, 82, 83. *See also* Gypsies, music
mythical references, 36–37
myths, 133
Orientalism, ix, 6, 7, 8–17, 166
in Picasso's vision, 163–72
popular culture, 19, 22, 23, 27
poverty and persecution, 21, 22
prehistoric dating, 102
primordial nature, xii, 166
Roman times, 11, 13, 35–36, 47
shrines and temples, 11, 102, 103, 106–8, 109, 111, 120, 122, 123, 126, 129, 136, 165
stagnant culture, 20–23
stereotype, 4–8, 9. *See also Pandereta*
syncretism of culture, 5–6, 17, 111
tradition, 158–60
writers, 24, 69
Anima Mundi, 168
Antequera, 102, 165
Aphrodite, 68, 73, 75, 103, 105. *See also* Mother-goddess
Aphrodite Kallipygos, 67, 71, 72–74, 76

Apuleius, 110, 117
Arabs. *See* Moslems
Archestratus, 59
Arganthonius, 38, 42, 43, 45, 50, 46,
    48
La Argentinita, 141
Ariadne, 160
Aristocracy, decline of, 19, 123, 143–
    44
Aristotle, 47, 171
Art of Flamenco, The (Pohren), 98
Ashbery, John, 164
Astarte, 11, 44, 74, 75, 103–9, 112,
    113, 114, 118, 121. *See also*
    Mother-goddess
Athenaeus, 58, 72, 73, 117
Atlantis, 41, 107, 133, 135
Attis, 77, 109, 110, 111, 112, 135, 136
Augustine, 111
Averroes, 9
Avienus, Rufus Festus, 11, 39, 40, 41,
    43, 54, 106, 121
    on Mother-goddess, 103–4

Baal, 112, 134
Baal-Hammon, 11
Baelo, 58, 60. *See also* Bolonia
Baetica, 11, 13, 49, 108
Baetis River, 37
Balzac, Honoré de, 164
Barbate, 64
Barca, Hamilcar, 49
Barcelona, 92, 165, 171
Baza, 105
Berbers. *See* Almohads; Almoravids;
    Moslems
Bizet, Georges, 7
"Black Legend," 16, 141
Black Sea, 53
Blake, William, 172
Blastophoenicians, 11
Bluefin. *See* Tuna
Bolero, 68, 81, 90, 93. *See also* Dance
Bolonia, 65. *See also* Baelo
Borrow, George, 7, 91, 95
Bos taurus Africanus, 138, 140
Bozo, Dominique, 164
Braque, Georges, 172
Braudel, Fernand, 60, 61
Brenan, Gerald, 7, 15, 16, 21, 23, 83
    on garden of Adonis, 116
Breton, André, 172
Breviarium Eborense, 112
Brown, Irving, 91, 92
Buleras, 129
Bull, fighting, 134. *See also* Toro
    Bravo
Bull, sacred, 102, 134, 155
    cults, 136
    customs, 137–38

rituals, 135–36
sacrifice, 23, 110, 135, 136, 137,
    140, 151, 154, 156, 166
statues and paintings, 136–37
symbolism, 135
Bullfighting. *See* Toreo
Buñuel, Luis, 24
Byblos, 112, 113
Byron, George Gordon, Lord, 7, 68,
    71, 74
Byzantines, 13, 14, 122

Caballero Bonald, J. M., 96
Cabra, 136
Cachucha, 93
Cadalso, José, 93
Cádiz, ix, 133. *See also* Agadir; Cai;
    Gadeira; Gades; Gadir
    ancient commerce, 52
    dancing, 87, 89, 93, 167
    Ford's perception of, 71, 74, 88, 89
    girls, 12, 67, 68, 72, 90. *See also*
        Gaditanae
    Gypsies, 18, 21, 90, 97, 98
    matadores, 148
    Phoenician trading post, 10
    popular culture, 145
    religions, 11, 14, 75, 107, 113, 136
    underworld, 62
Caesar, Julius, 108, 138
Cai, 133
Caló, 18
Camacho, Curro, 125, 126
Caña, 94
Canary Islands, 54, 57
Canciones de habib, 83
Cante jondo, 8, 23, 24, 87, 145
Caracol, Manolo, 98
Carambolo treasure, 45–46
Carlos II, 123
Carlos III, 146
Carlos IV, 146
Carmo, 109, 110
Carmona, 101, 102, 103, 109, 111, 136
Caro Baroja, Julio, 3, 11, 12, 15, 25,
    50, 166
Carriazo, 61
Carriazo, Juan de Mata, 44, 45, 46
"Carriazo Bronze," 30, 44, 45, 104
Cartagena, 58, 59, 105
Cartas marruecas (Cadalso), 93
Carthaginians, 38, 166
    attempt to unify Andalucía, 49
    bulls of Andalucía and, 138
    campaign against Iberia, 38
    fishing and commerce, 55
    force out Phocaeans, 10
    Gadir and, 40
    maritime activities, 43, 56, 57
    Oriental influence of, 14, 166

religious cults, 11, 105, 106, 108, 109, 111
Tartessos and, 42, 48, 50, 51
Carthago Nova, 105
Castanets, 76, 77, 78, 87, 90
Castilians, 15, 16, 21, 24, 85, 87, 123, 166
Castro, Américo, 16, 17
Çatal Hüyük, 102, 104, 134, 138
Catholicism. *See* Christianity
Celtiberians, 4
Celts, 4, 12, 32, 41, 42, 44, 104, 166
Cervantes Saavedra, Miguel de, 7, 61, 62, 78, 82, 86, 87, 88
Chacona, 90, 124
Un Chien andalou (Buñuel and Dalí), 24
Childe Harold (Byron), 68
Chinchines, 78
Chinese, 5
Christianity, 11, 15, 16, 17, 20, 136, 137
  cult of Virgin, 122, 127
  martyrs, 111–12, 115
  mystery cults and, 109, 110
Christians, 3, 8, 60, 82, 84, 91
Chrysostom, John, 82
El Cid, 15, 147
Cirlot, Juan Eduardo, 96
Cisneros, Cardinal, 16
City-states, 32, 49, 165
Columbus, Christopher, 61, 89
Columella, 69
Complete Aficionado, The (McCormick), 150
Conil, 61, 62
Constantine, 111
Córdoba, 9, 12, 13, 14, 59, 84, 85, 133, 136
Corridas, 27, 128, 140, 141, 142, 144, 151, 159, 165, 166, 168, 169
Cossío, José María de, 142
Costa del Sol, 11
Costillares. See Rodríguez, Joaquín
Coto de Doñana, 41, 125, 130
Covarrubias, Sebastián de, 87, 88, 89
Crete, 31, 44, 50, 80, 102, 104, 134, 135, 138, 139, 166
Crusade, 8, 14
Cubism, 163, 171, 172
Cúchares, 151
Curetes, 50
Cybele, 11, 77, 102, 103, 108, 109, 110, 111, 135, 136
Cypriots, 31, 42, 106, 166

Daimon, chthonian, 95, 96
Dalí, Salvador, 24
Dama de Baza, 105
Dama de Elche, 105

Dama de Galera, 105
Dance, 74–75. *See also Bolero; Fandango; Flamenco;* Gypsies, dance
  cult, 77, 79, 82, 91, 104
  in early Christian times, 82
  of *Gaditanae,* 67–74, 167
  manguindoy, 90–91
  religious, 74–80, 92
  zambra, 84
  zarabanda, 87, 88, 89
Dance, The (Lucian), 75
"Dance in Triana, A" (Estébanez Calderón), 94, 98, 99, 145
Dancing girls. *See Gaditanae*
Death, 153, 154, 155, 156
  culture of, 26–27, 96, 153, 158
Death in the Afternoon (Hemingway), 154, 157
De figuris Veneris (Forberg), 89
Les Demoiselles d'Avignon (Picasso), 162, 163, 169–71
Despeñaperros, 3, 136
Dictionary of Symbols (Cirlot), 96
Diogenianus, 112, 115, 131
Dionysus, 75, 76, 78, 92, 95, 96, 112, 126, 134, 135, 151, 155, 168
Diordorus, 47
La Diosa de Sevilla, 104
Dominguín, Luis Miguel, 167
Doré, Gustave, 7
Dos Passos, John, 7
Duende, 72, 78, 79, 95–97, 152, 153, 154, 157, 158, 167, 168, 169, 171
  chthonian daimon and, 95, 96
Dukh (Dook), 91, 95, 96
Dulce, Curro, 98
Dumas, Alexandre, 7, 8, 17
Durán, Rosa, 88

Earth-mother, 77, 103, 109. *See also* Mother-goddess
Ébora, treasure of, 46
Ecija, 136
Egyptians, 106
El Argar, 103
El Carambolo, 45, 50
Elche, 104, 106
El Dorado, 31, 46
Elephant, sacred, 109, 111
El Gárcel, 101, 102, 130
Eliade, Mircea, 155
Enrique IV, 60
Ephorus, 40, 41
Eratosthenes, 57
Erythea, 36, 37, 40
España: Árbol vivo (Fernández Suárez), 21
Essai sur les moeurs (Voltaire), 90
Estébanez Calderón, Serafín, 94
Etruscans, 42, 48, 51, 134

Eudoxus of Cyzicus, 56, 67
Euthymenes, 39–40

Falla, Manuel de, 98
Fandango, 68, 90, 93
Farallón Grande, 107
Felipe V, 123
Feria (Sevilla), 27, 90
Fernández Suárez, Álvaro, 21
Fernando (the Catholic), 137
Fernando III (*el Santo*), 21, 85
Fernando VII, 71, 146
Fernando and Isabel, 16, 85
Fertility rite, 76, 130, 135, 137, 139, 154
Fiesta, 128, 151, 154
    sense of life, 128, 151, 153, 158
Fiesta de los toros, 27, 139, 142
El Fillo, 94, 145
Fishing, xi, 12. *See also Almadraba;*
    Tuna
    ancient times, 52–60
    Christian times, 60–63
    famous historical ports, 58
Flamenco, ix, 8, 18, 19, 20, 21, 24, 71, 76, 78, 166, 167, 168. *See also*
    Dance
    analogue for ancient dances, 80–81, 93
    Arab influence, 83–84
    clans, 98
    dancers' similarity to priestesses, 80
    duende, 72, 78, 79, 95–97, 158, 169
    emergence of, 84, 86–88, 90, 92, 93, 94, 95
    essence of, 96–97
    as family tradition, 97–98
    Gaditanae and, 67, 78–80, 125
    gracia, 93
    guitar, 84
    Gypsies and, 18, 88, 97–99
    juerga, 93
    Oriental background, 83–85
    pilgrimage and, 120, 121, 124, 129
    polos, 93
    primordial spirit of, 81, 88, 92–93, 124–25, 153
    toreo and, 145, 152, 153
Flaubert, Gustave, 49
Fontes Hispaniae Antiquae (Schulten), 39
Forberg, Frederick Karl, 89
Ford, Richard, 17, 21, 22, 23, 37, 48, 49, 76, 88, 107
    on al-Andalus, 14–15
    on *almadraba,* 63
    on Andalusian culture, 6, 7
    on Andalusian religion, 117–20, 130, 131
    on Gades, 11, 67

on *Gaditanae,* 11, 12, 70, 71, 72, 73, 74, 89
    on loss of ritual, 116
    on *majos,* 22, 149
    on music and dance, 68–69, 88, 89, 90, 93–94
    on plight of Spain, 159
    on *toreo,* 146
    on *zarabanda,* 87
For Whom the Bell Tolls
    (Hemingway), 7, 138
Franciscis, Alfonso de, 72
Frazer, James, Sir, 74
French Revolution, 22
Fulton, John, 137, 149, 157

Gadeira (Gadira and Gadeirus), 37, 107, 133
Gades, 11, 36, 37, 41, 56, 67, 133. *See also* Cádiz; Gadir
    ancient dancing, 67–69, 81
    fishing headquarters, 57–58
    in Roman times, 57
Gadir, 10, 11, 14, 32, 35, 40, 41, 42, 43, 48, 54, 106, 107, 133. *See also* Cádiz; Gades
    center of maritime activity, 55–56
Gaditanae, 11, 12, 67–74, 76–78, 81, 82, 83, 84, 89, 94, 167
    connection with *flamenco,* 72, 78–80, 125
Galen, 59
Galera, 102, 105
El Gallo, Joselito and Rafael, 98
García Lorca, Federico, xi, 24, 25–27, 78, 128, 129, 130, 137, 157, 167, 168
    on *cante jondo,* 87
    on *duende,* 72, 78, 79, 95, 96, 152, 153, 154, 168
    on *flamenco,* 80, 98, 124
    on Gypsies, 85, 97–99
    on *toreo,* 152, 153, 159
    on *villancicos,* 84
García Lorca, Isabel, 25
García y Bellido, Antonio, 54, 55
Gargoris, 50
Garum, 55, 58, 59, 60, 67
Gatherings from Spain (Ford), 94
Gautier, Théophile, 81, 85
Geography (Strabo), 35
Germanic invasions, 12–13
Geryon, 36–37, 40, 133
    red cattle, 133, 134, 138
Geryoneis, 37
Gilgamesh, 135
"Girl of Cadíz, The" (Byron), 68
Glueck, Grace, 164
Godoy, 146, 147

Goya, Francisco de, 19, 133, 146, 147, 148, 149, 157
Granada, 14, 16, 18, 21, 24, 83, 85, 91, 98, 102, 105, 124, 142
Grazalema, 21
Greeks, 5, 37, 76, 80, 135, 166, 168
  deities, 11, 68, 73, 75, 103, 105, 106, 112. *See also* Aphrodite; Hercules
  duende and, 72, 78
  myth of Geryon, 134
  Tartessos and, 31, 35, 41, 42, 50
  trade with Andalucía, 10, 38
Guadalquivir, 3, 37, 41, 42, 43, 49, 113, 120, 122, 127, 134, 138, 167
Guadix, 18
Guernica (Picasso), 164
Guitar, 84
Gutiérrez Solana, José. *See* Solana
Gypsies, 85, 90, 166
  dancing, 68–69, 86–87, 88, 89, 91, 92, 145
  discrimination against, 85
  early, 18–19
  guardians of *flamenco,* 97–99
  influence, 20, 25
  music, 84, 86, 88
  Ortega family, 98
  pilgrimage, 129
  relationship to ancient dancers, 90, 92
Gypsy Romances (García Lorca), 97, 99

Habis, 50
Hacilar, 102
Hadrian, 108
Hagia Triada, 135
Hand-book for Travellers in Spain (Ford), 6, 89, 94
Hannibal, 49, 107, 108, 111
Hanno, 56, 57
Hebrews, 30, 31, 33–34, 166
Hemingway, Ernest 6, 7, 138, 139, 149, 153, 154, 157
Hercules (Heracles), 11, 31, 35, 36, 37, 106, 108, 109, 110, 121, 133, 136
  temple, 106–8
Hermandades, 123, 124
Herodotus, 37, 38, 107
Hesiod, 35, 36–37
Hieros gamos, 110, 111
High Living (Archestratus), 59
Hilaria, 110
Himilco, 56, 57
Hiram of Tyre, 10, 32, 33, 106, 107
Hispalis, 112, 115
Hispanophile Imperative, 6–7, 11
Holy Week, xi, 27, 117, 124, 125, 127–28, 130, 131, 154, 158, 167

Homer, 15, 35, 36, 38, 71
Horace, 68
Horse mackerel, 53, 59, 63, 64. *See also* Tuna
Hosea, 114
Huelva, 24, 42, 44, 46–47, 99, 102
Hughes, Robert, 164
Hugo, Victor, 164

Iberia (Michener), 6, 92
Iberians, 3, 4, 9, 35, 36, 38, 51, 53, 103, 163, 164, 169, 170
"Idea del teatro" (Ortega), 151
Iliad, 35, 36
"Illustrious Kitchenmaid, The" (Cervantes), 61
Industrial Revolution, 22, 23
Inquisition, 16, 85, 91, 141, 158
Irving, Washington, 7
Ishtar, 75
Isidore, Bishop, 82
Isis, 11, 90, 103, 118, 121
Israelites, 10
Itálica, 108, 136

Jerez, 18, 19, 21, 90, 97, 125
El Jerezano, 94
Jesuits, 62
Jesus (Gnostic), 172
Jews, 10–11, 13, 14, 16, 17, 20, 82, 84, 85, 106, 113
Jiménez, Juan Ramón, 24, 25
John of the Cross, Saint, 16
Jonah, 34, 133, 166
Johnson, Samuel, 6
Joselito, 98, 156
Jung, C. G., 74, 168, 172
Justa, 112, 115, 117, 121
Justinus, Marcus Junianus, 50
Juvenal, 14, 69, 76, 81

Ker, Walter C. A., 77

La Cueva de los Letreros, 130
La Cueva de Menga, 102
La Cueva de Romeral, 102
Ladrones, 23
La Mancha, 3
Latifundia, 12, 13, 21
Lebrija, 136
Leví, Judá, 83
Liber de mirabilibus auscultationibus, 47
Libro de Grandezas (Medina), 61
Libyophoenicians, 11
Livy, 6, 49
"Llanto por Ignacio Sánchez Mejías" (García Lorca), 98, 153
Lorca. *See* García Lorca, Federico

"Lorca and the Poetry of Death"
(Salinas), 26
Los Millares, 101, 102, 103, 121, 130
Lucan, 69
Lucena, 136
Lucian, 75, 110
Lydians, 78

McCormick, John, 150, 151
Machado, Antonio, 24
Macnab, Angus, 138, 139
Madariaga, Salvador de, 141
Madrid, 26, 81, 86, 102, 105, 138, 148
artists of 1920s, 24
corridas, 142
majismo, 19, 144
popular culture, 145, 146
Maenads, 91, 92
Magog, 33, 35
Magus, Simon, 172
Maimonides, Moses ben, 9
Mainake, 38
Majismo, 19, 143, 147
Majos, 19, 23, 145, 149
Málaga, 10, 11, 24, 104, 136, 141, 164,
165, 166, 168
Malagueñas, 94
Malraux, André, 7, 163, 168, 170, 171,
172
Maluquer de Motes, Juan, 44, 46, 51
Manguindoy, 90–91
Manual of Classical Erotology (For-
berg), 89
María Luisa, 146, 147
Marranos, 16
Martial, 59, 67, 68, 69–70, 71, 73, 74,
76, 77, 78, 79, 81, 87, 89
"Mask of Tharsis," 45
Matador, 133, 137, 143, 148, 149, 152,
153, 155, 160, 167
as archetypal figure, 156
Maugham, W. Somerset, 7
Medina, Pedro de, 61, 62
Medina Sidonia, 62
Medina Sidonia, dukes of, 60, 61
*Mediterranean and the Mediterranean
World in the Age of Philip II, The*
(Braudel), 60
Mediterranean pollution, 54, 64–65
Mela, Pomponius, 69
Melkart, 11, 106, 109, 110
Menéndez Pidal, Ramón, 79
Menestheus 133
Las Meninas (Velázquez), 172
Mérida, 108, 136
Mérimée, Prosper, 7
Michener, James, 6, 7, 92
Mining, 46–47
Minoans, 3, 32, 33, 42, 102, 104, 139
Mithra, 11, 111, 135, 136, 137

Mocádem of Cabra, 83
Moclín, 129
Molina, Ricardo, 18–19, 97, 145
Monte Salomón, 47, 48
Montherlant, Henry de, 7
Moriscos, 16, 20
Morison, Samuel Eliot, 61, 89
Morón de la Frontera, 92
Mosca, 91, 92
Moslems, 3, 8, 11, 84, 85, 86, 91, 122,
166
high culture, 13, 83
Orientalizers in Andalucía, 9, 13–
14, 15, 17
Mother Earth, 103. *See also* Earth-
mother; Mother-goddess
Mother-goddess, 101, 110, 135, 155,
167. *See also* Astarte
cults of goddess and consort, 106,
108–9, 110, 111, 112, 113–16
early representations, 105
forms, 103, 104, 106, 108, 109
of matriarchal society, 152
megalithic tombs, 102
Minoan influence, 102, 104
motifs, 102
Paleolithic roots, 101
in Picasso's work, 163, 168, 169,
170, 171
pilgrimage, 120–21, 123
rituals of Astarte and Adonis, 113–
15
syncretistic cults, 106–9
virgin, 117, 118, 119, 122–31
Muleta, 148
Musée Picasso, 164
"Museum Without Walls," 168, 169,
172

Nahr Ibrahim, 113
Nasrids, 14, 16
Necho (Pharaoh), 56
Noel, Eugenio, 137
Numidians, 11

Odyssey, 35, 36
Olé, 68, 88
Oppian, 53–54, 63
Ora Maritima (Avienus), 39
Ordóñez, Cayetano, 149
Orientalism, ix, 6, 7, 8–17, 166
Ortega family, 98
Ortega y Gasset, José, 23, 123, 126,
127, 128, 157
on *corrida,* 151
"Theory of Andalucía," 4–5, 8, 12,
19, 20, 127, 145
on *toreo,* 19, 140–41, 143, 144, 151,
154

Osiris, 112
Osuna, 136, 169

Pablo Picasso, Toros y Toreros, 167
Palais du Trocadéro, 169, 170
Palestine, 11
Pamplona, 139
Pandereta, 7, 8, 9, 18, 20, 24, 25, 75, 76, 78, 141. *See also* Andalucía, stereotype
Paris, 165
Paula, Rafael *de,* 152
Pausanias, 110
Payne, Stanley, 14
People of the Sierra, The (Pitt-Rivers), 21
Pérez de Guzmán, Alonso, 60
La Perla, 94
Persecution, 22
Petronius, 68, 69, 73, 74, 77, 81
Phocaeans, 10, 38, 41, 42, 43, 48, 50
Phoenicians 11, 28, 38, 48, 133
  deities, 44, 104, 105, 106, 109, 112, 113. *See also* Astarte; Melkart
  denigration of, 15
  fishing trade, 53, 55, 56, 57
  founders of Cádiz, 52
  Gadir and, 42
  Gypsies and, 18
  Oriental influence, 14
  puellae Gaditanae and, 74, 75
  Tarshish and, 32, 35, 41, 43, 50
  trade with Andalucía, 3, 10
  trade with Tarshish, 32, 35, 47, 166
  treasure of Ébora and, 46
Pícaro, 60, 61, 62
Picasso, Pablo Ruiz, 24, 25, 156, 157, 162
  Cubist insight, 163, 171
  exhibition at Museum of Modern Art, 163–72
  Gertrude Stein and, 163, 169, 170, 171
  Modernism, 171
  mother-goddess image, 163, 168, 169, 170, 171
  prototypical Andalusian, 165, 172
"Picasso" (Jung), 172
Picasso: A Retrospective (Rubin), 163
Picasso's Mask (Malraux), 163
Pilgrimage, ix, 12, 100, 118–19, 120–21, 123, 129, 167. *See also* Romería del Rocío
Pillars of Hercules, 32, 35, 37, 38, 53, 57, 58, 107
Pindar, 57
Pitt-Rivers, Julian, 21
El Planeta, 94, 98, 145
Plato, 41, 107, 135, 155
Pliny, 56, 59, 69, 81

Plutarch, 106, 110
Pohren, D. E., 89, 98
Polos, 93
Polybius, 47, 58, 59
Ponz, Antonio, 63
Popular culture, 19, 20, 22, 23, 143, 144, 145, 146, 155
Porcuna, 136
Poseidonius, 56
Poverty, 22
Preciosa, 7, 78, 86, 87
"Preciosa y el aire" (García Lorca), 78
Priapus, 73, 77
Los pueblos de España (Caro Baroja), 12
"Puella Gaditana" (Martial), 70
Puerto de Santa María, 71

Quiñones, Fernando, 71, 72, 79

Religion. *See also* Mother-goddess
  Christian, 109, 117–31. *See also* Christianity
  cults of goddess and consort, 75, 108–9, 110, 111, 112, 113–16, 135–36
  dancing and, 74–80, 92
  flamenco and, 124–25, 129
  martyrs, 111–12, 115
  Mithraism, 136
  mystery cults, 76, 77, 106, 109, 110, 111
  Oriental and Eastern cults, 106, 109
  pilgrimage. *See* Pilgrimage; Romería del Rocío
  prehistoric, 103
  primordial concept, 124
  Roman times, 106, 108, 109
  syncretistic cults, 106–9
Rembrandt (Van Rijn), 164
Rhadamanthys, 36, 133
Richardson, John, 164
Rilke, Rainer Maria, 7, 26, 80
Río Odiel, 42
Río Tinto, 42, 47, 48
Ríotinto, 47, 99
Rocío. *See* Romería del Rocío
Rodríguez, Joaquín, 145, 148, 149
Romalís, 67, 68, 87, 88, 94
Romances, 87, 93
Romans, xi, 5, 10, 13, 32, 48, 57, 76, 81, 122, 165, 166, 167
  Andalusian influence on, 49
  circus, 139
  conquest of Andalucía, 10
  cult of Attis and Cybele, 109, 110, 111, 112
  deities, 106
  fishing commerce, 55
  Hannibal and, 107, 108

Jews and, 11
Oriental cults and, 75, 126
puellae Gaditanae and, 69, 70, 71,
    82, 83, 167
Spanish gold as income, 33
Tartessos and, 43
theaters, 108
Romanticism, 6, 7, 19, 22, 23, 26, 67,
    68, 69, 72, 90, 130, 145, 146, 149,
    157, 166
of Goya, 147–48
Romería, 119. *See also* Pilgrimage
Romería del Rocío, ix, 100, 121, 123–
    26, 130, 131, 158, 167
Romero, Pedro, 145, 147
in Hemingway, 149
portrait by Goya, 132, 148, 149
Ronda, 12, 19, 94, 97, 136, 149
Rondeñas, 94
Rubin, William, 164
Rufina, 112, 115, 117, 121
Ruiz Picasso, Pablo. *See* Picasso

Saetas, 124, 128
"Sailors in a Bordello" (Picasso), 169
St. John of the Cross (Brenan), 16
Salammbo, 49, 103, 108, 112, 113,
    115, 117. *See also* Mother-goddess
Salinas, Pedro, 26–27
Salsamentum, 55, 58
Samians, 38
Sánchez Mejías, Ignacio, 98, 141,
    152–53
Sancho the Brave, 60
Sancti Petri, 107
Sanlúcar de Barrameda, 46
Santiago, 107
Santiago de Compostela, 8, 120
Santuario de la Virgen de la Sierra,
    129
Scaliger, Julius Caesar, 89
Schulten, Adolph, 31, 39–42, 43, 48,
    51, 104, 122, 139
Seguidillas, 87, 90, 93, 124
Seneca, 59, 69, 133
Sephardim, 11
Serranía de Cádiz, 20
Serranía de Ronda, 20, 21
Sevilla, xi, 4, 5, 24, 42, 44, 69, 115,
    124, 128
conquered by Fernando *el Santo,* 85
Easter in, 124, 130, 166
"Goddess of," 104
Gypsies, 18, 19, 21, 90, 94
Holy Week, 27, 125. *See also* Holy
    Week
love of pageantry, 116
megalithic tombs, 102
pagan rituals, 118

popular culture, 145
toreo, 142, 148
underworld, 62
Sevillanas, 90, 121
Sierra Morena, 3
Sierra Nevada, 20, 116
Silius Italicus, 107
Silvae (Statius), 78
Siret, Louis, 15
Solana, José Gutiérrez, 137
Solomon, 3, 10, 28, 32, 106, 107, 133,
    166
Song of Solomon, 114
South from Granada (Brenan), 15, 21
"Spanische Tänzerin" (Rilke), 80
Starkie, Walter, 7, 91, 95, 96
Statius, 78, 81, 86
Stein, Gertrude, 163, 169, 170, 172
Stesichorus, 37, 48
Strabo, 11, 15, 32, 33, 35–36, 37, 38,
    41, 47, 49, 50, 56, 57, 58, 67, 81,
    104, 134
Sun Also Rises, The (Hemingway), 149
Swinburne, Henry, 90
Syrians, 11, 15, 78, 106, 109, 112, 113

Talavera, 156
Tammuz, 112, 113
Tangier, 53, 61
Tanit, 11, 103, 105, 108, 111
Tarab, 95
Tarifa, 60, 62
Tarshish, 3, 28, 30, 133, 165, 166. *See
    also* Tartessos
in history, 31–51
mineral wealth, 32–35
symbolic importance, 35, 36
Tartessos (Schulten), 43
Tartessos, 3, 10, 16, 30, 77, 78, 103,
    104, 122, 133, 138, 166. *See also*
    Tarshish
apogee, 42, 44
"Carambolo treasure," 46
"Carriazo Bronze," 30, 44, 104
description, 40
fate, 48–49
fishing, 54–55, 57
in history, 31–51
location, 40, 41, 42
"Mask of Tharsis," 45
Minoan influence, 102, 104
mythology, 50
trade, 42, 54, 56
treasure of Ébora, 46
Taurobolium, 110, 136, 139
La Tauromaquia (Goya), 147
Tauromorph, 135
Telethusa, 67, 69, 70–74, 76, 78, 87,
    88, 89, 99, 112

"To Telethusa, Dancer of Gades"
(Alberti), 71–72
Teresa, Saint, 16
Tetuán, 62
Theater, 19, 144–45
Theodosius, 82
Theogony (Hesiod), 36
"Theory and Function of the *Duende*"
(García Lorca), 168
"Theory of Andalucía" (Ortega y
Gasset), 4, 145
Third of May, The (Goya), 148
Thomas of Aquinas, Saint, 9
Timaeus, 47
Tin trade, 54, 57
"Tomb of the Elephant," 109, 121
Tomkins, Calvin, 164
Toreo, xi, 12, 19, 23, 24, 27, 92, 159,
167
as archetype, 155–56
as art, 149–50
clans, 98
compared to English novel, 150
compared to Greek tragedy, 150, 151
corruption of, 157–58
creation of, 152
development, 138, 139, 140, 141,
142, 143
duende in, 95, 152, 158, 169
effect on Spanish social structure,
140, 143, 144
linked to *flamenco*, 92, 124, 152,
153
meaning, 150–57
Ortega family, 98
primordial spirit, 153
La Tauromaquia, 147
theater and, 144–45
Torero, 19, 20, 23, 98, 125, 140, 141,
142, 143, 145, 148, 167
Toro bravo, 138–40, 150
Torre, Manuel, 97
Trajan, 108
*Travels Through Spain in the Years
1775 and 1776* (Swinburne), 90
Triana, 88, 94, 97, 112, 125
Trocadéro, 170
Troy, 31, 32, 133
Tuna. *See also Almadraba;* Fishing;
Horse mackerel
bluefin, xi, 52–53, 58–60
pigs of the sea, 59
processing, 59
salt curing, 55
Turdetani, 37, 43, 46, 49, 51, 81
Turdetania, 35, 39, 47
Turks, 16, 62
Two Women at a Bar (Picasso), 163
Tyre, 11, 32, 33, 34, 42, 54, 57, 71,
106, 107, 108, 113
Tyrians, 10, 33, 54, 55, 106

Umayyad dynasty, 13
Underworld, 70, 103
of *almadrabas*, 61–62
Uphaz, 33
Urso, 169

Vandals, 12, 166
Van Rijn, Rembrandt. *See* Rembrandt
Vavra, Robert, 125
Vejer de la Frontera, 62
Velázquez, Diego Rodríguez de Silva y,
172
Velleius Paterculus, 32
"Venere Callipige," 67, 71, 72–74, 76
Venus. *See also* Mother-goddess
Callipygian, 67, 71, 72–74, 76
of Laussel, 134
Villa Item, 76, 77
Villancico, 83, 84, 87
Virgen del Rocío, 100, 119, 120, 122–
26, 167
Virgin
cult, 122–31
of the Dew, 120, 122
equated with goddess, 117, 118, 119
pilgrimages, 120
Visigoths, 12, 13, 166
Voltaire, 90

Wanderings in Spain (Gautier), 81

Yeats, William Butler, 168
Yerma (García Lorca), 129, 137
Yo Picasso (Picasso), 163

Zahara de los Atunes, 60, 61, 62, 64
Zambra, 84
Zapateado, 93
Zarabanda, 87, 88, 89, 124
Zincali, The (Borrow), 95
Ziryab, 84